W9-DEO-021

WITHDRAWN
WRIGHT STATE UNIVERSITY LIBRARIES

WORK AND TECHNOLOGY IN HIGHER EDUCATION

The Social Construction of Academic Computing

TECHNOLOGY AND EDUCATION
Raymond S. Nickerson, Series Editor

WORK AND TECHNOLOGY IN HIGHER EDUCATION
The Social Construction of Academic Computing

Edited by
Mark A. Shields
University of Virginia

LEA LAWRENCE ERLBAUM ASSOCIATES, PUBLISHERS
1995   Hillsdale, New Jersey   Hove, UK

Copyright © 1995 by Lawrence ErlbaumAssociates, Inc.
All rights reserved. No part of this book may be reproduced in any form, by photostat, microfilm, retrieval system, or any other means, without the prior written permission of the publisher.

Lawrence Erlbaum Associates, Inc., Publsihers
365 Broadway
Hillsdale, New Jersey 07642

Cover design by Mairav Salomon-Dekel

Library of Congress Cataloging-in-Publication Data

Work and technology in higher education : the social construction of
  academic computing / edited by Mark A. Shields.
      p. cm.
    Includes bibliographical references and index.
    ISBN 0-8058-0356-4 (alk. paper). — ISBN 0-8058-0357-2 (pbk. :
alk. paper)
      1. Education, Higher—United States—Data processing.
    2. Educational technology—United States.   3. Educational sociology—
    United States.   I. Shields, Mark A.
    LB2395.7.W67   1994
    378′.00285—dc20   94-2166
                                                                CIP

Books published by Lawrence Erlbaum Associates are printed on acid free paper, and their bindings are chosen for strength and durability.

Printed in the United States of America
10 9 8 7 6 5 4 3 2 1

Contents

Preface

Since the early 1980s, colleges and universities have become extremely important not only as computational research and development centers, but also as sociotechnical field sites for examining the relationship between technological innovation and sociocultural change. Yet, neither academic analysts of technological change nor the broader audience of computer professionals have a full understanding of higher education's catalytic role in shaping the so-called microcomputer revolution. This volume is a contribution to that understanding.

In contrast to previous publications about computers in higher education—most of which focus narrowly on technology deployment, use, and management strategies—the contributors to this volume adopt an expansive approach toward academic computing viewed as a social and cultural phenomenon. Conceptually and methodologically unique, this volume is the only collection of in-depth, mainly ethnographic studies of the "academic computing revolution"—its consequences, meanings, and significance. Most of the contributors are university-based social scientists who have been at the forefront of studying computing in higher education.

The contributions include several case studies, based on years of careful fieldwork and analysis, that document the open-ended, socially constructed, interpretively flexible character of computer-mediated academic work. Drawing on the core ideas of cultural anthropology, interpretive sociology, and the social construction of technology, the volume is also a contribution to the growing, multidisciplinary study of technology and society. The intended audiences are educators and social scientists concerned with computing and technology studies, as well as academic administrators who want to understand the sociocultural context of technological change as a basis for more informed decision making.

ACKNOWLEDGMENTS

Much of the research described in the following chapters was carried out at Brown University under the auspices of the Institute for Research in Information and Scholarship (IRIS). The bulk of that research was funded by IBM and the Annenberg/CPB Project, in addition to the Getty Trust Art History Information Project and the James S. McDonnell Foundation. Several individuals at Brown and IRIS were instrumental in facilitating the completion of that research. In particular, I want to thank Bill Beeman, Brian Hawkins, Marty Michel, Mike Pear, Bill Shipp, and Don Wolfe. Although some of them may disagree with our judgments about academic computing, they were all committed to the importance of in-depth analysis of technological innovation in higher education. I am grateful to Julia Hough for proposing this volume. The manuscript was completed while I was on the faculty of the School of History, Technology, and Society at Georgia Tech, where I enjoyed the multidisciplinary company of fellow humanists and social scientists. At Lawrence Erlbaum Associates, Hollis Heimbouch's support for seeing this volume through and Robin Weisberg's skillful editing were essential. Jeff Sherrill provided expert assistance in compiling the index. Finally, without Pascale Fillon-Shields' love, warmth, and forbearance, I would not have completed this undertaking.

Mark A. Shields

1

The Social Construction of Academic Computing

Mark A. Shields
University of Virginia

The 1980s were glorious years for academic computing enthusiasts and entrepreneurs in the United States. As Theodore Roszak (1986) pointed out, "with the advent of the microcomputer, a readily salable item, the computer industry went after academia with one of the most intense mass marketing efforts in business history" (p. 57). Massive discounts on microcomputers became available to students, faculty, and staff at hundreds of colleges and universities, while a few prestigious institutions were favored with unprecedented corporate grants of hardware, software, and dollars for computer support staff and technical research and development. "During the 1980s, the decade of the 'computer revolution,' our collective investment may have totaled as much as $16 billion" (Green, 1991, p. 6); in 1992 alone, colleges and universities spent more than $3 billion on information technology, a financial strain that has reached acute proportions at some institutions ("Recession Spurs Changes," 1992). Several campuses, of course, became more technologically affluent than others (Fiske, 1984; Tucker, 1983–1984; Waldrop, 1985), yet none went untouched by the so-called academic "computer revolution." In fact, by some measures, higher education may well have become one of the most computer-intensive organizational sectors of modern society. The diffusion of computers in U.S. households, for example, lags behind the diffusion of desktop computers and workstations on U.S. campuses (U.S. Bureau of the Census, 1991). Several institutions even require entering freshmen to purchase a microcomputer. "Has there ever been

1

another instance," Roszak (1986) asked rhetorically, "of the universities making ownership of a piece of equipment mandatory for the pursuit of learning?" (p. 58).

Along with the marketing of microcomputers in higher education, there was also an outpouring of ambitious intellectual visions about computing technology and higher education reform. Many of those visions embodied what were essentially utopian aspirations that the personal computer could deeply transform the quality of academic work and scholarship. Social reform through technological salvation has been a theme of American utopian thought and social movements in the past (Alexander, 1992; Segal, 1985). Arguably, the academic computing movement of the 1980s was one such contemporary utopian movement (cf. Kling, 1991a; Kling & Iacono, 1988, 1991; Morell & Fleischer, 1991; Winner, 1986) in which the personal computer became a key symbol (Ortner, 1973) of and a vehicle for higher education reform—a movement led by an unlikely (and some might say unholy) trinity of campus administrators, faculty, and key computer vendors. Armed with a rhetoric of liberation and transcendence to match their visionary activism, many campus administrators ebulliently proclaimed that higher education was in the midst of a revolution. "After almost a decade of relative stability," wrote a Cornell computer services director, "computing at Cornell University is entering a period of revolutionary change. This change is being fueled by the microcomputer" (Gale, 1983, p. 9). "The pace of the 'computer revolution' is illustrated by the fact that the term itself is already outdated," according to Carnegie-Mellon University's top computing administrator. "[T]he revolution we are experiencing is not a 'computer' revolution; it is an 'information processing' revolution" (Van Houweling, 1983, p. 35). It was commonplace, as well, to hear academicians speak in terms that prophesied an almost instantaneous transformation of institutional structure and culture through computing technology. Listening to these advocates, one might get the impression that teaching and learning had suddenly become empowering, whereas before it had been, merely, plodding. Of course, there were also more pedestrian rationales, emphasizing the instrumental and strategic importance of investing in computing technology to recruit faculty, lure students, enhance academic prestige, and attract institutional funding.

The most prominent (and prescient) academic skeptic was Harvard's Derek Bok (1985). His widely publicized 1985 "President's Report to the Harvard Board of Overseers for 1983–84" provided a rare moment of historical perspective:

> Experience should . . . make us wary of dramatic claims for the impact of new technology. Thomas Edison was clearly wrong in declaring that the phonograph would revolutionize education. Radio could not make a lasting impact on

the public schools even though foundations gave generous subsidies to bring programs into the classroom. Television met a similar fate in spite of glowing predictions heralding its powers to improve learning.

In each instance, technology failed to live up to its early promise for three reasons: resistance by teachers, high cost, and the absence of demonstrable gains in student achievement. There is as yet no clear evidence that computers and videodiscs will meet a happier fate. (p. 30)

Bok was a soloist out of tune with the chorus. Had he not been an eminent academic spokesman, Bok's cautionary reflections on computers in higher education would probably have gone unnoticed. Technological hubris and hyperbole were the order of the day. The voices of academic computing enthusiasts resonated the ebullient, transhistorical optimism of leading industry executives. Apple Computer's John Sculley (1989), forecasting the revolution's consequences ahead to the 21st century, summarized his vision in the following words:

[The new technologies] will allow us to set loose an avalanche of personal creativity and achievement. Once we have thousands of ideas to harvest, we may have the chance once again to create a second Renaissance, perhaps every bit as important as the first, in the early part of the next century. It would represent a rebirth and revival of learning and culture unleashed by new technologies. It would bridge the gaps between the arts and sciences. And it would signify the emergence of an integrated environment for instruction and research. (p. 1061)

The instrumental and symbolic appeal of computing converged to offer an almost irresistible case for the rapid computerization of academia. The computer represented, more convincingly than any previous educational technology ever had, the central mission of higher education: the creation, production, and transmission of knowledge. It is no coincidence that the spread of the machine was joined by a rhetoric of empowerment and transformation. Computers, went the constant refrain, would transform profoundly the way we work, learn, teach—even the way we socialize.

There can be no doubt, of course, that the dramatic growth of personal, or desktop, computing was a change of major proportions in academia during the 1980s. Nor can there be any question that unprecedented computational opportunities—most pervasively in writing and communication—were opened up by the new technology. But could these changes, collectively, bear the rhetorical baggage carried by calling them revolutionary? If not, how shall one characterize the rapid and thoroughgoing process by which computing became a ubiquitous, compelling, and indeed unavoidable practice of academic life? What does the study of academic computing contribute to the broader multidisciplinary social study of technology?

This volume seeks to answer those questions. It consists of a collection of original chapters written over a 5-year period spanning the late 1980s and early 1990s by researchers who were at the forefront of studying academic computing on their own campuses. That period, so recent in time yet so distant as computing history, was widely hailed as the academic computing revolution. But this is not just a volume about computing in higher education. It is also a volume on thinking about technology as woven into, and not simply superimposed upon, the praxis of everyday life—about "technology-practice" in historian Arnold Pacey's (1983) apt phrase.

As Bernward Joerges (1990) noted, "Sociology has not had much to say on technology per se" (p. 206). The advent of computing has changed that. Scholarly social science writing on computers—their uses, consequences, and meanings—goes back at least to the early 1950s, an era when Jacques Ellul (1964) in *The Technological Society* marveled at the "electronic calculating machine" capable of solving "equations in seventy variables, required in certain econometric research" (p.16). But not until the early 1980s was there an enormous growth in audiences for the genre: the ubiquity of computers had generated widespread demand for analyses of their social impacts and implications. Emblematic of that growth were three successful books by well-placed social scientists: Sherry Turkle's *The Second Self: Computers and the Human Spirit* (1984), James R. Beniger's *The Control Revolution: Technological and Economic Origins of the Information Society* (1986), and Shoshana Zuboff's *In the Age of the Smart Machine: The Future of Work and Power* (1988). Even earlier in the decade, before the publication and subsequent market success of those three books, other writers were making significant, albeit obscure and unheralded, contributions outside mainstream social science. Most notable was Rob Kling's (1980) intellectually ambitious codification of the computing-in-society literature, "Social Analyses of Computing: Theoretical Perspectives in Recent Empirical Research." Because it appeared in a major computing and information sciences publication, Kling's article did not capture the full attention of potentially interested social scientists (see also Kling & Scacchi, 1982).

By now, the social scientific literature on computing is voluminous (see the collection assembled by Dunlop & Kling, 1991). However, there is a meager social science research literature on *academic* computing (see Kiesler & Sproull, 1987; Shields, Graves, & Nyce, 1991, 1992). Most of the academic computing literature consists overwhelmingly of visionary speculation and personal testimonial. This volume tries to fill a gap by documenting and interpreting the role that computing has played in diverse contexts of higher education.

Most of the authors come from one of three major disciplines: anthropology, sociology, or political science. Collectively speaking, their approaches are best characterized in terms of ethnographic, phenomenological, or interpretive social science, in sharp contrast to approaches that fall within a rubric suggested by phrases like "human factors," "management information systems," or the "human–computer interface." ("The human–computer interface is easy to find in a gross way—just follow a data path outward from the computer's central processor until you stumble across a human being," Card, Moran, & Newell, 1983, p. 4). Thus, in contrast to perspectives that focus on actors as instrumentally adapting to technologically driven environments, the approaches reflected in this volume reverse the causal loop and reconceptualize its significance: In which ways do the experiences, interests, motivations, and goals of socially situated and culturally knowledgeable individuals influence them to adopt, use, and interpret the meanings of technologies that might thereby have an impact on them? Perspectives that screen out or deny the interpretive accomplishments of individuals are inadequate because they fail to recognize that technology's consequences are mediated through symbolically meaningful as well as structurally patterned exchanges.

In short, the authors emphasize questions of meaning more than function; they focus on social relations oriented more toward symbolic interaction than toward system integration; and, above all, they direct attention to the interpretively open, socially constructed, and negotiated character of technologically mediated action rather than any presupposed, fixed, or predictable technological impacts or imperatives. This volume not only demonstrates the intellectual vitality of constructionist approaches for understanding academic computing, but also suggests that such approaches may be fertile for developing better social theories about other technologies. If technological artifacts are the main components of what social scientists call "material culture," it is apparent that the tools of cultural analysis need to be applied more creatively to the study of technology.

No theoretical school or perspective offers a completely apt, let alone comprehensive, label for all of the contributions to this volume. Nevertheless, the social constructionist framework that provides a theoretical canopy may be traced to several distinctive but overlapping intellectual traditions in social theory and research. The three traditions of most direct relevance are: (a) cultural anthropology and ethnography, emphasizing the centrality of culturally defined symbols and their variegated meanings (see Dolgin, Kemnitzer, & Schneider, 1977; Geertz, 1973, 1983); (b) phenomenology and its sociological successors, ethnomethodology and symbolic interactionism, both of which stress the negotiated nature of multiple social realities, the relativity of "lifeworld" experiences, and the contingency and fragility of social structures (see Berger & Luckmann, 1966; Ihde, 1990); and (c) most recently the Social Construction of Technology (SCOT). This is an interdisciplinary movement, primarily European in origin, which has appropriated key motifs from the sociology of scientific knowledge to redefine radically the very character of technological innovation and change as inherently open-ended sociocultural, not simply technical, phenomena. The founding texts of SCOT are Bijker, Hughes, & Pinch (1987) and Bijker & Law (1992) (see also MacKenzie & Wajcman, 1985.) Readers familiar with any of these three traditions will find much in the following chapters that resonates with those central themes. Several of the contributions to this volume also touch upon the relevance of technology studies to broader foundational issues that perennially engage social theorists: linking micro and macro levels, reconciling system and lifeworld, interrelating agency and structure, and transcending the materialism–idealism dichotomy, as reflected, for example, in the works of Jeffrey Alexander (1983), Jürgen Habermas (1987), Anthony Giddens (1984), and Pierre Bourdieu (Bourdieu & Wacquant, 1992).

GUIDING THEMES

Having noted the key sources for our perspective on academic computing, it is now time to sketch the central themes that appear throughout the volume. Collectively, the chapters represent a critique of technological reification. The fallacy of reification is a pervasive tendency in both popular and academic discourse about technology. What all of this volume's contributors share is an insistence on avoiding this fallacy—that is, the tendency to reduce a complex, multidimensional phenomenon to a small subset of its component attributes and to make the latter essential and determinant, while residualizing the importance of the other dimensions. Typically, reification leads to one form or another of technological determinism, in which specific concrete, observable, and usually quantifiable aspects of an artifact—its technical attributes—are selectively isolated as independent variables, which are then said to account for the causal or explanatory power of the *whole* technology. In avoiding the fallacy of reification and its frequent correlate, determinism, the contributions to this volume exemplify three guiding conceptual themes, with the crucial proviso that the following generalizations apply to *academic* computing. They also may varyingly, but not necessarily, apply to computing technology in other settings as well as to other technological domains. The three themes are social constructionism, agency, and indeterminancy.

Social Constructionism.   Academic computing is socially constructed by a plurality of actors, not all of whom share the same interests in or attribute the same meanings to the artifact (computer) or the social process (computing) in which the artifact is embedded. The fact that interests and meanings are plural and variable means that the computer (and related terms, like *information technology* or *academic computing*) have no fixed, universal, operationally specific definition or significance among the plurality of relevant actors (e.g., students, faculty, administrators, technical staff, computer vendors, etc.). Social constructedness means that both the definition of the material artifact (e.g., *workstation, user-interface, network*) and its symbolic attributes (e.g., *appropriate/ cutting-edge, user-friendly/unfriendly, centralized/decentralized*) are rhetorically contested and thus subject to negotiation by the network of relevant actors. To use the terminology of SCOT, the technological frame "academic computing" is an interpretively flexible artifact within a given actor–network or system (Bijker, Hughes, & Pinch, 1987; Bijker & Law, 1992). An artifact may, at one level, be regarded as a "thing-in-itself"; but as an element of social structure and culture it is never a thing *by* itself. Rather, computers and other artifacts are material resources inscribed with meaning by "cultural schemas that inform their social use" (Sewell, 1992, p. 12).

Agency. Academic computing is a voluntaristic form of technologically mediated social action that is shaped (constrained, enabled) by structures that actors only partially control. In other words, individuals make computing choices but not under circumstances completely of their own choosing. The systemic conditions (e.g., the available hardware/software/network configurations, market and price structures, the social organization of work) that constrain or facilitate voluntaristic choice are, at any particular moment, taken as given dimensions of the technological paradigm, and thus not negotiable. At the same time, these conditions are themselves products of socially constructed definitions of the situation—the outcomes of previous choices—and are in turn susceptible to change on the basis of future choices. For example, a professor who decides to implement a computer-based instructional system in one of her courses is confronted with a myriad of existing conditions that make the innovation seem worthwhile yet simultaneously constrain what can be realistically accomplished through intentional action. The consequences (impacts) of implementing the innovation may, however, restructure those preexisting conditions and thus establish new parameters for voluntaristic choices and altered systemic constraints in the future. In Sewell's (1992) crisp formulation, "Agency . . . is the actor's capacity to reinterpret and mobilize an array of resources in terms of cultural schemas other than those that initially constituted the array" (p. 19).

Indeterminancy. There is no empirical, logical, or theoretical basis for presupposing that a technological "imperative" is at work in academic computing. Every contributor to this volume has probably winced more than once on hearing someone remark that such-and-such a technology has "impacts" on such-and-such a group, organization, or system. The language of impacts is not so much wrong as it is oversimplified and misleading; it fails to account for the fact that impacts are themselves social constructions and socially constructed (Hughes, 1983; Nye, 1990). It is pointless to talk about the impacts of computers unless we first know something about the nature of the social and cultural settings, or worlds, within which computers are *presumed* to have impacts. Accordingly, one must reject technological determinism as both a theoretical and empirical blind alley: the technical is indeterminant with respect to the social. Feenberg (1991), in a related vein, wrote about the "ambivalence of computer technology" (pp. 91–93). Rather than speaking the language of impact, imperative, or determinism, it is both more precise and more insightful to speak about "heterogeneously contingent" (Bijker & Law, 1992) interactions between technical, organizational, and cultural dimensions of technology-practice (Pacey, 1983) within particular sociotechnical systems.

Within the social constructionist school (broadly defined) it is important to note that sharp differences of logic and emphasis have already emerged, partly focused on how much empirical mileage can be gotten, theoretically, from a "thoroughgoing interpretivism" (Woolgar & Grint, 1991) in the social study of technology, including computing (cf. Grint & Woolgar, 1992; Kling, 1991a, 1991b, 1992a, 1992b; Woolgar, 1991; Woolgar & Grint, 1991). Kling's (1992a, 1992b) critique of constructionism argues for a more limited "reconstructive interpretivism" that avoids what he regards as "endless deconstruction" (1992a, p. 363). Other scholars, notably Winner (1993), have criticized social constructionists for ignoring technology's social consequences, for residualizing the significance of power in technological choices, and for invoking an implicit value-neutrality toward deeper philosophical and normative questions. Suffice to say that the contributors to the present volume carry interpretivism farther than most social studies of technology, but at the same time they do not shy away from value-relevant assessment and normative critique. Nor do they ignore structural constraints on voluntaristic choice. Constructionism does not deny "objective" material conditions or structured inequalities in the distribution of resources. Rather, it insists that the latter themselves are never simply given as rigidly fixed constraints; material conditions and structured inequalities can also be enabling factors depending on the actors and the situation. The key symbolism (Ortner, 1973) used by "computer revolutionaries" (Kling & Iacono, 1988, 1991) in the 1980s to construct an academic computing revolution helped to mobilize material resources from computer vendors on an unprecedented scale (see Shields, this volume). In the process previous inequalities in access to computing resources were rectified while new inequalities emerged. The severely constrained material conditions for funding computing in the early 1990s, however, are completely unlike those of the mid-1980s. Thus key actors' constructions of academic computing in the early 1990s employ different strategies of symbolization from those used by computer revolutionaries starting in the early 1980s: a tactical shift from "instrumental idealism" to "instrumental realism" (Shields, this volume).

It follows methodologically from our theoretical emphasis on the social relations and cultural meanings of technology that one must not only observe and analyze computing behavior (how users work and what they use computers for) but also understand and interpret the beliefs, practices, and norms that underlie—indeed, that encompass—their use patterns. In the words of Marshall Sahlins (1976), "No functional explanation is ever sufficient by itself; for functional value is always relative to the given cultural scheme" (p. 206). The functional, instrumental, or technical use-values of technologies are thus mediated by their sociocultural exchange-values; it is from the latter that attributions of impact and interpretations of their meaning and significance derive. Just as computers have no determinant impacts, functions, or imperatives, neither are their uses or meanings fixed or static but rather must be studied as a dynamic, ongoing process. For all of those reasons, most of the chapters in this volume are based on longitudinal, ethnographic field studies in a variety of academic milieux.

The contributors to this volume would probably endorse the conclusion of sociologist Alan Wolfe's (1991) assessment of artificial intelligence (AI):

> [F]ar from equating the kinds of intelligence associated with all organic systems, AI, in an admittedly backhanded way, actually reinforces the hypothesis of human distinctiveness by calling attention to the ambiguity-resolving, incomplete, and meaning-dependent features of human minds. Work in AI stimulates sociological theorizing in many directions; those traditions with antisystemic inclinations—such as ethnomethodology and symbolic interactionism—receive just as much support from AI as those who would use what we have learned about machine behavior to model what we know about human behavior. (p. 1093)

THE CHAPTERS

The next three chapters explore the nuanced multidimensional interplay between the material and symbolic, and technical and cultural dimensions of academic computing. Chapter 2, "Is Using a Computer Like Driving a Car, Reading a Book, or Solving a Problem?" by Peter Lyman, builds on his earlier ethnographic and phenomenological analyses of computing (see Lyman, 1984, 1988). For the most part, Lyman argues, computers are "rarely revolutionary" (p. 22) in education because they are used to accomplish traditional tasks in a more efficient way (e.g., writing with a typewriter vs. a word processor). Lyman describes three revealing instances from personal experience: a business faculty focus group on computerizing the library, a fifth-grade math class introduced to Logo, and college-level microcomputer literacy courses for novice users. In each case, the computer was introduced into settings where the existing social relations and symbolic meanings actually inhibited—perhaps even precluded—the production of novelty that was technically possible. "What is revolutionary about the computer," he suggests, "is the culture of the machine" (p. 21). As an agent of educational change, the culture of computing has introduced a new skill—problem solving—and its accompanying demands for reshaping certain work relations and attitudes toward technology. The new cultures of problem solving, in particular, imply "alternative ways of thinking about the nature of knowledge (operational vs. theoretical knowledge), its organization (the classroom vs. the workshop), and production (individual work vs. collaborative work)" (p. 34). Is using a computer like driving a car, reading a book, or solving a problem? Lyman suggests that it is all of these—and like a conversation, too. "A computer," he concludes, reflecting on the changing meanings of literacy, "is as much a cultural text as it is a machine, and even a machine is a cultural text in the hands of one who is technically literate" (p. 35).

In chapter 3, "Paradoxical Reactions and Powerful Ideas: Educational Computing in a Department of Physics," Sherry Turkle, whose 1984 book *The Second Self: Computers and the Human Spirit*, became the leading exemplar of the computer-as-symbolically-constructed-object perspective, analyzes the reactions of MIT physicists to Project Athena, perhaps the largest academic computing project ever undertaken. Athena's vision, she writes, conceived and implemented by MIT engineers and computer scientists, amounted to a high-technology "educational experiment without any specific educational thinking or philosophy beyond the idea of creating a technology garden and letting a thousand flowers bloom" (p. 39) (i.e., faculty-inspired instructional computing applications and experiments). In fact, however, many MIT faculty came to believe that the Athena architects really "wanted all the flowers to be roses" (p. 40). Athena's "technocentrism" and "narrowed view of computational and educational diversity" (p. 40) put it on a collision course with the pluralistic departmental computing cultures at MIT. Paradoxically, though, Athena's limitations "spawned a range of unintended cultural developments" (p. 41) touching on pedagogy, epistemology, and academic politics. Turkle focuses in depth on the Department of Physics, traditionally "reticent" about educational computing, yet whose "resistant" and tense partnership with Athena led to some "powerful effects" from "relatively mundane" instructional uses of computers. Athena, however, did "not properly see the physicists' achievements" (p. 42), and most of the Athena-funded physicists believed their successes came despite rather than because of Athena. In several subtle ways, Turkle's chapter reminds one that the computer, as a material *and* a symbolic object, is always "more than 'just' a tool" and that its definition as tool embodies and expresses not only a variety of uses but also an array of meanings.

In what could almost be dubbed, thematically, a companion chapter to Turkle's, chapter 4 by William Graves III, "Ideologies of Computerization," argues that computing can be seen as an arena in which contested "ideologies of computerization play [a critical role] in shaping the direction and outcomes of processes of sociotechnical change in diverse contexts and settings" (p. 68). He defines an ideology of computerization as "an imaginatively constituted understanding of the nature and consequences of using computers that emerges out of decontextualized reflections on the thing-in-itself" (p. 66). Graves focuses on three different cases of computerization: one in a corporate setting—a computerized publishing operation—and the other two in educational settings—an electronic catalog in a university library and a high school hypertext instructional project. A key feature of computerization ideologies is to authorize the notion that "the structure of use mirrors the logic of tools" (p. 71). They "attribute remarkable degrees of agency to machines" (p. 69) comparable to that imputed to human agents, thus conflating the distinction between programmable machine behavior (the logic of tools) and intentional human action (the logic of use). In diverse organizational cultures, particular computerization ideologies (usually reflecting managerial interests) become dominant typically by (falsely) imposing an " 'intrinsic' connection between the institutionally defined logics of work and of the structures and functions of the computing system" (p. 73). Yet, Graves argues, end-users may challenge the dominant ideology through various forms of resistance and counterlegitimation, a process (ironically) overlooked by most critics of management-centered computing designs. A major reason for this oversight is that both social-realist and neo-Marxist approaches to the study of organizational computing fail "to examine carefully and to treat seriously the situated understandings of social actors" (p. 76) and "the phenomenology of [their] computing experience" (p. 85) as they become involved in computerization processes. Graves argues convincingly that "*specific* ideologies of computerization are *essentially* contingent in that nothing intrinsic to . . . specific computing tools, the structure of institutions, the social organization of work, or the character of technology-mediated understanding can prevent the emergence of opposing ideologies that effectively challenge authoritative assumptions about the connection between the logic of technology and the logic of use" (p. 79). Contesting and resisting authoritative ideologies of computerization, Graves implies, are crucial if one is to avoid the stultifying embrace of technocratic rationalization.

The last four chapters examine computing in a variety of specific educational environments and disciplines. In "Stalking the Art Historian" (chapter

5), William O. Beeman explores the nature of art history as an intellectual craft and discipline in order to shed some light on the relatively unexamined subject of scholarly work routines. His analysis—based on "a compendium of observations, autobiographical statements and opinions from 18 prominent art historians, combined with a close study of two 6-month long art history research projects" (p. 92)—was the product of a collaboration between Brown University's Institute for Research in Information and Scholarship and the Getty Art History Information Program. The purpose of this unusual collaboration was to investigate the possibilities for developing and using information technology in art history research. His conclusions are not encouraging to those who believe that appropriately designed computer-based research tools can benefit scholars in any discipline. "Reproduced images seem to be useless for primary scholarly purposes in most cases in art history," he writes, although art historians (like other scholars) could well benefit from "improved international electronic communications" (pp. 101–102). But Beeman points out, "It is hard to know how interpretive processes could be much improved or changed through . . . technological intervention" (p. 102). Indeed, he concludes, "Interfering with the art historian's interpretive processes may well be detrimental to the field" (p. 102). Is art history a uniquely inappropriate discipline for computer enhancement, or does it represent one of several fields in which future technological innovations may find surprising challenges? Beeman's observations suggest that an answer to this question is far less important than an appreciation of the particular norms, practices, and work routines that prestructure scholarly work in any discipline affected by computer technology. Readers interested in following up on Beeman's observations should consult the text of the full study (Bakewell, Beeman, Reese, & Schmitt, 1988).

In chapter 6, "Computers and Pedagogy: The Invisible Presence," Patrick McQuillan poses this question: In courses that incorporate computer-based educational (CBE) materials, is the computer a necessary and unique factor contributing to improved student performance or is it merely a passive carrier of an instructor's pedagogical strategies? Using data gathered in an ethnographic study of a Brown University English literature course—part of that university's Intermedia Project (Beeman et al., 1988)—McQuillan examines the effect of developing hypertext-based materials on an instructor's pedagogy and his students' learning processes and outcomes. He presents an unusual (and fortuitous) quasi-experimental before-and-after comparison of teaching and learning in the course. Although the instructor developed the hypertext materials and was ready to use them in the course, technical problems prevented him from delivering those materials to his students via the expected computer medium (a network of interactive, multitasking workstations). McQuillan's meticulous analysis and interpretation of the data suggest that the computer, in a phrase, is "good to think with." That is, its absence was tantamount to an "invisible presence," insofar as the instructor's pedagogical strategies successfully incorporated the intellectual content and logic, if not the hypertextual format and medium, of the courseware he had developed. "Thus, though Intermedia as a *computer tool* did not produce pedagogical innovation, Intermedia as a *conceptual tool* did" (p. 128). McQuillan concludes with some reflections on the relevance of his case study to the debate about the benefits of CBE. Readers familiar with the works of Landow (1992) and Bolter (1991) on hypertext will find McQuillan's chapter and the one that follows especially pertinent.

James M. Nyce and Gail Bader, in chapter 7, "To Move Away From Meaning: Collaboration, Consensus, and Work in a Hypermedia Project," report on their ethnographic study of two Rhode Island high schools (one a private girls' school, the other public and coed) that were the sites of a pilot project using Apple Macintoshes and Hypercard to enhance the teaching of American history and literature in secondary school curricula. The project— American Culture in Context: Enrichment for Secondary Schools (AC-CESS)—involved four high school teachers not only in the instructional use of an interconnected, interlinked hypermedia corpus but also in its design and development, a model inspired by Brown University's Intermedia Project. Nyce and Bader focus on the teachers' shifting views and assessments of the corpus and its educational values during the last 2 years of the 3-year project, and on the assymetrical relationship between machine-based "links" and knowledge-based "connections" that the links are supposed to represent. The original collaborative model was compromised by the participants' "beliefs about teaching and [about] their subjects, the nature of their particular schools and their students" (p. 136). The authors argue that "the ability to make [Hypercard links] was seductive and to some extent misleading because it hid . . . the need to agree on the meaning (or associations) embedded in those [links]" (p. 136). The teachers' inability to arrive at a pedagogical consensus about which interdisciplinary associations should be taught was replaced by a technical consensus about how links should be made. Although each of the teachers came to this redefinition, none of them was aware of shifts and changes in their own thinking about ACCESS. Nyce and Bader conclude that these unrecognized shifts and changes really reflect tacit, significant, yet unaddressed questions about meaning and significance in the constitution of disciplinary (and interdisciplinary) knowledge. In other words, "trivial" technical discourse and decisions about what Hypercard links can or should be made in a corpus mask an underlying irresolution and ambiguity about the contested epistemological connections that might or could be made to represent meaningful and significant knowledge.

In chapter 8, "The Social Ecology of Student Life: The Integration of Technological Innovation in a Residence Hall," James Larkin, Kenneth Anderson, and Anne McClard describe their ethnographic case study of a

computer network in a freshman residence hall at Brown University in the
late 1980s. Throughout their chapter, one is struck by the seamless web
formed by technology, work, play, and learning in the dorm. Their central
conclusion that "[c]omputers do not seem to revolutionize the way students
live and work but rather fit within existing individual and group social
patterns" (p. 142) is supported by their use of richly detailed sets of qualitative
and quantitative data. Along the way, one learns a great deal about not only
how students use and think about computers, but how the whole texture of
computing depends on the microcultural environment in which it is embedded as well as the temporal, spatial, and interpersonal demands (and
pleasures) of student life. The authors describe the students' subtle and
shifting notions of work, play, learning, and how computers and networking
are integrated into that culturally constructed matrix of practices and meanings. Above all, the authors conclude, "Individual computing choices [of
students] cannot be understood simply as a product of individually defined
motives and interests . . . [but rather are] developed and carried out . . . with
regard to the motives and interests of others" (p. 158). The thick description
in this chapter amply reveals the power of ethnography as a method for
investigating computing and everyday life. And it stands as another cautionary tale for system planners who implicitly presume that a kind of
inherent, unifying technologic can impose a new order of norms and relationships defined by a distinctive sociocultural logic.

In the concluding chapter, "The Legitimation of Academic Computing in
the 1980s," I examine the evidence for an academic computing revolution in
the 1980s and find it thin indeed. Focusing on the Scholar's Workstation
Project at Brown University, a case study that exemplifies the transformative—indeed, utopian—aspirations of academic computing enthusiasts, I
argue that the project articulated a compelling (yet ultimately unattainable)
vision of computing in higher education. The vision embodied a technologically based instrumental idealism that resonated well with American cultural
values and was a normative precondition for legitimating the computerization of academia in the 1980s. Technocratic-managerial decision-making
models of technological diffusion have little relevance in explaining that
process. Weighing the consequences of the so-called revolution, I conclude
that there is almost no evidence for major transformation. Appropriating
Marx's distinction between the means and the social relations of production,
I argue that *"Although there was a computational revolution in the means of academic
production, it was not accompanied by a revolution in the social relations of academic
production"* (p. 175). As access to computer resources has expanded, cross-
institutional inequities have developed; instructional computing has failed to
produce the pedagogical benefits that its proponents promised; professors
still control the curriculum in much the same way as before; administrators
are by-and-large more conservative, technocratic, and entrepreneurial; and

the academic reward system ("publish-or-perish") provides scant incentives (and often major disincentives) for faculty to devote time and attention to instructional computing innovations. "[D]espite unprecedented technical innovations in the means of academic production, the diffusion of microcomputers on American campuses has scarcely reformed, let alone revolutionized, higher education. Instead, probably the net effect thus far has been to reinforce prevailing stratification systems, institutional values, and hierarchies of authority" (p. 181). There is some evidence that the aforementioned trends have contributed to a routinization of academic computing discourse, "a deflationary rhetoric, a contingent pragmatism, a strategy of 'situational adjustment' "—in short, discourses emphasizing "instrumental realism" to counterbalance nearly a decade of idealism. Nevertheless, the concurrent revival of utopian discourse about computer networks suggests that "instrumental idealism and instrumental realism will coexist in dialectical tension" (p. 184).

CLOSING REMARKS

An apt, if infelicitous, alternative subtitle for this volume could have been: "The Unintended Consequences of Purposive Technological Change." With the benefit of hindsight, it is apparent that the computerization of academia in the 1980s failed to produce most of the consequences intended by academic computer revolutionaries. That should not surprise us. Sociotechnical change, in the main, is more unpredictable than predictable, even when intended consequences are intentionally pursued. Indeed, one characteristic that might entitle it to be called an academic computing revolution was its unpredictability. As I argue in this introduction and as the contributors document in the chapters that follow, unpredictability is a consequence of the absence of a technological imperative. And the notion of a technological imperative is itself a reifying background epistemology about how technologies, decontextualized from social relations, supposedly transform elements of social structure and culture. As an antidote to technological reification this volume seeks to recontextualize academic computing within the domains of cultural anthropology and sociology, and thereby exemplify the theoretical fruitfulness of empirically rich sociocultural analyses of technological action.

REFERENCES

Alexander, J. C. (1983). *Theoretical logic in sociology: Vol. 1. Positivism, presuppositions, and current controversies*. Berkeley & Los Angeles: University of California Press.

Alexander, J. C. (1992). The promise of a cultural sociology: Technological discourse and the sacred and profane information machine. In R. Munch & N. J. Smelser (Eds.), *Theory of culture* (pp. 293–323). Berkeley & Los Angeles: University of California Press.

Bakewell, E., Beeman, W. O., Reese, C. M., & Schmitt, M. (General Ed.). (1988). *Object, image, inquiry: The art historian at work.* Santa Monica, CA: The Getty Art History Information Program.

Beeman, W. O., Anderson, K. T., Bader, G., Larkin, J., McClard, A. P., McQuillan, P., & Shields, M. A. (1988). *Intermedia: A case study of innovation in higher education.* Unpublished report to the Annenberg/CPB Project, Brown University, Institute for Research in Information and Scholarship.

Beniger, J. R. (1986). *The control revolution: Technological and economic origins of the information society.* Cambridge, MA: Harvard University Press.

Berger, P. L., & Luckmann, T. (1966). *The social construction of reality: A treatise in the sociology of knowledge.* Garden City, NY: Anchor/Doubleday.

Bijker, W. E., Hughes, T. P., & Pinch, T. J. (Eds.). (1987). *The social construction of technological systems: New directions in the sociology and history of technology.* Cambridge, MA: MIT Press.

Bijker, W. E., & Law, J. (Eds.). (1992). *Shaping technology/building society: Studies in sociotechnical change.* Cambridge, MA: MIT Press.

Bok, D. (1985, May/June). Looking into education's high-tech future. *Harvard Magazine, 29–38.*

Bolter, J. D. (1991). *Writing space: The computer, hypertext, and the history of writing.* Hillsdale, NJ: Lawrence Erlbaum Associates.

Bourdieu, P., & Wacquant, L. J. D. (1992). *An invitation to reflexive sociology.* Chicago: University of Chicago Press.

Card, S. K., Moran, T. P., & Newell, A. (1983). *The psychology of human–computer interaction.* Hillsdale, NJ: Lawrence Erlbaum Associates.

Dolgin, J. L., Kemnitzer, D. S., & Schneider, D. M. (Eds.). (1977). *Symbolic anthropology: A reader in the study of symbols and meanings.* New York: Columbia University Press.

Dunlop, C., & Kling, R. (Eds.). (1991). *Computerization and controversy: Value conflicts and social choices.* San Diego: Academic Press.

Ellul, J. (1964). *The technological society.* New York: Vintage.

Feenberg, A. (1991). *Critical theory of technology.* New York & Oxford: Oxford University Press.

Fiske, E. (1984, May 13). Computers in the groves of academe. *The New York Times Magazine,* pp. 40, 41, 86, 87, 90.

Gale, D. (1983). Cornell's strategy for the microcomputer revolution. *EDUCOM Bulletin, 18*(3/4), 9–11, 15.

Geertz, C. (1973). *The interpretation of cultures.* New York: Basic Books.

Geertz, C. (1983). *Local knowledge: Further essays in interpretive anthropology.* New York: Basic Books.

Giddens, A. (1984). *The constitution of society: Outline of the theory of structuration.* Berkeley & Los Angeles: University of California Press.

Green, K. C. (1991, January/February). A technology agenda for the 1990s [Editorial]. *Change,* p. 6.

Grint, K., & Woolgar, S. (1992). Computers, guns, roses: What's social about being shot? *Science, Technology, & Human Values, 17*(3), 366–380.

Habermas, J. (1987). *The theory of communicative action* (Vol. 2). Boston: Beacon.

Hughes, T. P. (1983). *Networks of power: Electrification in western society, 1880–1930.* Baltimore: Johns Hopkins University Press.

Ihde, D. (1990). *Technology and the lifeworld.* Bloomington: University of Indiana Press.

Joerges, B. (1990). Images of technology in sociology: Computer as butterfly and bat. *Technology and Culture, 31*(2), 203–227.

Kiesler, S. B., & Sproull, L. S. (Eds.). (1987). *Computing and change on campus.* New York: Cambridge University Press.

Kling, R. (1980). Social analyses of computing: Theoretical perspectives in recent empirical research. *Computing Surveys, 12*(1), 61–110.

Kling, R. (1991a). Computerization and social transformation. *Science, Technology, & Human Values, 16*(3), 342–367.

Kling, R. (1991b). Reply to Woolgar and Grint: A preview. *Science, Technology, & Human Values, 16*(3), 379–381.

Kling, R. (1992a). Audiences, narratives, and human values in social studies of technology. *Science, Technology, & Human Values, 17*(3), 349–365.

Kling, R. (1992b). When gunfire shatters bone: Reducing sociotechnical systems to social relationships. *Science, Technology, & Human Values, 17*(3), 381–385.

Kling, R., & Iacono, S. (1988). The mobilization of support for computerization: The role of computerization movements. *Social Problems, 35*(3), 226–243.

Kling, R., & Iacono, S. (1991). Making a "computer revolution." In C. Dunlop & R. Kling (Eds.), *Computerization and controversy: Value conflicts and social choices* (pp. 63–75). San Diego: Academic Press.

Kling, R., & Scacchi, W. (1982). The web of computing: Computer technology as social organization. *Advances in Computers, 21*, 1–90.

Landow, G. P. (1992). *Hypertext: The convergence of contemporary critical theory and technology.* Baltimore: Johns Hopkins University Press.

Lyman, P. (1984). Reading, writing and word processing: Toward a phenomenology of the computer age. *Qualitative Sociology, 7*(1/2), 75–89.

Lyman, P. (1988, March/April). The computer revolution in the classroom: A progress report. *Academic Computing,* pp. 1–5.

MacKenzie, D., & Wajcman, J. (Eds.). (1985). *The social shaping of technology.* Milton Keynes & Philadelphia: Open University Press.

Morell, J. A., & Fleischer, M. (1991). The impact of computer systems: Revolution or incremental change? In J. A. Morell & M. Fleischer (Eds.), *Advances in the implementation and impact of computer systems* (Vol. 1, pp. xii–xxiii). Greenwich, CT: JAI Press.

Nye, D. (1990). *Electrifying America: Social meanings of a new technology, 1880–1940.* Cambridge, MA: MIT Press.

Ortner, S. B. (1973). On key symbols. *American Anthropologist 75*, 1338–1346.

Pacey, A. (1983). *The culture of technology.* Cambridge, MA: MIT Press.

Recession spurs changes in college market for computer technology. (1992, December 9). *The Chronicle of Higher Education*, pp. A15–A16.

Roszak, T. (1986). *The cult of information: The folklore of computers and the true art of thinking.* New York: Pantheon.

Sahlins, M. (1976). Utility and the cultural order. In *Culture and practical reason* (pp. 205–221). Chicago: University of Chicago Press.

Sculley, J. (1989, September). The relationship between business and higher education: A perspective on the 21st century. *Communications of the ACM, 32*(9), 1056–1061.

Segal, H. P. (1985). *Technological utopianism in American culture.* Chicago: University of Chicago Press.

Sewell, W. H., Jr. (1992). A theory of structure: Duality, agency, and transformation. *American Journal of Sociology, 98*(1), 1–29.

Shields, M. A., Graves, W., III, & Nyce, J. M. (1991). Technological innovation in higher education: A case study in academic computing. In J. A. Morell & M. Fleischer (Eds.), *Advances in the implementation and impact of computer systems* (Vol. 1, pp. 183–209). Greenwich, CT: JAI Press.

Shields, M. A., Graves, W., III, & Nyce, J. M. (1992). Computing and the social organization of academic work. *Journal of Science Education and Technology, 1*(4), 243–258.

Tucker, M. S. (1983–1984). The star-wars universities: Brown, CMU, MIT (Computers on Campus: Working Papers). *1983–84 Current Issues in Higher Education, 2*, 3–24.

Turkle, S. (1984). *The second self: Computers and the human spirit.* New York: Simon & Schuster.

U.S. Bureau of the Census. (1991). *Computer use in the United States: 1989.* (Current Population

Reports, Series P-23, No. 171). Washington, DC: U.S. Government Printing Office.

Van Houweling, D. E. (1983). Information processing futures for higher education. *EDUCOM Bulletin, 18*(3/4), 35–40.

Waldrop, M. M. (1985). Personal computers on campus. *Science, 26,* 438–444.

Winner, L. (1986). Mythinformation. In *The whale and the reactor: A search for limits in an age of high technology* (pp. 98–117). Chicago: The University of Chicago Press.

Winner, L. (1993). Social constructivism: Opening the black box and finding it empty. *Science as Culture, 3*(16), 427–452.

Wolfe, A. (1991). Mind, self, society, and computer: Artificial intelligence and the sociology of mind. *American Journal of Sociology, 96*(5), 1073–1096.

Woolgar, S. (1991). The turn to technology in social studies of science. *Science, Technology, & Human Values, 16*(1), 20–50.

Woolgar, S. & Grint, K. (1991). Computers and the transformation of social analysis. *Science, Technology, & Human Values, 16*(3), 368–378.

Zuboff, S. (1988). *In the age of the smart machine: The future of work and power.* New York: Basic Books.

2

Is Using a Computer Like Driving a Car, Reading a Book, or Solving a Problem? The Computer as Machine, Text, and Culture

Peter Lyman
The University of Southern California

What kind of tool is a computer, that we expect it to be an agent of change? A tool is conventionally thought to be an object which is animated by human expertise. But this tool is has already given its name to this historic era, "the computer revolution," is named after a human mental capability, "computation," and is often called a "brain." Yet computers are only machines, and in higher education, are ordinarily used as a medium for writing and communication, not computation. What makes this tool an agent of change, or revolutionary?

Certainly the presence of a machine in higher education has not been revolutionary since the industrial revolution. It would not be surprising if a machine which changes the skills which are fundamental to education—computation, writing, and communication—were revolutionary. Yet it is perfectly possible to replace a typewriter with a personal computer and word processing program without changing the organization of educational work or its content.

But two aspects of this machine are new: it is a symbolic engine, using words and numbers to communicate with its user, thus it is the only machine that we must read; and because it uses symbols it contains a culture, and is a medium for introducing new practices and values into the traditional cultures of higher education.

The computer, both hardware and software, contains two distinctive kinds of educational cultures, derived from engineering: (a) the understanding of creative work as the product of a workshop in which work is collaborative; and (b) the understanding of knowledge as procedure and performance, rather than as fact or theory. Thus, the culture of the computer is changing the definition of a text into a group product or resource, not the personal property of an individual author. It is creating new kinds of texts, such as databases or hypertext. And it is changing the relationship between writing, editing, and publishing. These changes are not discrete; they are the consequence of a new educational culture, the culture of problem solving.

THE COMPUTER AS MACHINE AND AS TEXT

Let us initially explore the nature of the computer as a tool by engaging in a short thought experiment, comparing our engagement with computers to other tools which we engage in skilled ways. Is using a computer more like driving a car or reading a book?

It is hard to learn to drive, but in time the many laws that govern the road, habits that govern the car's machinery, and social forms that shape the culture of driving settle into a subsidiary awareness, and the mind can focus on other things or daydream, at least until something unusual happens to recall the focal awareness of conscious attention to the problem of driving. It is also hard to learn to read a book, but although the interpretation of printed signs eventually settles into subsidiary awareness, the focal awareness often enters into a kind of dialogue with an author. As our hands effortlessly turn pages and eyes scan the words in a kind of physical performance, the printed page becomes a medium for thinking. This picture leads to the definition of car and book as different kinds of objects: one engaging the body, the other engaging the mind; one requiring physical skill, the other requiring cultural skills.

Such a picture is somewhat misleading, being based on an arbitrary opposition between human attention and the artifacts we have made and use. There are many ways people might engage a tool, whatever its design or function, whether smart or inanimate. A recent car accident might make a driver painfully aware of the rules of the road, and a mechanic might listen to a car engine with a diagnostic mind that in some sense is engaging in a dialogical or literate relation with a machine. Or proofreader or typist might see only signs on the printed page, not ideas, or a bored student might daydream while reading. Although we are always free to daydream, it is when we engage with tools in dialogical thought, as when we read, that the tools might have the power to bring about the intellectual and social changes that are implied in phrases like "the computer revolution."

And it is possible that computers might have the power to change us even when we engage with them unconsciously, as when we relate to a tool through the performance of a skill like driving or typing. Although skills are tacit and embodied forms of knowledge, they are still forms of knowledge. As Michael Polanyi (1958) defined skill, "The aim of a skillful performance is achieved by the observance of a set of rules which are not known as such to the person following them" (p. 49). Although skills are ordinarily tacit forms of knowledge, we become aware of them as knowledge when we are learning to use tools or when tools are broken. This is true in a trivial way with a tool like a typewriter because a typist rarely fixes a typewriter, but fixing a car requires a diagnostic sense of the machine and a mode of action that resembles a performance in its marriage of thought and action.

Like other machines, computers may be used to discipline human activities, but unlike other machines they also *informate*, "generating new streams of information" that require human responses (Zuboff, 1988, p. 9). A smart technology provides even more extensive opportunities for "reading the machine" the way one might read a book. Although this distinction is necessary to the concept of a computer revolution, it is not sufficient because even smart machines may be treated like machines; even today most computers are used as efficient typewriters, not smart machines. Thus, an essential component of the definition of a skill is cultural and intellectual and is contained in a conceptual model that defines and regulates our relationship to the machine (cf. Young, 1981).

What is revolutionary about the computer is the culture of the machine. Computers are both machine and text, in that the logic of the machine is literally a text that has been instantiated in microcode. Nearly every novice begins by treating computers as machines, in using the typewriter as a conceptual model, but soon either learns the need to engage the machine as text in a problem-solving behavior or becomes furious that the machine is making demands upon his or her attention. In many ways computer experts treat a computer like musicians treat a musical instrument: an artifact that is properly an extension of the body and mind; a medium governed by a written code that is not merely operated but requires a virtuoso performance governed by a sense of timing and personal expression and that is almost always part of a collaborative social experience.

And finally, tools are not randomly distributed in society, nor are kinds of relationships to tools: There is a sociology of tools, suggested by the fact that some schools teach "keyboard skills" to students and other schools teach "programming tools," or that some computers are used to supervise and discipline human work and others are designed to empower the worker. Thus, although the printed book was initially defined as a mass produced version of the manuscript, considered sociologically the book was more than a more efficient means to a traditional end, for it made possible a cultural transformation by so increasing storage and distribution of knowledge that it made possible a middle class of mental laborers. The analysis of technology requires more than "the history of a technique," in the words of Febvre and

Martin, for the print revolution "has to do with the effect on European culture of a new means of communicating ideas within a society that was essentially aristocratic . . . an elite which, apart from the aristocracy of blood, included those who had moneyed wealth, political position or prestigious intellectual reputations. How did the printed book facilitate the rule and the activity of these men?" (1976, p. 12)

In the analysis of a technology, one must reflect upon the society whose purposes are reflected in the design of the tool and in the way a tool is used to distribute and redistribute discipline and power. The mainframe computer brought cybernetic command and control to the military and to large hierarchical corporations. This heritage is reflected in the keyboard of the microcomputer with its control key and command structures, even as the microcomputer is used to decentralize information and organization.

To return to the question: Which kind of tool is a computer, and in which ways do people engage with computers that they expect them to be a medium of educational change? Like the print and industrial revolutions, the image of the computer revolution suggests that a new technology is an agent of change. For the reasons suggested previously, I analyze the computer as an agent of intellectual change from the point of view of a new skill, the skill of problem solving. Theorists about the computer often treat problem solving as a mental activity, epitomized by the skill required in playing chess (cf. Newell & Simon, 1963). Just as focusing on chess as a logical activity ignores the fact that the exercise of this skill occurs within and requires a social relation, a contest between two players, so thinking about problem solving as a mental activity ignores the social context within which it is practiced, that I define as a workshop relationship between master and apprentice. In exploring the ways that computers encourage educational change, I focus on the nature of the skills that are introduced and the social relations within which those skills are exercised.

TECHNOLOGY AND SOCIAL CONTEXTS

I have been observing campus computing as an ethnographer for the past 8 years to discover how and when information technologies introduce fundamental changes in the organization of educational work and how and when do they fail to do so. Because computers are generally used as a more efficient means to a traditional task, they are rarely revolutionary. Computers are often used as typewriters that do not penalize revision, as more powerful calculators, as a communications medium more spontaneous than a letter but more formal than the telephone, or as a more powerful card catalog. In these cases, the possibilities of reorganizing work are limited by conceptual models derived from print and by a need to protect authoritative relationships at work. These dynamics are illustrated by three examples from my fieldnotes in which computer technology has failed to change educational settings.

The computer is an object whose social definition is being contested in these encounters: It may be defined as a machine, or tool, or as "an object to think with." Embedded in these definitions are different visions of social relations, of work, and ultimately of knowledge.

The Faculty Focus Group

A group of senior faculty in a major business school were asked to help plan the information technologies for a new building and library. To begin the focus group discussion, the faculty were shown two videotapes that depicted what the technologies of the future might look like, one a hypertext-based multimedia windowing system, the other a portable computer with an electronic research assistant. The discussion that followed was instructive but not very futuristic.

The faculty viewed computers as machines not as "productivity tools," because new tools imply the necessity to learn new skills, that was perceived to be a distraction from the content of scholarly work. To the extent that computers require intellectual attention, the way a book does, they take time away from the content of scholarly work. Technology was defined as "efficient" only to the extent that it would retreat to subsidiary awareness, like a machine. Thus, these professors often still used the first computer and word processing software they had learned.

The faculty's conceptual models for interpreting the possible role of new technologies in their work were derived from their current social relationships to support staff—librarians, research assistants, and secretaries—not their relationships to machines. After viewing the "knowledge navigator," a computer that acts as a secretary, one faculty member commented that he would still prefer a human secretary, but if it would be too expensive, he would accept an electronic assistant. Another commented that the danger of new technologies is that they upset the authority structures that govern the office; for example, a networked laser printer would give secretaries equal priority with faculty.

These two orientations towards computers—that computers should be "cars" not "books" and that computers essentially automate services better provided by people—merged in the idea that a new mission for the library was to train graduate students in the use of new technologies. Technological change was viewed as generational, not part of a lifelong process of learning like reading.

The Fifth Grade

Last year my daughter's fifth-grade teacher invited me to teach a class on Logo, the computer language the children had been studying that year. Seymour Papert created Logo, and in *Mindstorms* (1980) described Logo as a playful environment within which children can be empowered as learners by programming a turtle to draw interesting shapes. Implicitly Logo lets children explore the world of mathematics in an environment that encourages experimentation. *Mindstorms* makes it clear that Logo is more than a new tool for teaching mathematics, it is intended to encourage a revolutionary pedagogy that fundamentally changes the role of teachers and challenges their monopoly of right answers.

I began the class by describing Papert to the children, so that they could get a sense that computers are not just machines but are also texts that reflect the purposes and personality of their creators. I began to ask the children about the command vocabulary of Logo, to make sure that they understood how to use the language. I asked them to solve a few problems, showed them how to pace out geometric shapes to get new ideas, and asked them how they would create the primitives if they didn't exist. As they gathered Papert's purposes, the children became excited, turning classroom space into a workshop as they paced out shapes to figure out command sequences, engaging in group discussions.

Only one child had understood Logo as a problem-solving environment as Papert intended it to be, a place free of the pedagogical structures that inhibit their own natural explorations of mathematical problems. For most, however, Logo consisted of a series of computer commands and not a medium for ideas. Thus, when I asked the class how to make the turtle disappear, they were stumped, until one girl thought of the command "penup." She had translated Logo into a task, like memorizing multiplication tables. It was not a metaphor, it was a machine.

It is not that the children lacked imagination, but they had no conceptual models for making machines an environment for play and were not used to working in school without instructions or supervision. Logo had been presented to them within a culture of schoolwork, in this case, as a class assignment structured by the social relationships typical of fifth grade pedagogy. Problem solving was not part of the school pedagogy, not only because it does not fit the "right answer, wrong answer" structure of school knowledge but also because the school's ratio of one teacher to 36 students precluded the kind of workshop consulting that Logo requires. Rather than changing the school, Logo was transformed into school knowledge, a set of tasks to be memorized, because the social organization of the classroom and the authority relation between teacher and children could not be changed.

Computer Literacy Courses

Computer literacy courses were initially an encounter between technical culture that regards microcomputer technology as a revolutionary social force, and faculty who regard the computer instrumentally as a tool or machine.

Computer experts call the knowledge that enables them to assert mastery over the computer "problem solving." Problem solving includes heuristics ("powerful ideas"), attitudes about control ("giving commands"), and social relations ("consulting") that transform the relationship between human and machine from work into play. Experts learn problem solving in a workshop environment in which they form apprentice relationships to one another. Yet when they teach novices to use computers, they often create a pedagogy they would not tolerate for themselves, teaching in classrooms and assigning written documentation. In consequence, experts are perplexed that novices treat the computer like machines rather than as a source of pleasure and often seem disappointed that the introduction of the computer seems to have little revolutionary impact on the work of the faculty.

Yet the faculty themselves were more comfortable in classrooms; like students everywhere, they found that the social distance from their teachers protected them from humiliation. (Several commented that it was probably good for their own teaching that they were reminded what it was like to be a student again, one commented, "You look around and all the other boys are the most famous professors you know.")

And like students everywhere, their pedagogical goals were different from those of the experts. Experts define problem solving as the skill of learning skills, not simply as the acquisition of a new skill. The more the learner is focused on learning specific tasks, the less transferrable the skill to new settings. In approaching the computer as a means to a work related task, like word processing, novices take an instrumental approach that leaves them without strategies for coping with unexpected events or for learning new computer software.

Computers and Social Relations

In each case, computers implied new social relations that were in tension with those of the educational settings into which they were introduced. In the first case, computers were not socially neutral: they were a substitute for humans and were defined as appropriate for certain social roles belonging to young faculty and graduate students, signifying their lack of resources to hire human support staff. In the second and third cases, computers were intended as a medium for the introduction of technical pedagogy, problem solving, into educational settings with other pedagogies.

SKILLS AS KNOWLEDGE AND PERFORMANCE

Problem solving is not information that is necessary to make a machine work or to use the computer in an instrumental way as a tool; it is an attitude

toward technology that profoundly questions our conventional understanding of our relationship to machines and our notions of learning and
knowledge itself. As a skill, problem solving requires the willingness to
restructure work itself as much as the ability to manipulate a technology to
serve work; it is this, more than the nature of computers, that is the obstacle
in each of these cases.

We tend to underestimate the importance of skills because by their nature
skills become unconscious or tacit forms of knowledge. Michael Polanyi
described swimmers who unconsciously yet skillfully keep themselves afloat
by regulating their breathing—not emptying their lungs when breathing out
and inflating them more than usual when breathing in. One expert swimmer
tried to discover what made him swim and was puzzled to discover that
"whatever he tried to do in the water, he always kept afloat" (1958, p. 49).

Technical skills are a kind of performance requiring that theoretical principles be transformed into embodied practices, so that mindful attention can
be directed toward the task at hand, not toward the tool. Thus, technical skills
are accomplished by practicing rules that are not known as such to the person
following them. As a kind of "know-how," skills are not subject to the rules
of verification that gives knowledge structure and validity. Skills have low
prestige in academic settings for this reason, although computing often finds
a home in the performing and plastic arts because of the kinship in attitude
concerning skills. Problem solving requires a willingness to engage with an
artifact in a skilled dialogue that raises the tacit dimension of know-how to
critical examination.

Broken Tools or Objects to Think With?

To users with only an instrumental interest, tools become invisible as they are
used because they disappear from attention; as attention is focused upon the
task at hand (as the eye fixes upon the nail, not the hammer), the tool tacitly
becomes an extension of the body. After the use of the tool has become
habitual, it becomes an object of attention only when it doesn't work, and we
think of it as broken. One novice said, "The computer is like a car. I don't
want to pay any attention to it; if it doesn't work, I'll take it to someone who
can fix it." Yet the tool that the novice defines as "broken" is defined by an
expert as "a problem," an object of analytic attention.

When the tool becomes visible to a novice, the tacit expectation of invisi-
bility has been violated, and the response is often anxiety, frustration, or rage.
The anger directed at computers reveals much about the human–tool relationship; if anger is awakened by a violation of one's sense of justice or
self-esteem by another, how is it possible that a computer is tacitly given the
agency necessary to arouse anger? Because we experience tools as extensions
of our body, their "disobedience" has the power to resonate with the disorder

we feel in our selves and our lives (Turkle, 1980). The anger of novices is the most distinct point of vulnerability for both user and expert. One consultant told me:

> People often come here with a high level of anxiety because they have a problem they can't solve; but although they are frustrated they don't seem to get angry too often. There are a few exceptions, and they really hurt. You don't want to go back to work the next day. Programmers and technical services people don't ever have to face that.

But most fundamentally, most people only want to "use" tools and not to think about them; to nonexperts, thinking about tools is a distraction from the problem presented by the content of the work.

To the expert, the computer is never broken; it presents problems to be solved. Problem solving is essentially a process of communication with an "other," although one that interacts rather than speaks. Seymour Papert described tools as "objects to think with," not just to use. This is how he described playing with gears in his childhood in an attempt to understand the mathematical ratios that governed them:

> Before I was two years old I had developed an intense involvement with automobiles. The names of car parts made up a substantial portion of my vocabulary: I was particularly proud of knowing about the parts of the trans-mission system, the gearbox, and most especially the differential. . . . Playing with gears became a favorite pastime. I loved rotating circular objects against one another in gearlike motions . . . I became adept at turning wheels in my head and at making chains of cause and effect: "This one turns this way so that must turn that way, so . . ." (Papert, 1980, p. vi)

This kind of play consists of an attentive search for clues to illuminate the laws that govern the mechanism and is the essence of the inductive reasoning of problem solving. It is the essence of problem solving that differentiates it from asking questions but gives it kinship with playing games and music. It is a kind of performance that unifies order and spontaneity. And, in fact, this is the pedagogical core of problem solving, for it defines knowledge opera-tionally, in terms of the procedures necessary to produce knowledge, not theoretically or in terms of its content.

Whereas a machine has a purpose built into its mechanism, and a tool requires the novice to acquire skill to realize this purpose, a computer is a field of play only to an expert. One teacher of computer literacy to faculty groups told me, "Humanists will use it as a tool, not get into programming, that is, as a plaything. They will use the computer as a tool, not as a source of pleasure. Programming gives one access to the computer as a plaything, as a source of gratification. The pleasure is getting something to work."

The novices most successful in learning the computer were performing arists—creative writers, poets, painters, musicians, dancers. Their conceptual models were acts of performance rather than objects produced. All thought of themselves as craftsmen, not scholars, and had learned their craft by example in workshops. One told me, "The computer is threatening to scholars because they want to conserve the traditional forms of knowledge; as artists we want to change them." Yet there is a sense of craft in all forms of scholarship that resembles the engagement between Papert and gears, as one English professor described:

> I love script, manuscript, and handwriting. I write letters longhand when I really do want to communicate with someone. I love the physical process: I like to write, physically. I like shaping my paragraphs and sentences on the page. I revise and insert endlessly on the page and I get a pleasure, a sort of sculptural pleasure, out of inserting and revising with my hands. I love the words that I use, and like to have immediate contact with them. I love the English language and love the words as they are, letter by letter, and the shape of them, and how I make them when I write them. And I don't want to lose touch with that.

There are obvious differences between a mathematical engagement with gears and a linguistic engagement with words that parallel the differences between scientific and humanistic cultures. For one thing, the love of language is not only sculptural (a love that is disrupted by the mechanistic discipline of the keyboard). All written words are potentially spoken and thus potentially human communications. And, although every machine also reflects its culture of origin, it remains mute even when used, thus is only in the social world as a silent presence.

Problem Solving as Play

Experts and children both often approach learning the computer by defining it as an object for play. Children often focus on the computer program as a field for play, exploring in a random way but forming a picture organized around their own experiments. Problem-solving children learn to beat computer games by losing, discovering when and where the program is "dumb" or predictable. Given the information that in WordStar Control-K will "kill" a word, one child tried out the whole alphabet as commands to see which worked and what they did, building a inductive picture of the program (including its undocumented features).

Play, then, is an inductive mode of learning, whereas work or school tends to be deductive. One high school student described playing on an Apple II during lunch everyday and told me, "It was the only time I was allowed to define my own problems and discover how to solve them in four years."

When the computer is defined solely as an instrument for production, the user focuses upon learning only the information that is a means to that end. Problem solvers might begin exploring with a picture of the tasks the computer is to do but explore the limits of each command. Told that DOS requires a date, one novice who became a problem solver began by exploring the limits of the dates MS DOS would recognize in order to understand its syntax.

The physical and mental engagement produced by skill and attention to clues produces a feeling of integration that experts call play and that they compare to playing music or playing with games. This feeling of "flow" is an experience of intense concentration and a distinct slowing of time sense that is produced by a feeling of control and pursuit of a noncontradictory goal (Csikszentmihayli, 1979, p. 260). This kind of engagement is not play in the sense of spontaneous activity, it is a feeling of control that is possible when playing games in which the player's attention is focused within an environment of a known set of rules that have been mastered. Problem solving is a kind of game to experts, a "field" of rule-governed play that is a contest for mastery between their skill and the machine.

Several of the computer programmers were also musicians, and said that making music served as a powerful metaphor for their relationship to the computer. In performance, the musical instrument and player interact in a manner that cannot accurately be described as a human–tool relation. Sudnow commented, "If I watch my hands on a typewriter I don't recognize their movements . . . but the sight of my piano-playing hands is familiar" (Sudnow, 1978, p. xi). Problem solving is performance, whether it is a matter of fixing the program or creating a program, and in performance the tool never entirely becomes tacit.

A performance is always a social act, even when the medium is silicon. I interviewed a group of computer center programmers who have written a mainframe operating system that has been adapted over the years to a wide variety of individual user's needs. Because it was an interdependent system, each partial solution had created greater systemic inconsistency. When one programmer was asked to explain its organization, he told a series of stories rather than introducing any global organizational principles. Each story consisted of a catastrophic system failure, the programmer who had been assigned to fix it, and the clever solution he had invented. *As a whole, the operating system had a history rather than a structure.* The history of fixes is displayed onscreen on each module and roughly parallels the status system of the members of the programming group. Because the system consists of a history of fixes, documentation is often not very helpful in solving problems with a mainframe system: The documented features of a system are only the solutions that the operators consider reliable tools, not the undocumented features that are powerful but may pose problems for nonexperts.

Central to all of these dimensions of skill is the operational definition of knowledge as performance, without an experience of separation between performer and tool or content and procedure. Computer knowledge is *operational knowledge* in that the content of knowledge cannot be separated from the program with which it is produced. The concept of performance also suggests why there is a kinship between computer technology and the arts and why computers and the arts are estranged from the humanistic disciplines. This is illustrated by Papert's comment that in some respects "scientific knowledge is more similar to knowing a person than similar to knowing a fact or having a skill" (Papert, 1980, p. 135).

PROBLEM SOLVING AS COLLABORATIVE WORK

If computer skills are understood to be operational knowledge enacted in a performance, then in an important sense technical knowledge must be taught by example. Although the rules governing technical knowledge are taught in schools, they are often taught from a theoretical point of view and deductive method that devalues the tacit embodied knowledge and the aesthetic dimensions of expert performances. Problem solving consists in part of connoisseurship, an aesthetic dimension of judgment learned by example and applied by instinct; the idea of "an elegant solution" or "powerful idea" are examples. These aesthetic judgments represent the instinctive form in which the tacit rules that govern performance, but are not consciously attended to as rules, are enacted. Thus, even when taught by example in workshops, technical expertise is taught by experts for whom expertise is a performance based upon tacit knowledge that they themselves may not accurately be able to describe (cf. Feigenbaum & McCorduck, 1983, pp. 81–83).

How, then, is problem solving learned? When asked to define problem solving, one expert answered, "knowing how to ask questions." Problem solving as knowing how to ask questions, grows within a social setting within which learners can discover their own problems and find experts willing to teach them. Becker (1972) contrasted three aspects of on-the-job learning to learning in schools:

(i) The apprentice is thrown into the "tangled complexity" of the work from the first day, instead of being introduced to knowledge in a logical order and from a theoretical perspective within a classroom.

(ii) Apprentices make a curriculum for themselves by choosing problems from those ready at hand in the workplace; in schools the curriculum is defined by the experts, and problems presented with solutions in a step by step manner.

(iii) In a workshop, training is left to the apprentice's own initiative; "If an apprentice is any good he will make you teach him."

When asked to describe what he needed in order to learn a new system, one of the experts told me, "One should have a teacher to ask questions of now and again." In a genuine apprentice relationship a novice finds problems and teachers in a diffuse way by hanging around the work.

Problem solving is not simply the mastering of a skill but learning how to master skills; thus, there are no firm institutional roles of master and apprentice. Within computer centers, problem solving is taught and learned by consulting, the social relation established when one person asks another for help. In one of the computer centers I studied, it was well known that "Jeff," who had the reputation of being the best programmer in the group, was available to answer questions when he was smoking a cigarette in the hall; when he was in his office, he was working. A consulting relation is established when one expert becomes an apprentice by asking another for help, "Could you come take a look at what is happening?"

Consulting is a voluntary relationship established between peers for the purpose of learning and is governed by rules of appropriate learning and teaching behavior. Although formally equal, consulting communities are ruled by status hierarchies created by knowledge and pranks. Pranks, which generally involve programming tricks that must be solved in order to access one's computer files, are the way programmers test each other's status claims. Those best at problem solving have the highest status and are quickly promoted.

Consulting developed as a relationship between technical experts both within computer centers and with experts outside; it has become a general pedagogical strategy for. teaching technical skills. Asking for help is not considered a mark of inferiority in computer centers, as long as it doesn't happen too often or the problems are inappropriately simple.

One expert told me that people from the humanities seemed to find asking for help a kind of humiliation:

> As much as they need the help, many of the humanists have trouble asking for help"
> *Why do you think so?*
> Perhaps they feel they ought to know. Do they turn to other kinds of professionals when they need help? Do they ask questions of reference librarians? I don't know what they are used to doing when they need help.

This expert argued that one of the major differences between technicians and humanists was that technicians knew they were dependent upon each other. Consulting functions best as a peer relation, as in user groups in which information and techniques are shared between people with the same kind of computer and software. For example, one faculty member wandered into another's office, watched him write for a while, and then said, "Do you know how to set tabs?" "No," the other said. "You'll need that pretty soon," the friend said and showed him how.

Demonstrations are a pedagogical compromise between classroom instruction and consulting. In demonstrations, the consulting relation is reversed: The teacher acts, the students observe; however, the students pose questions, and the teacher demonstrates problem solving behavior as well as gives answers. Typically, the class consisted of lectures on the commands necessary to work the program, handing out written documentation, and demonstrations followed by question and answer periods. When asked a question, "What would happen if you said . . .," the instructor said, "Let's see," rather than answering directly and tried out the student's approach. If it worked, he yelled, "Pow!" and swung his fist in the air. If the experiment failed, he diagnosed what might have happened and demonstrated how one might figure out how to make it work. When I asked the instructor why he taught this way, he said, "I'm really only comfortable teaching in a consulting mode." Another said, "I just want the class to understand that there's basically nothing you can do which is going to hurt anything . . . except your sense of efficiency."

Problem solving is first of all the ability to recognize a problem and secondly, the ability to define it in a way that leads to a solution. In the words of one expert, novices "tend to think they're in trouble when they aren't, or that they aren't in trouble when they are." Between "false alarms" and "garden paths" is the kind of attention to clues that may well be a kind of "feel." To name a problem well requires a sense of the difference between the normal trouble a computer user might experience and of unusual trouble. Having asked for help and having named the problem, the apprentice sits down at his workstation and shows the problem to the master, who stands behind watching. The coach observes the practice of the learner rather than question in an explicit way that would create a kind of authority that computer experts try to avoid. The purpose of this pedagogy is to let the apprentice discover the solution as is illustrated by this interview question:

> *When you consult, you put the student at the workstation and watch over their shoulder. Why?*
>
> I can see when the student is about to make a mistake and can choose to let the problem occur. We let them make only the mistakes they can learn from. If you let the student see the problem, you can help them learn how to correct it perhaps give advice about how to solve it.

Advice might consist of restating the problem by giving the minimal information necessary to let the apprentice discover the solution, pointing out a clue, or introducing a "powerful idea." A "powerful idea" is essentially a conceptual model for problem solving; one expert defined powerful ideas as "simple notions that let you do a lot of things in a lot of different contexts." A typical powerful idea might be the "stepwise procedure" by which problems are analyzed, a procedure that isolates one variable at a time. One expert showed a novice how to make a printer work by changing the ribbon, then replacing the ribbon in place and printing a file, then printing the same file on another printer until the trouble was isolated.

Thus, problem solving is a mental skill that requires a social context that might be called consulting and that occurs within a workshop setting. In introducing computing into the curriculum, one introduces problem solving both as skill and as social relation; the former is explicit, the latter is implicit and, as described previously, requires a reorganization of work. This may occur at an epistemological level as well, when operational knowledge replaces theoretical knowledge. It is most likely to become visible at a political level, when the formally egalitarian and achievement-oriented culture of the workshop comes in conflict with hierarchical settings such as the classroom.

CONCLUSION

If we are living in the era of a "knowledge revolution" or are entering an "information society," what is more likely to change than the institutions of higher education which produce and consume knowledge and information? Although the information management capabilities of computers have made possible multinational corporations, and their analytic and imaging capabilities have made possible scientific and engineering breakthroughs, thus far relatively few changes have occurred in the practices of creating knowledge or teaching it or in the organization of higher education. But social changes are not made by tools in and of themselves; many revolutionary technical ideas have not made for social change in the past, because they were in fundamental conflict with their social contexts. In the conclusion, I review some of the ways that computer technologies are raising new issues for education.

What is a Computer Revolution?

Although it is popular to think of technical change as social progress—to think of a digital society now replacing a print society just as centuries earlier a print society replaced an oral society—this picture fundamentally distorts the nature of real choices. Today spoken, print and digital communication coexist together. The problem is to learn how to choose wisely between the knowledge media with which one might communicate: when to speak face to face, when to write, when to use E-mail, when to use the telephone. What are the strengths and costs of different media as representations of truth? Which information do they communicate well; which information do they sacrifice?

Similarly at an institutional level the organization of knowledge must be reconsidered. Up to now the organization of learning has had a spatial location that is a haven from the world of work—classroom, the library, and the campus itself. But the possibility of storing knowledge digitally and distributing it on networks might separate the process of learning from these traditional sites. Both at an individual and institutional level computer technologies suggest fundamental changes in the organization of daily life. The culture of problem solving suggests some alternative ways of thinking about the nature of knowledge (operational vs. theoretical knowledge), its organization (the classroom vs. the workshop), and production (individual work vs. collaborative work). The culture of problem solving may not be the final culture of an information society, but at present it is defining the terms of debate with the institutions based upon print.

Is Know-How Knowledge?

The culture of problem solving is in tension with the present emphasis upon giving knowledge a theoretical foundation but reinforces those disciplines in which knowledge is founded upon practice or performance.

The ethos of problem solving in computer centers is the spiritual descendent of the tinkering of inventors at the turn of the century. Like Ford and Edison, many computer experts are inventors more than scientists; tinkerers practiced the art of invention by bricolage, not through the systematic rule-govered experimentation of science. Problem solving is a more sophisticated understanding of technical thinking than is tinkering, but the two share the view that the process of thinking is founded in a task orientation; this epistemological orientation has recently become the foundation of expert systems research (Newell & Simon, 1963, p. 280).

Tinkering as such does not produce systematic knowledge, for problems are not defined by intellectual criteria but by the failure of a tool to work. Thus, a solution is likely to be local and may well create inconsistency in the system as a whole. This is the cause of tension between "hackers" and computer scientists, who promote "structured programming" (Turkle, 1980; Weizenbaum, 1976). Computer experts reject authority based upon academic credentials or institutional order and give status to master practitioners of "the hack" (cf. Levy, 1984, pp. 26–36), the ability to fix problems. When asked to define the most distinctive characteristic needed for technical work, one group of computer center managers answered, "flexibility," defined as the ability to master new technologies without formal training by using problem-solving skills. Thus, computer center staffs often include experts without graduate credentials or more frequently, experts who have changed careers and bring professional credentials from other fields of expertise. Computer centers have cultures of their own, balancing the task orientation and time structure of creative work, often at night. Yet increasingly computer centers are subjected to the discipline of a profession with standard work procedures, daytime office hours, and organizational structure of the office (cf. Levy, 1984; Turkle, 1984). For all of these reasons, computer center experts have an anomolous position in the organizational structure of the university between academic departments and data processing departments and the ambiguous status of "problem-solving expertise" itself between craft knowledge and science.

Historically, institutions of higher learning claimed a monopoly of the right to certify degrees by placing craft knowledge on a scientific basis, replacing tinkering with experimentation and pragmatic results with theory. This in part also justifies the pedagogy of higher education, primarily teaching by lecturing to students who do not gain practical experience in their fields until they leave the institution and go to work. Of course, this domination of practice by theory is not absolute, because science courses and arts courses have laboratory components. And it is precisely in these fields that the problem-solving culture of computing has been most likely to resonate and produce new pedagogies.

The Computer as Machine, Text, and Culture

Which kind of tool is a computer, and in which ways do people engage with computers that they expect them to be a medium of educational change?

The computer suggests that a picture of history as a dialectic of nature and culture is fundamentally flawed. Intelligent artifacts like the computer are both object and culture and are becoming a dominant feature in the human environment. Using a computer is both like driving a car and reading a book and for that matter, like a conversation with another person. A computer is as much a cultural text as it is a machine, and even a machine is a cultural text in the hands of one who is technically literate.

The greatest challenge that the presence of intelligent artifacts poses to education is the reconsideration of the meaning of the word literacy. Part of this redefinition, as is implied previously, is reuniting the relationship between theory and practice and grounding educational knowledge in doing and making things as well as reading and talking about things. Such a reunion would have two other important consequences. First, it would recognize the truth that knowledge is a social product by bringing legitimacy to collaborative work, although this would require fundamental change in the system of intellectual property that is focused on individual ownership (cf. Lyman, 1984, 1988). Second, it would reduce the dependency of learning upon a separation between the social world of work and educational worlds based on campuses and thereby encourage the development of skills with which life-long learning might occur.

REFERENCES

Becker, H. S. (1972). A school is a lousy place to learn anything in. *The American Behavioral Scientist, 16*(1), 85–105.

Csikszentmihayli, M. (1979). The concept of flow. In B. Sutton-Smith (Ed.), *Play and learning* (pp. 257–274). New York: Gardner Press.

Febvre, L., & Martin, H. (1976). *The coming of the book* (D. Gerard, Trans.). London: Verso Editions.

Feigenbaum, E. A., & McCorduck, P. (1983). *The fifth generation.* Reading, MA: Addison-Wesley.

Levy, S. (1984). *The hackers.* New York: Doubleday.

Lyman, P. (1984). Reading, writing, and word processing. *Qualitative Sociology, 7*(1/2), 75–89.

Lyman, P. (1988). Sociological literature in an age of computerized texts. *The American Sociologist, 19*(1), 16–30.

Newell, A., & Simon, H. A. (1963). GPS, a program that simulates human thought. In E. A. Feigenbaum & J. Feldman (Eds.), *Computers and thought* (pp. 279–293). New York: McGraw-Hill.

Papert, S. (1980). *Mindstorms.* New York: Basic Books.

Polanyi, M. (1958). *Personal knowledge.* Chicago: University of Chicago Press.

Sudnow, D. (1978). *The ways of the hand.* New York: Simon & Schuster.

Turkle, S. (1980). Computer as Rorschach. *Society, 17*(2), 15–24

Turkle, S. (1984). *The second self: Computers and the human spirit.* New York: Simon & Schuster.

Weizenbaum, J. (1976). *Computer power and human reason.* San Francisco: W. H. Freeman.

Young, R. M. (1981). The machine inside the machine: Users' models of pocket calculators. *International Journal of Man–Machine Studies, 15*, 51–85.

Zuboff, S. (1988). *In the age of the smart machine.* New York: Basic Books.

3

Paradoxical Reactions and Powerful Ideas: Educational Computing in a Department of Physics

Sherry Turkle
Massachusetts Institute of Technology

PROLOGUE: THE ATHENA AESTHETIC

Massachusetts Institute of Technology (MIT) has been known for its contributions to computer science since the 1950s. MIT scientists were central to the early development of cybernetics; its graduates founded computer companies that made Boston's Route 128 an internationally recognized center of research and development. However, even by 1980, MIT had not yet confronted the challenge of using computers to do its own job: the use of computers in university education.

In some ways this was surprising. MIT had made an early commitment to research on the use of the computer as a cognitive tool. In the early 1960s, its Project Mac developed time sharing as a technical means for personal use of the computer for intellectual expression long before personal computers existed as physically independent objects. By the mid-1960s, the community in and around Project Mac, including undergraduate and graduate students who had easy access to time-sharing terminals, was using computers to write, communicate, and explore ideas.

But the Project Mac community was a minority, a computer elite within the School of Engineering. The idea that all students, all studies, and all teaching would take on new forms in a computer-rich environment had its first implementation at other universities. It was only in 1983 that MIT embarked on Project Athena, a large-scale experiment in the use of computers in the undergraduate curriculum.[1] At MIT something like this could never be small: Athena was built around a $50 million gift of equipment from International Business Machines (IBM) and Digital Equipment Corporation and an institutional commitment to raise an additional $20 million to support faculty development of educational applications.

The ideas for what Athena should be grew out of priorities that had developed over many years within the School of Engineering.[2] The engineering faculty believed that for MIT to take a leadership position in educational computing it was necessary to establish a new, networked, uniform, and graphically sophisticated computer utility. In their view, this computer utility—the engineers referred to it as the "system of pipes"—would be the sufficient condition for innovations in education because MIT faculty would develop educational software once the computer system was in place. There would be "a thousand flowers." And MIT being MIT with its entrepreneurial, even "Darwinian" spirit, it was expected that these flowers would not simply bloom, they would compete, and the best would thrive.

The School of Engineering originally tried to raise the money to make this vision a reality within its own domain. However, when IBM and Digital made their very large offers, the MIT administration insisted that the resources be spread throughout the institution. In an undertaking of this scale, it was not acceptable for there to be "haves" and "have-nots." And so a

---

[1]This study of the Physics Department was part of a larger project on the educational impact of Athena. In Spring 1986, the Project Athena Study Group, an MIT faculty committee chaired by Professor Jean de Monchaux, Dean of the School of Architecture and Planning, mandated a study of the impact of Athena on teaching and learning. Four departments were chosen as case studies: Architecture and Planning, Chemistry, Civil Engineering, and Physics, with Sherry Turkle and Donald Schön as principal investigators. The field studies began in April 1986, were completed in Fall 1987, and were reported in Turkle Schön, Nielsen, Orsini, and Overmeer (1988). This chapter draws on a chapter I authored in that report, "Athena in Physics," and is based on field research by myself and Brenda Nielsen (including observation and interviews with faculty and students) and on a roundtable discussion with department members that served as a feedback session after they had read an early draft of this chapter. Early drafts profited from comments by all members of the research team and by Seymour Papert, Director of the Learning and Epistemology Group in MIT's Media Laboratory. All persons quoted have had an opportunity to review their quotations.

[2]Two important MIT documents for tracing the developing vision of an Athena-like activity are "Report of the Ad Hoc Committee on Future Computational Needs and Resources," April 1979 (committee co-chairs Weston Burton and Michael Dertouzos) and Joel Moses, "Report on Computers and Education for the School of Engineering," October 1982. Other data on the growth of the Athena vision come from conversations with its central architects, among these Michael Dertouzos, Professor of Electrical Engineering and Director of the Laboratory of Computer Science, Robert Logcher, Professor of Civil Engineering, Joel Moses, Professor of Electrical Engineering, and Gerald Wilson, Dean of the School of Engineering, that took place in the context of the larger study of Athena at MIT (see footnote 1).

vision of an experiment in educational computing drawn up by and for the School of Engineering became a program for all of MIT.

The computer is an exemplary culturally constructed object, an object that different people and groups of people apprehend with different descriptions and invest with different attributes. In their guidelines for Athena, its engineer–architects inscribed their image of the ideal MIT computer culture, a culture that was modern and state of the art, built around a networked community not of simple users but of highly fluent computer professionals. To this community MS-DOS would be unacceptably low-tech and the Apple lower still, truly a computer for the "rest of them."

Thus, Athena was first of all characterized by its emphasis on high technology. Athena began as an educational experiment without any specific educational thinking or philosophy beyond the idea of creating a technology garden and letting a thousand flowers bloom. Every educational application of technology is a marriage of idea and tool. The architects of Athena were engineers and computer scientists. They believed that the idea would be the easy (and inexpensive) part; with the right tools in the hands of the right people, the ideas would come. This meant that the heavy investment of time and money was targeted for the development of the technical infrastructure; MIT faculty were expected to create the educational applications as something of "an exercise for the left hand." From the earliest days of Athena, this materialist perspective, corresponding to a toolmaker's view of innovation, clashed with a more idealist one—that it was the idea behind the educational application that needed the infusion of new resources. Despite the language of a thousand flowers, the engineers' desire for technical leadership and system coherency placed severe constraints on the kind of educational proposals that Athena would entertain. For one thing, there were constraints on the computer languages that Athena projects could use. Four languages were allowed, with the notable absence of BASIC, the language in which most currently available educational software was written and Logo, a language at the center of a long tradition of MIT research in computers, education, and learning epistemology. And there were constraints on the computer operating system: It had to be UNIX, deemed by the engineers to be state-of-the-art, although MS-DOS and the Apple Macintosh systems were already on their way to becoming the common coin of rapidly and spontaneously growing MIT personal computer cultures.

When a professor of music who had used the Logo language on personal computers to teach composition and analysis for over a decade was denied Athena funding, she was told by Athena's director that her work was not in an acceptable language and her insistence on continuing with Logo was technically indefensible: "All computer languages are equal in the sense that a program to accomplish a given task can be written in any of them," he said.

From an engineering point of view, he was right. But she was not an engineer. From her point of view, from the perspective of her research on the epistemology of learning, it was more important that different computer languages encouraged different kinds of thinking and concept formation. Similarly, when proposals came in from historians in the School of Humanities and Social Sciences to use Athena funds to create data bases and bibliographical resources, Athena found such applications too mundane, too far from the technological cutting edge.

So a second and related characteristic of the Athena vision was a necessarily narrowed view of computational and educational diversity. The much-vaunted image of a thousand flowers reinforced its architects' belief that Athena was about freedom and decentralization, but there was another reality. Over many years, the School of Engineering had developed a computer culture with its own intellectual aesthetic, with its own ideas about what was important and what was trivial. What was important was cutting-edge technology and "big," high profile, technology-driven ideas. What was important was making a big difference in the teaching of the core undergraduate subjects. When this vision was projected onto MIT as a whole, it translated into guidelines for acceptable diversity in Athena proposals. For example, to keep the project focused on undergraduates, Athena resources would not be made available to graduate students. To keep the project focused on instruction, Athena would not support research, not even for undergraduate theses. To keep the project focused on the technological future, Athena would not support word processing. Athena tried to encourage faculty initiative by offering small development grants but was best designed to identify, encourage, and reward large flagship projects that used advanced technology to develop software for large lecture courses.

The Athena architects talked about a thousand flowers, but from the point of view of many MIT faculty members, they wanted all the flowers to be roses. Behind the mandate for diversity were assumptions about which kind of diversity would be acceptable. And even a call for every species of flowers in a garden will be perceived as constraining if one is talking to constituencies who want to plant shrubs.

Athena was announced as a 5-year experiment. During that time, it did not meet the expectations of its architects. Although there were significant, even stunning achievements in individual departments, the dream of a coherent network was thwarted by technical difficulties. And the dream of intellectual diversity within the constraints of technical coherency met with an even more profound challenge. Because computers extend the power of the mind and affect how people think and work, the machines become intimate intellectual partners. Experiences with computers naturally become woven into the social fabric and creative styles of individuals and groups. In the context of scholarly disciplines, what might seem like a technical preference (for a computer language or programming style or operating system) often expresses deeper intellectual values. It soon became clear that disciplines and subdisciplines within the Institute wanted to build their own computer cultures with their favored languages, machines, operating systems, and styles of educational innovation. Computers became enmeshed in cultural forces that refused to be easily denied or sidestepped.

A centralized and technology-centered approach to change simplifies such issues of context to open a window for decisive action, but such simplification brings with it a special vulnerability: an underestimation of the influence of psychology, history, tradition, and culture. In the case of the introduction of computers in education, the vulnerability is costly. It meant that Athena was able to recognize and claim as successes those achievements that took place within its intended framework, for example, intelligent tutors in civil engineering and interactive, multimedia foreign language environments, whose educational ideas were embedded in advanced technical applications. However, other significant effects of the Athena experience could not be recognized as successes. In the 1980s, Athena was a major context for the further development and growth of rich and diverse computer cultures at MIT, including and especially those that grew up around the officially "Athena outlawed" Macintosh and DOS systems. And Athena was the context for the disciplines to grapple with a technology that raised fundamental questions about styles of learning even about their objects of study. One of the ironies of the Athena experience was that the project, by defining itself in terms of specific technologies and a narrow view of diversity, could not recognize, nurture, or indeed, claim credit either for the development of an increasingly pluralistic computer culture or for these intense and productive intellectual debates.

Thus, Athena deserves close study not only for what one can learn from its technological successes and failures in its *intended* direction but also and especially as an environment that spawned a range of unintended cultural developments. It presents a cautionary tale about the limits of technocentrism and centralized planning in educational computing that has implications for thinking about the introduction of computation in a wide variety of organizational environments. Central to this story is the problematic nature of mandating diversity. Notions of diversity tend to express cultural values. One person's or one group's diversity is another's constraint.

Athena provides a place to study the tension between the diversity of computational practice and a procrustean computer ideology that has a hard time recognizing diversity outside of its toolmaker's framework. This chapter begins to explore this tension as it was played out in an MIT academic department with a strong history of commitment to educational innovation, the Department of Physics. The case of Athena in physics is noteworthy because it so clearly illustrates how computational ideologies can blind potential innovators to powerful educational effects. From the point of view of Athena's architects, the Department of Physics was a reticent, indeed resistant, partner. However, when one steps outside that frame, one can see success rather than resistance: In physics, the Athena experience raised old theoretical issues in new and more concrete forms and led to a clash of intellectual cultures whose sparks raised fundamental epistemological issues.[3] The first section of this chapter describes the historical reticence of this department towards educational computing and how Athena provided an impetus for several of its members to move beyond it. The second section examines the institutional paradoxes: Athena could not properly see the physicists' achievements, and although funded with Athena money, most of the physicists were left feeling that they achieved their successes in spite of rather than because of the project.

COMPUTERS IN PHYSICS: BEYOND THE DATA PROCESSING CULTURE

Since the 1960s, computers have been an essential element in physics research. Because of physicists' need to process large amounts of data, FOR-TRAN was the language of choice and became deeply embedded in the physics culture. Thus, most physicists' ideas about computers grew out of experiences in a particular and very limited kind of computer culture: the data processing culture.

Although in recent years, the speed and interactivity of personal, dedicated computers have provided possibilities in data collection and analysis that have little to do with the "number crunching" of the FORTRAN culture, its domination was resonant with a general reticence about computers among physicists. In the data processing world, the researcher stands at a considerable distance from the tool. At MIT, a number of distinguished members of the Physics Department felt that this kind of distance was appropriate for keeping computers in their proper place. Indeed, some actually saw computers as posing a threat to serious work in physics. Professor emeritus Victor Weisskopf, who had been chairman of the department for many years, feared that computers take physicists too far away from the steps between problem and solution. When colleagues would show him their computer print-outs, he was fond of saying, "When you show me that result, the computer understands the answer, but I don't think *you* understand the answer." Professor Herman Feshbach who followed Weisskopf as department chair had co-authored a classic text on methods in mathematical physics with MIT

---

[3]This chapter covers Athena activity in physics from the beginning of the project until Fall 1987.

colleague Phil Morse. Within the department, its implicit message about a hierarchy of methods was summarized in a way that made it clear that computers were for second-class minds, or as one MIT physicist put it, "If you are really gifted at solving problems in mathematical physics, you might have as a corollary that somebody who has to resort to a computer to solve problems is not as clever as somebody who can solve them with mathematical techniques."

But the story of computers in the discipline of physics cannot be so simple because only a small subset of "real world" physics problems are soluble by purely mathematical, analytical techniques. Most require experimentation where one does trials, evaluates forces, and fits data to a curve. Not only does the computer make such numerical solutions easier, but in a practical sense, it makes many of them possible for the first time. Professor Anthony French whose own work in science education went back to the 1960s when he collaborated at MIT with Jerrold Zacharias on a new physics curriculum for high schools, stressed that computers could put even beginning students in touch with a physics that they would otherwise only be able to read about. "The chief difficulty of teaching elementary physics is that it tends to be presented as a set of absolute truths. Students don't see the things that go outside these oversimplified models; they are simply not things you can handle in simple terms. But the computer makes that possible."

Here French acknowledged that computers undermine certain oversimplifications, but he feared they have the opposite effect as well, encouraging subsitutes for direct experience. "In general, students come here innocent of any particular acquaintance with the real world, the physical world. . . . So, if there is anything at all that can be achieved by direct experience, I would want to go for that rather than for the substitute."

This theme of the computer's dual effects as a tool that both masks and reveals nature ran through the feelings physicists brought to the opportunities presented by Athena. This was true for both faculty and students. Like their professors, physics students talked both of the new possibilities for numerical solutions and the dangers of reality substitutes that mask nature. One said, "Using computers as a black box isn't right. For scientists who are interested in understanding phenomena and theorizing, it's important to know what a program is doing. You can't just use them to measure everything." For another, computers speed things up too much: "When you plot data with the computer, you just see it go 'ZUK' and there it is."

For both faculty and students, computers are good when they make it clear that the world is characterized by irregularities that demand a respect for measurement and its limitations. And computers are bad when they interfere with the most direct possible experience of that world. The faculty teaches that it is always better to get your hands dirty and speak reverentially of the power of direct, physical experiences in their own introductions to science, of "learning Newton's laws by playing baseball." Demonstrations, although seductive, are dangerous when they take you away from direct experience. And the faculty fears that if simulation becomes too easy, students will turn away from the messy reality to which they owe a first allegiance. In this context, simulation is only acceptable when there is nothing else to work with.

For although baseball may be a medium for learning Newton's laws, there is no such direct access to quantum physics and special relativity. This is where technology is grudgingly granted its necessary role. French described the "amazed" reaction of the "technologically skeptical" senior theorists when presented with a film that represented wave packets propagating as a function of time and fragmenting on collision:

> You see this thing moving along and doing remarkable things. That's something the likes of which had never been seen. It is difficult to calculate that without a computer. Seeing it as a moving picture is also wonderful. There's been published recently a handbook, a picture book of quantum mechanics which includes, among other things, some of these wave packet collision things, but to see them just static doesn't begin to give the effect of watching a screen and seeing these things actually happen.

Edwin Taylor, a researcher in the MIT Physics Department, had like French, collaborated with Zacharias in the 1960s. When Athena resources became available, Taylor proposed a computer project in the spirit of that film on wave packets. But now, Taylor argued, the computer's interactivity would make it possible to go beyond the passive experience of *watching* a film to an experience of actually *living* in the quantum world. Taylor's goal was to create an computer environment where students could develop intuitions about the world of invisible physics in the same sense that they develop intuitions about the world of classical physics: by manipulating its materials. Metaphorically speaking, computers would make it possible for students to play baseball in the quantum world.

One of Taylor's relativity programs simulates what it looks like to travel down a road at nearly the speed of light. Shapes are distorted; they twist and writhe. Objects change color and intensity. All of this can be described mathematically, but without the computer they cannot be experienced. Taylor shares his colleagues' reticence about demonstrations, so his students are required to use his programmed worlds as utilities for problem solving. But for many of his colleagues, this safeguard did not go far enough.

Professor Martin Deutsch exemplified the opposition to Taylor's Athena work. Deutsch's feelings about simulation are negative and impassioned. Deutsch feels that simulations always function as black boxes. As such, they run counter to his style and to what he considers most important in physics education: "I like physical objects that I touch, smell, bite into. . . . The idea of making a simulation . . . excuse me, but that's like masturbation." Deutsch characterized his views as extreme and characterized Taylor's work as good—but disliked the genre. Indeed, he laughingly accepted a characterization of it as a "good thing of the bad kind." Deutsch feared that students would watch it "as they would a movie" and come to believe that something will happen in the real world because they have seen it in the computer model. When such opposition mounted, the Physics Department refused to make a commitment to use Taylor's programs in its large introductory courses, a decision that led Athena to cancel Taylor's funding because of its emphasis on developing software for large lecture courses.

From the official Athena perspective, the resources given to Taylor was money not well spent because it did not lead to a "big" change in undergraduate teaching. But within the Physics Department, the long debate about whether to use Taylor's programs in introductory courses became an important forum for discussion of whether the "culture of simulation" poses a threat to science. An engineer is satisfied with a simulation, went the dominant view, and a physicist wants to be in touch with the real. Some faculty likened all "canned" or prepackaged programs to viruses that could inject the scientific culture with engineering values. Others grudgingly accepted that in the case of quantum physics simulation may be a necessary evil, but the talk inevitably turned to "how one thing might lead to another," and computers might be used to demonstrate something that could be done in a traditional laboratory setting. And here, the concensus was that computers had to be kept in their place. Demonstrations would always be anathema, "the stuff of engineering education."

An interchange between physicists John Negele and Robert Ledoux spoke eloquently to this issue. Negele described how a physicist must come to grips with how light behaves both like a particle and like a wave:

Negele: If you have a dike, and two little openings, the waves of water will propagate through those two little openings. They'll form little rings, which will then interfere with one another, and you'll see the results of these two wave fronts coming out, interfering with one another. That's a very clear wave front. If you think about shooting bullets through these two holes, you know the bullet goes through one or through the other. Now, you're being told as a student of quantum mechanics that sometimes you're supposed to think about light in one way and sometimes you're supposed to think about it the other way. And so a very important experiment comes to mind. You take this case of two slits and decrease the level of illumination so you're very sure photons are only going through one at a time. You would be tempted to say, "Well, by gosh, this is going through one at a time, they are managing to diffuse. It's a fantastic experience for a physicist who is beginning to think about quantum mechanics. And I think many of us have the same reactions, that to simulate that on the computer . . .

Ledoux: It's a cheat.

Negele: It's almost sacrilege.

In the Physics Department, work on computer-resident quantum micro-worlds continues as does the debate about the proper role for simulation. The debate is increasingly impassioned and interesting as the available programs become more sophisticated and force new distinctions among demonstrations, simulations, and models. What is the epistemic status of an interactive simulation? Is it unfair to reduce a microworld to the status of a simulation? Not so long ago such questions were only philosophical. The computer presence makes it possible to address them empirically and to study the educational effects of different styles of computer use.

Such study was the idea behind the Freshman Seminar proposed to Athena in its earliest days by Professor Robert Hulsizer. Hulsizer's original proposal was ambitious: to use the seminar to rethink the freshman physics curriculum in light of what computers had to offer. When Athena's rules for funding proposals for the School of Science made it impossible for Hulsizer to receive salary support that would release him from other teaching duties and give him the time to develop such a curriculum, he scaled down his project.[4] The seminar took on a more modest goal: to teach students to use computers for numerical problem solving. Hulsizer ran the seminar for 2 years. When he retired in 1985, two junior faculty members, Robert Ledoux and Stephan Meyer, were asked to take it over. Ledoux's formulation of its continuing purpose: "To let students learn how to use the computer, show them the power of solving problems numerically, the power, you might say, of 'just plotting stuff.' "

For years MIT faculty have complained that their students' ability to deal with scale is deteriorating and that the microchip is at least partly to blame. The slide rule, goes the received wisdom, demanded that its user specify the placement of the decimal point in his or her answer; the calculator makes no such demand. Ledoux subscribed to this theory; he felt that his students "have gotten lazy; they don't want to do things by hand and they don't want to include units in their calculations."

Thus, when Ledoux was asked to teach the Freshman Seminar, he rede-

---

[4]In faculty interviews, it became clear that many faculty saw a refusal to fund faculty salaries and to thus grant faculty released time to do Athena work as "Project Athena Policy," especially during the early years. They were interpreting decisions by one or more of the faculty review committees that gave this as a rationale for not funding proposals. Athena's executive committee, however, never officially adopted this policy that emerged nevertheless, as what Donald Schön referred to as a "policy-in-use."

signed it to emphasize scale and physical measurement. A return to the slide rule was not a practical option, but Ledoux wanted to use the computer to increase student awareness of the uncertainty and error involved in any experiment. He wanted to create a computational analog to "back of the envelope calculations" where "you need to understand the scale you are working in, the units you are using, the number of significant digits that make sense." He pointed out that when it comes to understanding scale and error, failure to get things straight while at MIT can translate into "a space shuttle blowing up." Because the stakes are so high, the faculty have to serve as "mind police."

> In any model you have to state error. It's an unpopular but fundamental topic. I think it is something in which MIT education is very deficient. . . . I've never heard a student say, "I took a course in error analysis." I've never seen that. . . . There may be some in applied math, but for physical measurements, you have to learn it through a lab. So we try to provide that service. We're ideologues in this; we're preachers.

In one Freshman Seminar exercise, students interact with a computer program that simulates a ball dropping in space. Students may vary the ball's weight and the height from which it is dropped. Students learn about measurement and error when they are asked to account for the effects of forces that are factored out of "pure theory," for example, friction and wind drag. One student in the Freshman Seminar testifies to the success of this exercise when he says, "When you have to consider these forces that otherwise you ignore in dealing with plain [analytical] theory, it changes things radically. You really try to make the connection between theory and data. It's not someone else's experience. You have to make it work for yourself." Ledoux noted that when students are asked to measure the acceleration due to gravity and state the uncertainty, "this blows their minds totally."

> People are used to textbooks. They are used to computers. They understand that the computer is marvelous to take data and reduce it, but what does it mean to have an error? If someone said, '$g = +9.81$,' that's totally meaningless. 9.81 plus or minus what? And so we try to drill into them the whole idea of error analysis.

In the Freshman Seminar, the computer is being used for a "paradoxical effect": a tool usually associated with rules and precision is used to bring students closer to the messiness and irregularity of the real world. "When students plot points for the first time, they literally understand what the physical screen is, what the graphics screen is, and how to actually put points on the screen," said Ledoux. "So, if a curve drawn on the screen and a theoretical curve don't look the same, students are in a position to investigate the screen's resolution. If the two things overlap, they may differ at the tenth of a pixel level, which you can't see." And yet, this tenth of a pixel level may be critical. "If the space shuttle blows up it may be the margin of error that makes all the difference." It is important to note that to use technology for this purpose, the physical computer must be made transparent—this intellectual aesthetic demands direct contact with the physics behind the machine.

Similar intellectual values stand behind computer use in Martin Deutsch's Athena-funded Junior Physics Laboratory. For this laboratory, Deutsch wrote computer programs that will not accept a data point without the specification of an error factor. To remove this feature, said Deutsch, students "have to take affirmative action. The default is always to put an error in." Whereas some computer cultures celebrate the computer's opacity—one doesn't need to know what is going on inside the hardware or software to use a spread sheet or word-processor—Deutsch used the computer to argue for an aesthetic of the transparent in the physical sciences. Whereas some computer cultures celebrate abstraction and simulation, Deutsch used computers to promote a revaluation of the concrete.

Deutsch became interested in computers in the 1960s when he discovered the PDP-1. For a few years, he devoted himself to that machine, writing programs in machine language, getting involved in its internal architecture, "having a good time." Then for 10 years, he had nothing to do with computers until he met the Apple 2E. "I bought a 2E and I said, 'This is going to change my life.' " And it did. "For the first time in my life, I could write."

Deutsch did not work through problems by making a plan and following it through from top to bottom. He preferred to assemble the elements and "sculpt" a solution. The combination of this sculpting style of work and a perfectionistic nature had always made writing painful to the point of near impossibility. Deutsch found it too linear a process for his associative style. The computer presented a new opportunity:

> A person like me can never write anything. By the time I had five sentences down, I'd start correcting them. And by the time I'm through correcting them, I've lost the train of thought. So I used to do things like use a tape recorder, put it at the far end of the room, hang up the microphone, walk over to the other end of the room so I couldn't get to the machine in time to stop it, you see, and start talking. Because once you have a draft, you can work on it. And of course, the word processor solves all that. You can just put it in any old way and then start working on it.

Deutsch used the sculpting style, a concrete "playing with" the materials at hand not only for writing but for doing science. The abstract and formal have long been privileged in science, its canonical values have put a premium on objectivity defined as the observer's distanced relationship with the object of study.[5] But Deutsch described his work in physics in terms that privilege the

---

[5]For a discussion and critique of this position from a feminist perspective see Bleir (1986), Harding and Hintikka (1983), and Keller (1985).

concrete and a closeness to the object.[6] Recent writing in scientific ethnography has gone far to reveal such concrete thinking in science-in-practice despite idealized, after-the-fact reconstructions of the discovery process.[7] Deutsch made no such after-the-fact reconstructions. He admitted to using a style reminiscent of what Claude Lévi-Strauss (1968) called *bricolage* or tinkering, a "science of the concrete."[8]

The bricoleur scientist does not move abstractly and hierarchically from axiom to theorem to corollary. Bricoleur scientists construct theories by arranging and rearranging, by negotiating and renegotiating with a set of well-known concrete materials. Whereas hierarchy and abstraction show up in how structured programmers use a "planner's aesthetic," bricoleurs rely on negotiation and rearrangement of their materials. The bricoleur resembles the painter who stands back between brushstrokes, looks at the canvas, and only from this contemplation, decides what to do next. Bricoleurs use a mastery of associations and interactions. Unlike the planner, where mistakes are missteps, theirs is a navigation of mid-course corrections. A paradigmatic bricoleur, Deutsch admitted that he "never reads the literature first. I first try to solve the problem." Not surprisingly, Deutsch used the concrete, sculpting style in computer programming as well.

In both the popular and the technical culture there has been a systematic construction of the computer as the ultimate embodiment of the abstract and formal. Deutsch illustrated another side to the computer's intellectual personality. It can support a bricoleur's style of concrete thinking that runs into conflict with standard ways of doing things within the established computer culture. Deutsch is not alone. A close look at programmers at work makes it clear that the practice of computing supports a pluralism that is denied by the social construction of the machine. Despite widespread stereotypes about computers encouraging or even enforcing one style of use (a "top-down," planned, and structured style), computers can become partners in a variety of intellectual approaches, including some that like Deutsch's, deal with the world of formal systems by using objects rather than the rules of logic to think with.[9]

Unlike many of his colleagues whose experiences with computers had been limited to batch processing and FORTRAN, Deutsch's background led him

---

[6]On the theme of closeness to the object as a style of doing science, see Keller (1983).

[7]A sample of relevant studies is provided in Knorr-Cetina and Mulkay (1983). See also Knorr-Cetina (1981) and Latour and Woolgar (1979).

[8]Lévi-Strauss (1968). In his contrast of bricolage with Western science, Lévi-Strauss ignored the significant aspects of bricolage in the latter. Recent writers have written about Western science in a way that begins to redress this imbalance. See, for example, Feyerabend (1975) and Hanson (1958). In a less formal vein, see Feynman (1985).

[9]For a more explicit discussion of computer style and the issue of personal appropriation, see Turkle (1984) and Turkle and Papert (1990).

to see them as personal tools that can flexibly enter the researcher's intellectual space and support a variety of intellectual styles. He had used them to get
into a new relationship with words and saw little reason why they couldn't be
used to get into a new relationship with scientific data. But this would not
follow from a model of computer use where the scientist fed data into a
machine and used a FORTRAN program to get it out.

For Deutsch, the most valuable instrument in the laboratory is his Swiss
army knife, a simple, understandable, and all-purpose tool. Other people
want to use the most up-to-date tools. Deutsch wants to use the most
transparent ones.[10] He generalized his ideas about the knife's intellectual
power, and in the realm of computers, this translates into a preference for
general purpose computers that allow one to "look under the hood."
Without transparency, Deutsch claimed one loses a sense of one's material
and how it is being transformed by technology. And when one loses a sense
of the intermediate steps, then, he said "You are an engineer, not a scientist."

When Deutsch approached his colleagues about using personal computers
as intellectual tools in the service of a more transparent physics, he felt
misunderstood. "They didn't know what I was talking about. Everybody
knew what a computer was. It was in a computer center where you submit
your stuff in the evening and pick it up the next day. And I said, 'Look, this
is really going to change. We're really going to have new things.' "

In the early 1980s, Deutsch created an ad hoc committee on computers
within the Physics Department to "stir the pot," to create an awareness of the
new possibilities. And just at this point, Athena was announced. Deutsch
thought that its preoccupation with networks were off the main point of
what computers could do for education. What he saw as exciting was an
opportunity to bring computers into students' lives as direct, personal, and
transparent tools. Deutsch's idea was simple: introduce personal computers
into the physics laboratory required of all majors in their junior year. His goal
was to make computers the Swiss army knives of the Junior Laboratory.

Deutsch began with the assumption that the most dangerous thing in a
laboratory is a black box, an incompletely understood procedure or piece of
equipment. Ideally, "each apparatus should be simple enough so that the
student can open it and see what's inside." For practical reasons, students
can't design all of their instruments for themselves, but they should be able to
feel that they *could* have. Deutsch's educational philosophy is based on his
learning style: It emphasizes intellectual ownership through working in a
transparent environment.

As Deutsch saw it, his lifelong battle against the black box is a "rear-guard
action" because, "as techniques become established, they naturally become

---

[10]For an explicit discussion of the relationship between bricolage as a style and a preference for
transparent understanding, see Turkle and Papert (1990).

black boxes." But "it's worth fighting at every stage, because wherever you are there is a lot to be learned if you keep the box open that you will surely miss if you close it." Deutsch made the computer a new weapon in his battle by writing data collection and analysis programs that could be transparent to their users. One such program was for the Stern–Gerlach experiment on space quantization.

When an electron travels around an atomic nucleus, a magnetic field is set up. Classical physics predicts that if influenced by another magnetic field, the orientation of the electron will be deflected. One expects a continuum of deflections depending on the strength of the external magnetic field and the magnetic momentum of the atom itself. But quantum physics predicts that only two positions occur and the Stern–Gerlach experiment demonstrates this space quantization. A beam of silver atoms is passed through a magnetic field and then onto a film plate. The atoms form smudges form which their orientation can be determined. Originally in a mixed state, once they enter the magnetic field, the silver atoms are arranged into the two orientations predicted by quantum theory.

Before the computer was used to collect the data for this experiment, students had to move the magnets manually, read the meter, and record measurements with a painfully slow pen-recording device. The process was laborious. Deutsch said that "you could never quite figure out what was going on because it would take fifteen minutes to do any one thing." Now in the laboratory, the computer is attached to an apparatus that collects data from the film smear, and it does the calculations necessary to determine the shape of the orientations. Two peaks appear, indicating the two magnetic moments predicted by quantum mechanics. Because of the computer's speed, the peaks appear in a dramatic fashion. For Deutsch, this makes the experiment an illustration of what he thinks is most important about science. "It brings together something profound and something mundane—that combination, it's like love! The mundane part: something as simple as remembering to degauss the magnet in the experiment. The profound part: the space quantization. That the mundane and profound go together—like washing dishes and love—it's one of those things that is hard to learn"

Deutsch wrote all of his transparent Junior Laboratory software by himself; some of his students had trouble with its "homebrew" nature, finding the system truly transparent only to its author. But even the students who criticized the software's bugs and lack of documentation appreciated how Deutsch's efforts protected the immediacy of their contact with data. "The software was designed so you can still see the raw data. We're still doing our own data analysis. It's a tool that doesn't change the data fundamentally, just does the things you'd know how to do anyway." And students reported how powerful was the experience of using the computer to analyze data in the Junior Laboratory. For example, one recalled how before the computer, access to the data in an experiment in resonance fluorescence was through Polaroid photographs taken of an oscilloscope. "Before you could only get a qualitative understanding. There was less data on the photo than you have on the computer. Now, you can get an exact fit of the data to the function and see the deviations and how much of it doesn't fit an exact curve. Seeing that the data fits in spite of the variations is part of the allure of physics."

Here again, as in the case of the Freshman Seminar, there is a paradoxical effect. The tool so long associated with precision allowed an appreciation of the messiness of nature. And as in the case of the Freshman Seminar, the tool so many feared would force an alienation from the real brought students closer to it because they were able to get their hands dirty playing with data. Speaking of the resonance fluorescence experiment, Deutsch commented that the computer enabled laboratory physics to "come alive"; students could get closer to underlying experience. With the computer, "a student student can take thousands of curves, and develop a feeling for the data. Before the computer, nobody did that because it was too much work. Now you can ask a question, and say, 'Let's try it.' "

In the Junior Laboratory, computers allowed a subject as abstract as quantum mechanics to be directly experienced through a hands-on exercise. Computers provided a window to theory through glimpses of physical phenomena that opened science up to intuition. Some of Deutsch's students used this new point of contact as a supplement to traditional mathematical understanding. But other students, particularly those who like Deutsch himself are bricoleurs by intellectual temperament, said that they had a sense of "really understanding" for the first time.

Computers offer a great deal to bricoleurs. Computational objects belong to both the world of ideas and things and can offer concrete physical access to formal systems. Computers make it possible to manipulate the abstract as though it were concrete. When Deutsch talked about his writing, he was describing an intellectual style that puts a premium on the manipulation of the tangible. What is true of text can be true of a mathematical curve.

The Junior Laboratory was funded by Athena, but its intellectual aesthetic stood in sharp context to Athena's ideas about the importance of "big ideas" and big technology in educational computing. Through that evaluative prism, Deutsch had a "small idea": relationships with modest, transparent computers could have positive pedagogical effects. Deutsch wanted to use the computer in a low-tech and unobtrusive way, as an extension of current laboratory practice. Deutsch had no technical feats to report, his students needed no special place or special machines. Athena hoped for courseware that could be used around the Institute and could become influential when shared with other universities and colleges. Deutsch produced no over-arching abstractions, nothing easily exportable. His intellectual investment was in a different kind of process: helping students develop a personal relationship with a new tool. From the point of view of Athena, Deutsch's experiment was almost invisible.

The quantum microworlds, the Freshman Seminar, and the Junior Laboratory were very different from each other; each project was marked by the intellectual personalities of the faculty who ran them. Their diversity suggests that educational innovation involving computers requires the widest latitude for diverse intellectual styles. Taylor's computational aesthetic involves an opaque machine. For him, only the quantum processes need to be made more transparent. In contrast, Deutsch and Ledoux stress computational transparency. In the use of computers for simulation, Deutsch and Taylor find little to agree on. But each is committed to using computers in education. To be successful, the organizational framework in which such innovations are carried out must be able to accommodate, respect, and reward their differences. The architects of Athena took diversity as a goal, but they expected the diversity would be in the *content* of educational software written according to a certain abstract model of what would constitute an innovation. The experiences of intellectual disciplines with computers suggests something different: a diversity of diversity, a need for a more fundamental pluralism.

The positive side of the Athena experience in physics was that individuals used its resources to explore a range of issues within their own intellectual culture. The side of the story that reads as a cautionary tale raises the question of why each felt that his work was actually inhibited by the Athena organization, that he had done his work *in spite of* its constraints. How did the organization evolve in a way that gave faculty the sense that to exploit intellectual opportunity one had to use Athena resources but circumvent Athena culture?

THE INSTITUTIONAL PARADOX: MANAGING INNOVATION

The roots of this paradox lie first of all in Athena's history. Designed in the School of Engineering, it developed priorities appropriate to that school's disciplinary needs and the interests of its corporate sponsors, in particular, the emphasis on building an advanced computer utility that had system coherency at its heart. The decision to accept hardware gifts from two vendors and to make Athena Institute-wide intensified the engineers' focus on system coherency. They wanted equipment that had been built originally for incompatibility to run on the same network and to serve courses across all subject matters.[11] Of course, the ideal of coherency was given an educational

---

[11]Because of the gift from two vendors, MIT was divided into two camps. The Schools of Science and Humanities and Social Sciences received IBM equipment; the engineers received machines from Digital.

as well as a technical rationale. With system coherency, a student's one-time investment in learning would provide access to the full range of Institute-developed educational software. Because it was the faculty who were to write the software and this required money, Gerald Wilson, Dean of the School of Engineering, made a commitment to raise an additional $20 million to support faculty proposals in all the schools.

The presence of money to spend set up a logic of its own. From the point of view of the engineering faculty at the center of Athena, one couldn't just give it away, and one couldn't give it directly to departments because they didn't yet understand the technical system. The engineers turned to the model they knew best, a federal system along the lines of the National Science Foundation. There would be requests for proposals and faculty review committees within each of MIT's schools—Engineering, Science, Humanities and Social Science, and Management. There would be a central Athena administration that would insure that all proposals conformed to technical rules that would insure system coherency and to administrative rules that would insure Athena's commitment to major change in under-graduate education. I have already discussed some of these rules. What is important to note here in this discussion of paradox is how many of them went counter to longstanding MIT customs and to MIT's own institutional sense of its greatest strengths. For example, despite a widespread feeling that computers were most valuable as productivity tools to be used in personal workspaces, the Athena machines would only be allowed in centralized public clusters; despite a MIT tradition of integrating research and teaching, Athena resources would not be available to students for research use, not even for senior theses; despite the close integration of undergraduate and graduate education, Athena would not be available for graduate courses or graduate students; despite the fact that most students and faculty relied on computers for wordprocessing, Athena would not support such a mundane application. And of course, despite MIT's sense that decentralization and entrepreneurship had made for its historical strengths, Athena was built as a hierarchical structure. From the point of view of those at the center of Athena, none of these rules were "really" constraints. They were simply technical requirements for keeping the system maximally available to undergraduates and firmly pointed toward future developments in educa-tional rather than research computing. From the point of view of one computer culture, its computational aesthetics always seem natural, like the simple expression of the computer's true nature. Put somewhat differently, for an engineer, these constraints were empowering, they allowed you to get things done. From outside the engineering culture, these constraints were inhibiting. In the history of Athena, things looked different from the center and the periphery.

The School of Engineering had raised the money for Athena. It had the understandable feeling that it should be somehow thanked for its efforts. Yet when the central administration decided to take that money and distribute it around MIT as a whole, the engineers became the "them" in a division between "us and them." From the center, hard work on the part of the engineering faculty had led to free resources for everyone. But other faculty complained that the project had been negotiated and finalized without any consultation with the Institute faculty as a whole. Athena was presented as a fait accompli. Faculty comments were disgruntled. Athena seemed an uninvited guest or an unwanted gift. "They are going to tie us to mainframes"; "They are going to give us terminals"; "They are going to commit us to a system which they know is the only right one to use"; "This gift reminds me of someone who brings two ex-smokers a crystal ashtray as a housewarming present." In the School of Science, and perhaps most particularly within the Department of Physics, Athena brought the added irritation of engineers telling scientists what to do.

As independent and successful scientists, the physicists were accustomed to setting their own educational priorities. Martin Deutsch spoke of their "instinctive negative reaction to anything that smells at all like something that will regulate or control our activities, because basically our success, when it comes, comes from the fact that we disregard such things." His colleague John Negele went further. He felt that Athena's rules and regulations did more than discourage independent-minded scientists, they actually insured that nothing important would happen at MIT.

Independent of Athena, Negele had been thinking about new ways to teach computational physics, but soon after Athena was announced, he decided that "at MIT conditions were not right" for him to pursue this demanding intellectual job. In his view, although Athena said that it wanted to encourage "big ideas," it tended to see such ideas as byproducts of powerful technologies. Thus, it would provide and support hardware but did not see its job as providing the kinds of support traditionally considered necessary for "intellectual" advances, most significantly time and intellectual freedom. To make this point, Negele contrasted his Athena experience with that of a colleague who became involved with educational computing at California Institute of Technology. "At Cal Tech," said Negele, "conditions were right."[12] He continued, "At the same time as the first meetings were occurring here with Project Athena, his [the colleague's] chairman at Cal Tech told him that they were interested in a serious effort to get some serious intellectual involvement

---

[12]It is important to note that Negele reported a version of the situation at Cal Tech based on the experience of one colleague whose freedom he envied. But Cal Tech itself has been involved in serious battles over the rights to educational software produced using its resources. Negele's version of the "Cal Tech Plan" is most usually read as a screen on which he can project his vision of the ideal institutional structure for innovation in educational computing.

of physicists using computers in undergraduate education. He didn't want menus which gave students a convenient way of doing repetitious exercises."

The Cal Tech chairman didn't ask for a proposal that followed a fixed set of technical rules and regulations but provided two assistants, a computer office workstation, and a year off from regular teaching. Negele's colleague at Cal Tech used these resources to develop a textbook and computer exercises that Negele now uses in his MIT course on computational physics. "He could use whatever computer language he wished, and was told that whatever he created, he would own, hardware, software, a book, whatever." And he was guaranteed that when he was done, students would take the course he developed because it would be on a "short list" of courses that satisfied a new computational requirement.[13]

Negele's narrative directly criticizes Athena's model of how to manage innovation. In Negele's view, careful work went into designing the system, but insufficient attention was paid to creating the personal and organizational conditions for the kind of intellectual work that interested him. Negele didn't need a sophisticated network; he needed time and intellectual freedom. But at least as the Physics Department came to understand policy, Athena would not grant faculty released time from teaching by paying academic year salaries, the same constraint that had frustrated Robert Hulsizer's original plans to revamp the undergraduate curriculum.[14] Negele chafed at defending his proposal to a funding committee made up of people outside of his field. He couldn't have an Athena machine in his office and of course would not own any marketable products that came out of his Athena work.

Negele's narrative also describes a clash of intellectual cultures. Within the MIT engineering culture, one becomes successful by getting grants to develop advanced technical systems with widespread applications. The architects of Athena had a materialist view of what was required to produce successful products. It was difficult for them to believe, as did Negele, that breakthroughs would come from time spent on educational research, on *thinking* rather than tool building. From Negele's idealist perspective, the Athena ideology of a thousand flowers was not so much a call for diversity as a vote of no confidence about educational research. If one doesn't believe that

---

[13]Although 35 sophomores signed a petition asking Negele to teach computational physics, only 10 of them were able to fit this elective into their schedules because the Physics Department had just added a new required subject for majors. Cal Tech required students to take courses that used educational computing, whereas at MIT, Athena courses are electives, and with rare exceptions, electives are doomed to low enrollments. Negele suggested that subjects that use educational computing be made requirements for graduation. "Students could choose among what was available—the architecture students might tend to go one way, the physics students another." But as students "made one or more natural couplings," the faculty who had put in the time and effort would know that there was a clientele for their work.

[14]See footnote 4.

such research could lead to any concensus about its quality, it makes sense to simply let individual faculty members do their own thing.

Finally, Negele's narrative raises questions about the balance between centralization and decentralization in the management of educational innovation. In the intellectual climate of the Physics Department, Athena was experienced as disrespectful of the faculty's knowledge, autonomy, and right to be consulted on matters of intellectual substance.

Negele recounted that when Athena was first presented, he and a group of colleagues asked the chairman of the MIT faculty why there was no real faculty participation in its planning. Negele reported that the reply to their question described a closed door: The chairman of the faculty "had asked about this and had been told that the negotiations with the vendors, with IBM and DEC, were too sensitive to allow the faculty to get involved." Negele began working with Athena as early as he could but felt that the key decisions had already been made by an inner circle of engineers. "They created a huge number of committees and I was a real sap, and it took me about a year to figure out what these committees were about. These committees were to give the impression of involving faculty. But there was no substance. Nearly every major decision had already been taken."

For example, while he was serving as a member of a technical issues committee, the Athena restrictions on computer languages and operating systems were brought up for discussion. Negele insisted that the restrictions were not technical issues but a form of censorship inappropriate in a university. "It was as though they were saying, 'These are the approved books and these other ones have too much secular humanism in them or whatever.' "

> If my department chairman told me what book I must use to teach a course, I would hand in my resignation. As a professor of physics, I believe I am the person who can make the best judgment as to what textbooks to use when I teach a course. Now who are these people at Project Athena? And who do they think they are that they should tell me what languages I'm allowed to use to teach a course and what languages I'm not allowed to use?

Negele said that the result of his objections was that he was asked to "cool it." He was made to understand that this question, for better or worse, was closed.

In fact, Athena later softened many of its restrictive policies. The language restrictions were softened because of technical difficulties and increasing pressure to get things running. The ban on word processing was lifted in the face of massive violations and student protest. When surveys of how students actually used Athena showed that despite official discouragement, over 80% of all use was for wordprocessing, the system relented.[15] The policy-

---

[15]From 1985, Athena commissioned surveys of patterns of student use, done by Karen Cohen, Principal Research Associate. They appeared as "Project Athena Impact Study Reports."

in-practice about not granting faculty salaries was never Institute wide but a provisional decision on the part of the allocations committee in the School of Science, and it, too, changed. But such relaxations of the rules were several years in coming. Certainly, in physics, the rules about salary, languages, and operating systems contributed to an environment openly hostile to Athena. As Negele saw it, they led his colleagues to a basic assumption that "Athena is something they don't even want to *hear* about. They think it's such a stupid, ridiculous, terrible mistake. They aren't even going to waste their time talking about it. In physics, Athena created conditions for things *not* to happen." In his view, the centralized Athena administration was insensitive to the educational needs of the departments, for example when it prohibited use of the system for senior theses and undergraduate research.

> There was a great resistance to using Athena machines for senior theses. They were supposed to be used for large courses. That was crazy. At that time, there was nothing of intellectual substance that had been developed for large courses, but yet there was a whole generation of students coming up with senior theses and UROP [undergraduate independent research] projects.

When Negele evaluated the Athena experience as a whole, he noted that no textbooks have been produced and that in his opinion, the majority of proposals, although "nice," "don't blaze the way. They don't put MIT in a position of intellectual leadership in a way that I would like to see." Negele believed that the straightforward acknowledgment of a missed opportunity would be a good first step towards doing things better. Not surprisingly, his ideas about doing things better are firmly opposed to where Athena began. He thought one should "abolish all those silly rules." Indeed, one might look at the "Negele Plan" as a suggestion that MIT switch to what he has understood as the Cal Tech Plan: Identify faculty members who are willing to experiment, put a machine in their offices, give them each a machine to take home, give them a semester or a year off to work, and tell them that they own their products. In other words, give faculty incentives that will make it worth their while to be taken away from their major research interests. In addition, show confidence in the strength and integrity of intellectual communities by decentralizing funding decisions. That power should go to departments. "A chairman knows his faculty." In sum, take the emphasis off technology and put it into people and their ideas.

As things turned out, Athena projects in the Physics Department would have proceeded more smoothly if the emphasis had not been on cutting-edge technology.[16] Taylor fought for the right to use only the "bottom end" of

---

[16]This was not true in all departments. In chemistry, for example, projects suffered because the most advanced equipment was late or never arrived. See Sherry Turkle and Brenda Nielsen, "Chemistry," in Turkle et al. (1988).

Athena equipment because he wanted his relativity software to be easily exported to other universities that would not have such advanced machines. Ledoux and Meyer fought Athena for the right to use BASIC in the Freshman Seminar. Because its purpose was not to teach a new programming language but numerical problem solving, they wanted students to program in this familiar and Athena-disapproved language. Only after long negotiation did Athena grudgingly agree to support an IBM version of BASIC for the seminar. But the physicists wanted "Quick BASIC, Microsoft Version 2," arguing that it was better suited to their educational purposes. "We would have been fools not to use it," insisted Ledoux. In the end, the Physics Department purchased its own Quick BASIC for the Freshman Seminar, but this meant that Ledoux and Meyer had to update and maintain the software themselves. "It takes manpower to do something that Athena doesn't support," said Ledoux. "It is a manpower that Athena doesn't provide." Again and again the physicists insisted that there was a high cost to using Athena: lost time, wasted energy, and the widespread sentiment that to make an Athena project work, one had to circumvent Athena.

Athena created a climate in which the choice to use BASIC or Logo or currently available technology was read as a sign of failure. Faculty felt like "second class citizens" if their innovations were not technical but "simply" educational. Athena was supposed to be about freedom and diversity, but here again there are the questions: "Diversity for whom?" "Freedom for whom?" "Freedom from whom?"

From the point of view of the engineers at the center of Athena, freedom meant escaping from the "confines" of IBM PCs and "impoverished" computer languages like BASIC. From the point of view of most Athena users on the periphery of power, such freedoms meant new constraints. From the perspective of the center, a funded Athena proposal provided money and undisturbed work. From the point of the periphery, Athena restrictions violated intellectual freedom. And as for the privilege of working undisturbed, Alan Lazarus, Chairman of the Physics Department's Education Committee, made it clear that for those who had worked on the Freshman Seminar, the fact that Athena "left them alone" was read as a distressing lack of support.

Lazarus commented that Athena's concession to allow BASIC in the Freshman Seminar served to intensify rather than abate his faculty's hostility: "We finally got them [Athena] to agree that it was okay but then they disowned us. They said, 'Here are the terminals, but don't expect us to keep them up to date, or put new operating systems on them. You're on your own.' This put people off rather severely."

Athena seemed not to care what we did with the terminals or what we had developed. Nobody came around and said, "What have you guys done, show us, give us a demonstration." We have invited people over, but nobody, as far as I know, came. We mentioned this to the people at Athena and they said, "We have no provision for that sort of thing." It was clearly "Here they are, good-bye." It was not the kind of mutual working together it should have been.

In the Physics Department, different faculty were disappointed with Athena for different reasons. From the physicists' perspective, the problem with Athena was not that it was "one-sided" but that its technological emphasis made it virtually "none-sided." Deutsch, Ledoux, and Meyer were working on a small scale, experimenting with technically mundane uses of the computer in the service of encouraging a new and more transparent relationship with tools of measurement. They felt undermined by Athena's distaste for the small, the homebrew, the low-tech, and for BASIC. Negele's interest in computational physics, Hulsizer's in new curricula, and Taylor's in quantum microworlds fit better into Athena's "big ideas" category. But they also felt let down. Taylor could not meet Athena's demand that he get his materials into large courses. Decisions about changing the curriculum in large courses demands concensus within disciplines, yet the Physics Department case study demonstrates that computers are just as likely to sharpen debates within them. For Negele and Hulsizer, the problem with Athena was its notion that educational ideas would follow from technical advances, that educational issues could be dealt with in one's spare time. Thus, despite the achievements of faculty working within it, in the Physics Department, Athena suffered from its reputation of pleasing none of the people all of the time.

The story of Athena's first 5 years reflects tensions that characterize MIT as a whole: the tension between a powerful School of Engineering and a distinguished faculty in the arts, sciences, and humanities who often feel marginal to institutional priorities; the tension between a powerful, centralized provost's office and its diverse, independent, and entrepreneurial constituencies; the tension between a faculty promoted for its research contributions and the demand for innovative teaching. Athena was a new stage on which these larger institutional tensions were played out. Thus, it is not surprising that it brought to the surface a range of issues that must be addressed by the institution and not only in the context of computing. For example, the Athena experience dramatized that if educational innovation is to occur, junior faculty must be give greater incentives to participate in it. Martin Deutsch commented that he was free to throw himself into Athena work because as an older and very senior member of the department he could come to it "without ambition." He continued, "I don't have to write two papers a year, three papers a year, I don't have to write any papers a year if I don't feel like it. It's easy for me . . . in a funny way, and that goes into many things. It's easier when you're sort of pulled out a little bit, out of the struggle. I could afford to play."

In the Physics Department, major Athena commitments were made by people marginal to the department such as Taylor who holds a research appointment and must therefore survive on the kind of "soft money" Athena provided and by "elder statesmen" such as Deutsch and Hulsizer. The younger faculty who participated were assigned to their roles. Elder statesmen and marginals are naturally limited in their ability to effect lasting change, and the younger recruited faculty will cycle out when their assignments end. Not only is educational computing marginal to their research careers, but they can't afford to make it more central. The incentive system will ultimately punish them if they remain involved for too long.

Although Project Athena won a new visibility for educational innovation at MIT, that doesn't translate into promotion and tenure within a discipline. To sustain educational innovation in a research institution, either senior faculty have to commit to ongoing responsibility or the incentive system has to change to reward junior faculty who do educational research. At the very least, experiments in educational computing need support staff trained in the various disciplines who can take the burden off the faculty in the production and maintenance of software. What does not work is the Athena solution where it was assumed that a serious experiment in education could be done as an "exercise for the left hand," something for faculty to do on the side, something that junior faculty would have no problem fitting in alongside their disciplinary research programs. This model denied the difficulty of educational innovation, saw such innovation as possible without serious research, and allowed the incentive system to remain unquestioned and unmodified.

EPILOGUE: POWERFUL IDEAS OR PARADOXICAL EFFECTS

Physicist Judah Schwartz holds a joint appointment at MIT and at the Harvard Graduate School of Education where he heads a program in educational technology. He was involved in an Athena-funded software development project for an experimental freshman curriculum and served as chair of a faculty subcommittee that examined the impact of Athena on the residence system. Schwartz began a conversation about Athena by recalling a lecture by Barbara Tuchman on "How I Write My Books." "The first sentence out of her mouth," said Schwartz, "was 'First you have to have an idea.' " He continued:

> You need to have an idea, a powerful idea, in order to do something that is
> conceptually interesting. Physicists have been using computers forever and will
> continue to use computers forever. It doesn't make a conceptual difference in
> what they do and so they are very casual about computer use, and I think
> properly so. The question of how to make a conceptual leap is much subtler, and
> with far fewer answers. It's something whose major intellectual impetus derives
> from trying to understand something about how people learn about abstraction
> and the building of quantitative models. MIT doesn't have such an enterprise.

Schwartz was correct when he said that the Athena experience in physics
proceeded without what he would classify as powerful ideas, for example,
new models of how people learn about abstraction. But in fact, it ended up
challenging the notion that for something interesting to happen one needs to
start with *that kind* of powerful idea just as it challenged its own starting
assumption that the ideas that would matter in educational computing would
grow out of advanced technical innovations. What was seen in physics is that
powerful effects could follow from relatively mundane uses of computers.

First, in the Freshman Seminar, numerical problem solving with the
computer presented a challenge to the traditional textbook physics, skewed
towards those problems that can be solved analytically. As such experiences
become widespread, there may be change in what is considered "high" or
prestigious physics, a position currently occupied by the "pure" (i.e., mathematical) approach. And in this setting, the computer brought students closer
to the real by forcing a new consideration of error and the limitations of
measurement.

Second, in the Junior Laboratory, when computers relieved the tedium of
data collection and data plotting, students were able to implement thought
experiments that gave theory a concrete and more intuitive dimension. For
some, these new possibilities were a supplement to traditional mathematical
understandings. For others, they seemed to present a new and privileged path
of access to science because they offered the ability to play with the abstract in
a concrete, almost tangible form. In the Junior Laboratory as in the Freshman
Seminar, students were put in a better position to honor the scientist's
primary allegiance to nature's messiness because they were better equipped to
handle uneven and anomalous data. Before the computer entered the laboratory, if a student's one round of an experiment yielded only anomalous data,
the student could not bring his or her experimental result in relation to theory
but would have to rely on prepackaged, idealized data. The computer made it
possible to generate a richer and more representative data set.

Finally, looking at the Athena experience in the Physics Department as a
whole, it is clear that even with relatively mundane and low-tech uses of
computers, different people made them their own in their own ways, using
different intellectual approaches and different points of contact with what the
technology has to offer. Martin Deutsch used a "different" computer than

did John Negele or Edwin Taylor. The physical machines may have been the same; the machines in the mind were not. The fact that computers invite their personal appropriation suggests that the most productive uses of educational computing will demand an epistemological pluralism, an acceptance of the validity of multiple ways of knowing and thinking.

From the time that it was announced as an MIT-wide plan, Athena declared ambitious educational and epistemological goals, for example, to use computers to "help students learn more creatively and fully" by developing "new conceptual and intuitive understanding."[17] But in fact, many MIT faculty simply expected computers to help them do what they already did faster and better. According to this line of reasoning, the computer is "just a tool" that would help students do the old things more efficiently. Important educational effects would follow, but it was expected that they would take place *away from* the machines. For example, when computers speeded things up in the laboratory, students would have more time to study underlying theory and mathematics outside of the laboratory. Thus, despite its official rhetoric, as an educational experiment Athena proceeded with a widespread and conservative hypothesis that if things were going to change, it would not be by much or at least not in significant qualitative ways.

The story of Athena in physics challenges this hypothesis because computers not only enabled students to do the old things more quickly, they opened up new ways of thinking. And even doing an experiment more quickly (in the Junior Lab the time for performing experiments was reduced by a factor of five to six) led to significant qualitative changes as students were able to run through many variations of the same experiment, developing a new feeling for what was going on. Students experienced a greater ownership of theory because they had the feeling that they were confirming it for themselves.

By being a magnificent tool, the computer became more than "just" a tool. Most surprising of all, this machine that is most commonly thought of as the ally and embodiment of the abstract showed its vocation as an actor in the revaluation of the concrete. The story of Athena in physics makes it clear that it is naive to launch experiments in educational computing that expect diversity in content but not in the form and feeling of computer use.

REFERENCES

Bleir, R. (Ed.). (1986). *Feminist approaches to science.* New York: Pergamon.
Feyerabend, P. (1975). *Against method: The outline of an anarchistic theory of knowledge.* London: NLB.
Feynman, R. (1985). *Surely you must be joking, Mr. Feynman.* New York: Norton.

---

[17]"Project Athena Faculty–Student Projects," *MIT Bulletin*, March 1985.

Hanson, N. R. (1958). *Patterns of discovery.* Cambridge: Cambridge University Press.

Harding, S., & Hintikka, M. B. (Eds.). (1983). *Discovering reality: Feminist perspectives on epistemology, metaphysics, methodology, and philosophy of science.* London: Reidel.

Keller, E. (1983). *A feeling for the organism: The life and work of Barbara McClintock.* San Francisco: Freeman.

Keller, E. (1985). *Reflections on gender and science.* New Haven: Yale University Press.

Knorr-Cetina, K. (1981). *The manufacture of knowledge: An essay on the constructivist and contextual nature of science.* Oxford: Pergamon.

Knorr-Cetina, K., & Mulkay, M. (Eds.). (1983). *Science observed: Perspectives on the social studies of science.* London: Sage.

Latour, B., & Woolgar, S. (1979). *Laboratory life: The social construction of scientific facts.* Beverly Hills, CA: Sage.

Levi-Strauss, C. (1968). *The savage mind.* Chicago: University of Chicago Press.

Turkle, S. (1984). *The second self: Computers and the human spirit.* New York: Simon & Schuster.

Turkle, S., & Papert, S. (1990). Epistemological pluralism: Styles and voices within the computer culture. *Signs: Journal of Women in Culture and Society 16*, 1.

Turkle, S., Schön, D., Nielsen, B., Orsini, M. S., & Overmeer, W. (1988). *Project Athena at MIT.*

4

Ideologies of Computerization

William Graves, III
Bryant College

IT'S THE IDEA, NOT THE OBJECT, THAT COUNTS . . .

In the fall of 1988, Brown University was riding an economic and political wave of "academic computing" on its way to becoming, hopefully, one of the premier "Star Wars" universities of the 21st century. One of the earliest direct effects beyond the university was the initiation of a hypertext development project in a local secondary school, a project that was modeled on and supported by Brown University's own Intermedia Project.[1]

George Landow (1990), the English instructor/developer on the Intermedia Project, recently summarized the "power" of this computing technology in words that echo his presentation of Intermedia to the administration and faculty of this secondary school on the eve of their commitment to a very similar development project: "Hypertext, by blurring the distinction between author and reader, allows, encourages even demands new modes of reading, writing, teaching and learning" (p. 407).

Teacher response to Intermedia and the idea of hypertext was decidedly mixed. In the midst of much animated discussion over the wisdom of

---

[1]Interested readers will find a detailed ethnographic study of the Intermedia Project in Beeman et al. (1988), Graves (1989), and Nyce and Bader (chapter 7, this volume) that describes this secondary school project—Project ACCESS. I discuss the first year of Project ACCESS in more detail in a later section of this chapter.

embarking on this secondary school experiment, I conducted my first interview with the headmistress of this secondary school. The interview was intentionally unstructured with the strategic use of open-ended "probe" questions, for I hoped to get a broad sense of how she was interpreting her teachers' diverse responses to the recent announcement of this project.

The dominant theme of her story repeated and embellished a confident claim I had heard in other settings and contexts—hypertext as an "open-ended," "flexible," and "nonhierarchical" medium would promote "independence of "thought" and "creative intellectual exploration" in students.[2] In spite of the fact that she had no practical experience with hypertext, a few demonstrations, conference presentations, and trade reviews had convinced her that this computing tool embodied "empowering" characteristics and capabilities. Consequently, all questions I posed about her understandings of the relationship between the structure of hypertext and student learning she answered with more detailed descriptions of what she understood hypertext could do, rather than what students or teachers did or could do.

A second major theme of her reflections on hypertext was equally interesting. Discussions of the possibilities of hypertext at faculty meetings, she told me, had provided faculty with a "nonthreatening way" of discussing differences in teaching styles and selection and use of instructional materials. Before the arrival of hypertext, the administration had sought the support of faculty in developing an evaluation metric for teaching performance, but the faculty were reticent to discuss each other's teaching in such a context.

Apparently, as long as the focus of discussion was imagined uses of hypertext, faculty were willing to draw strategically on their own teaching experiences and preferences in order to support or to challenge any imagined use of hypertext. In effect, by endorsing or rejecting any proposed use of hypertext, faculty members were indirectly evaluating particular styles of teaching, objectives, modes of student evaluation, and choices and uses of instructional resources.

The headmistress' discussion of hypertext provides two good examples of what I call an *ideology of computerization*—an imaginatively constituted understanding of the nature and consequences of using computers that emerges out of de-contextualized reflections on the thing-in-itself. Imaginatively and analytically detached from the concrete contexts of its design, development, marketing, and use, a particular form of technology as a thing-in-itself becomes an infinitely manipulable symbol. Thus, it can be employed strategically to define problems, answer questions, organize ideas, resolve dilemmas, mediate contradictions, structure practices, and even to forecast the future.

Reflecting on hypertext provided the headmistress with a means of tran-

---

[2]For a decidedly utopian use of these and related ideas to argue for the critical role of hypertext and other types of new academic computing tools in promoting the contemporary utopian vision of "globalization," see Sculley's (1991) address to the Association of Computing Machinery.

scending and, thus, redefining as a technical problem a chronic dilemma traditionally framed as a series of questions about moral responsibility—how to get secondary school students more actively involved intellectually and creatively in the educational process. Reflecting on hypertext also provided faculty and administrators with a transcendent technological idiom for dealing with a sensitive cultural contradiction that could not be ignored—outside authorities were pressuring the school to adopt general standards for evaluating teaching performance, yet the culture of the school had always embodied strong principles of individual autonomy with respect to styles of teaching and use of instructional resources.

In both cases, ideologies of computerization provided administrators and faculty of this secondary school with a perceived nonthreatening idiom for reconstructing moral dilemmas in ways that, ironically, encouraged analytic detachment from the very sociocultural conditions that had promoted the definition of such dilemmas in the first place.

Turkle (1984) showed us how the computer becomes, in essence, a mirror for end-users. However, at a more distant remove from the concreteness of the computing experiences of Turkle's end-users, ideas about and representations of computers become not mirrors of the self but lenses on the world beyond the self.[3] I find such lenses—ideologies of computerization—to be pervasive elements of utopian and anti-utopian visions of so-called "postindustrial society." More importantly, I find them to be constitutive features of many computer planning, development, implementation, and evaluation projects.

Notable representatives of the "social realist" systems-analytic approach to studying computerization have taken critical stock of the widespread practice of treating computer systems as analytically isolable from the settings in which they are designed, developed, marketed, implemented, and used (cf. Kling, 1980, 1987; Kling & Iacano, 1989). They will surely recognize the social and cultural phenomena I discuss in this chapter as typical of the kinds of a priori understandings they have critiqued as confounding rational technological choice.

However, if, as I suspect, many of the social realist systems analysts presuppose the possibility of a determinate correspondence between technically defined means and socially defined ends, then I want to argue that their sociotechnical analyses rest ultimately on the substitution of one contestable

---

[3]Only after finishing this chapter did I become aware of Ihde's (1990) extremely interesting project to construct a phenomenological typology of technology-mediated experience. In terms of his proposed typology, Turkle's (1984) analyses of the relationship between self and computer deal exclusively with "embodied relationships to technologies." My notion of ideologies of computerization, on the other hand, treats as strategically inseparable two types of phenomenological relations that Ihde, as I understand it, would treat as analytically distinct—"hermeneutic relations" and "alterity relations."

ideology of computerization for another. With respect to recent neo–Marxian critiques of computerization, I argue this more forcefully and in more detail later. In particular, I suggest that these analysts of computerization have been surprised by the actual outcomes of processes of computerization because they have tended to rely too heavily on the logical implications of their own ideologies of computerization (e.g., most notably, Hirschhorn, 1984, 1989; Zuboff, 1988).

I argue that because ideologies of computerization are pervasive features of all types of discourse directly and indirectly related to processes of computerization, we need to treat them much more seriously. We need to pay greater attention both to their nature and to the magnitude of the role they may play in directing and shaping concrete cases of sociotechnical change.

In the remainder of this chapter, I begin a broad, if sketchy, interpretive exploration of the nature and role of ideologies of computerization within situated processes of sociotechnical change. In particular, I am interested in questions related to nontechnical perceptions and understandings that serve to legitimate specific ideologies of computerization, as well as to the types of knowledge and interests that promote successful challenges to the legitimacy of such ideologies. In short, I seek to understand the dynamic of sociotechnical change as a dynamic powered essentially by a contest of technologically mediated meanings and definitions, rather than as a dynamic powered by behavioral responses or adaptations to the physical presence or technoeconomic character of specific tools.

Although I examine most closely computerization within educational settings, I do not limit my analyses and discussions to such settings. I believe that many of the issues central to mainstream analyses of corporate automation and new office technologies are of equal importance to studies of a wide range of computerization efforts in educational contexts. In particular, I want to examine three very different cases of computerization, one in a corporate setting and two in educational settings, in order to argue for the importance of analyzing the critical role ideologies of computerization play in shaping the direction and outcomes of processes of sociotechnical change in diverse contexts and settings.

THE ARCHITECTURE OF IDEOLOGIES OF COMPUTERIZATION

Central to any ideology of computerization is the assumption that the essential properties and capacities of computers direct or determine patterns of thought and action at the individual and collective levels of experience. In their most commonly encountered forms, ideologies of computerization appear as general assessments of specific computing tools on the basis of technical specifications and configurations under imagined and, quite often, unspecified conditions of use.

Hardware and software reviews in such mainstream trade journals as *PC Magazine, Byte Magazine,* and *Mac World* present the clearest examples of this type of ideology of computerization, which Dunlop and Kling (1991) identified as a systematic failure to distinguish between "computability" and "usability." While claiming that such trade reviews are "helpful in teaching about the strengths and weaknesses of various programs," Dunlop and Kling also offered the important observation that popular hardware and software reviews do not discuss the types of settings and social conditions that would make specific products "most effective—or even usable at all" (p. 21). In other words, there is an implicit assumption in many popular reviews that the nature of the technology itself transparently specifies the appropriate conditions for its successful adoption and effective use.

In their most clearly deterministic forms, ideologies of computerization depend on, yet move far beyond, a basic technological essentialism to attribute remarkable degrees of agency to machines. The "essential" structures and functions of these machines are implicitly or explicitly equated with human powers of understanding and action. In such widely read popular accounts as Alvin Toffler's *The Third Wave,* for example, computing technologies are cast as determinants of revolutionary social transformations precisely because their "communicative" and "intelligence" functions are presumed to be equal to (perhaps greater than?) human powers of communication and understanding. The course of human history is radically changed because human beings have intelligent partners (or, in some accounts, omniscient overlords) for the first time:

> In all previous societies, the infosphere provided the means for communication between human beings. The Third Wave multiplies these means. But it also provides powerful facilities, for the first time in history, for machine-to-machine communication and, even more astonishing, for conversation between humans and the intelligent environment around them. (Toffler, 1980, p. 178)

As illustrated by Toffler's enthusiastic utopianism, one well-known difficulty with all determinist ideologies of computerization is the common-sense conflation of such complex and problematic categories as *interaction, communication,* and *conversation,* on the one hand, and *intelligence* and *electronic data processing,* on the other.[4] Conflating these categories effectively blurs important distinctions between human action and machine behavior, thus enabling

---

[4]Suchman's (1987) analyses of specific types of human–machine interaction demonstrate the importance of distinguishing among notions of interaction, communication, and conversation. Her work nicely complements Dreyfus' (1972) earlier analyses of impasses in artificial intelligence that result from failures to acknowledge qualitative distinctions between embodied human understanding and disembodied electronic processing. More recently, Nyce and Graves (1990) and Graves and Nyce (1992) found that these same conceptual difficulties continue to thwart attempts to develop "expert" or "knowledge–based" diagnostic systems for clinical neurologists.

the proliferation of radical utopian and anti-utopian visions of a world transformed by machines functioning as independent agents rather than as humanly directed means to humanly conceptualized ends.

Some skeptics of the uncritical attribution of agency to computers have perceived a much more serious social problem than philosophical confusion. To cite a prominent early critic, Feenberg (1991) pointed out that in the 1950s Norbert Wiener, one of the founders of cybernetics, warned of the ultimate irrelevance of debates over the capabilities of computers: If decision-making machines have no capacity to learn, we are not wise to place much reliance on them; if, on the other hand, such machines do have the capacity to learn, we still must decide on the acceptability of their decisions. In short, Wiener saw the uncritical attribution of agency to computers as resulting in dangerous abdications of human responsibility:

> For the man who is not aware of this, to throw the problem of his responsibility on the machine, whether it can learn or not, is to cast his responsibility to the winds, and to find it coming back seated on the whirlwind. (Wiener, 1950, cited in Feenberg, 1991)

Wiener's warning is important because it partially unmasks a critical structural feature of all ideologies of computerization—the intrinsic connection between notions of computer agency and notions of human responsibility that such ideologies presuppose. Although Wiener and numerous anti-utopians envision the extreme case of human beings abdicating complete responsibility for decisions as the logical outcome of granting agency to computers, there are more common and less extreme scenarios. These latter involve strong expectations by designers, developers, and administrators that end-users structure their patterns of decision making in conformity with presumed essential capacities of their computing tools. In effect, end-users are urged or directed to abdicate responsibility to the technology in the sense that they are expected to subordinate their notions of choice to the presumed logic of their tools.

Over the past decade, an increasing number of faculty, students, and nontechnical staff in colleges and universities aggressively promoting academic computing have been dependent to a greater or lesser extent on a new cadre of technical support specialists. These specialists are being hired by academic institutions to promote the computerization of activities that support instruction and research. For those who are interested in the potential of new technologies but have little experience, the advice, guidance, and support these technical specialists routinely provide is valuable and often key to the attainment of computing objectives.

At the same time, I and many other technically unsophisticated users periodically become aware of strong expectations that we subordinate our notions of choice to the presumed logic of particular computing tools. We become most aware of the character and force of these expectations when we feel we have successfully incorporated a tool into our work routines, yet technical support staff advise us either that we are "underutilizing" its "capabilities" or that we are using an "inefficient" system, the "wrong" application, or an "inappropriate" technical feature for the particular objectives we seek to attain.[5] In such cases, their ideological message to us is clear— we have not grasped the "intrinsic" connection between the logic of our work and the logic of our computing tools.

CHALLENGES TO THE LEGITIMACY OF IDEOLOGIES OF COMPUTERIZATION

A specific ideology of computerization can only achieve absolute legitimacy and, thus, unchallenged authority when all participants in the computerizing setting accept that there is not only a natural logic intrinsic to their tools but also a natural analogy by which the structure of use mirrors the logic of tools.

The problem in actual processes of computerization, however, is that end-users can and do sometimes challenge these institutional definitions either by actively resisting or effectively agitating for alternatives to authoritatively structured notions of choice. As the anecdotal case presented here illustrates, even within the most highly centralized, totally computerized organizations that appear to present end-users with no means of effectively resisting the organization's dominant ideology of computerization, end-users can still initiate action that constitutes a significant challenge to that ideology.[6]

Case 1: The Keyboarders' Challenge and Its Consequences

I once worked as a data-entry operator in a highly centralized, totally computerized publishing operation. Sitting behind 20 dumb terminals in an "open-bay" office, we were trained to do basic keyboarding and simple editing on a complex typesetting application. However, we were never systematically taught this typesetting application and we were never pro-

---

[5]At the height of the Faculty Workstation Project at Brown University (see Shields, Graves, & Nyce, 1991, 1992), a small, overworked technical support staff struggled to provide large numbers of faculty with "cutting-edge" UNIX workstations and the basic skills to use them. Throughout this period, we often heard technical staff use the term *end-user failure*, sometimes jokingly but sometimes seriously, to describe these types of cases.

[6]Attewell (1991) provided a valuable review of the phenomenon of employee resistance to so-called "electronic sweatshops." Both he and the sources he cited, however, adopt managerial perspectives that do not consider seriously the implications for sociotechnical change of effective end-user challenges to authoritative ideologies of computerization.

vided with any information about the mainframe, its operating system, or any other applications. Furthermore, the highly structured data-entry interface rendered both the typesetting application and the operating system opaque to the "keyboarders," as we were then called. In short, management had carefully constructed a maximally controlled computing environment for typists with minimal skills and no presumed interest in computers.

Through the character of its training program, interface design, and institutional definition of essential tasks, this publishing organization effectively promulgated one authoritative ideology of computerization, the legitimacy of which ultimately depended on the keyboarders' accepting as natural and necessary an unambiguous, intrinsic connection between the institutionally defined character of their work and the apparent logical structure of their tools. In fact, most keyboarders did accept without question the legitimacy of this state of affairs. Nevertheless, a serious challenge did finally emerge that led to a sustained critical questioning of the dominant ideology of computerization.

On the eve of the "microcomputer revolution," television, radio, and print media were vigorously promoting the notion that "computer literacy" was the key to high-paying jobs in the new economy (cf. Chesebro & Bonsall, 1989). We keyboarders knew that several of the respected old timers were taking this idea seriously. They had enrolled as part-time students in a local vocational school and were taking computer and information sciences (CIS) courses. In contrast to a number of us who were part-time or casual labor with little or no long-term commitment, these full-time keyboarders were beginning to think of ways to make their jobs more interesting, more highly skilled, and, most importantly, better paid.

At staff meetings, these senior keyboarders began to raise informed questions about hardware and software. Management gave them polite but cryptic answers. They openly agitated for an e-mail system. Management smoothly refused, citing vaguely defined fiscal and technical constraints. Finally, one or two of these people began "hacking" their way through the interface to explore the system.

Resisting all challenges to the authority of its ideology of computerization, the organization responded guardedly and cautiously. We were informed that a new system of bonuses for individual productivity was being created. A new surveillance program had been installed that would "count keystrokes per hour," so that "highly productive" individuals could be "more effectively rewarded." We keyboarders received this idea with a great deal of suspicion. In less than a month, an outside hacker had been recruited by the old timers to sabotage the surveillance program.[7]

---

[7]An engineering colleague of mine argues that there was a high probability of collusion between keyboarders and programmers within this company. His argument is based on his personal knowledge that data-entry interfaces of this type under normal operating conditions are

Management was never able to identify the saboteurs. Furthermore, the sabotage was so obvious, so effective, and so threatening that the bonus/surveillance project was scrapped with no explanation. Not long after the sabotage we were given our own internal e-mail system. However, we were now sensitive to the possibility that management would monitor the system to obtain information on the sources of hacking and sabotage, so we all agreed that "computing" would be a forbidden e-mail topic. A collective attitude of resistance was beginning to crystallize.

Providing us with an e-mail system may have been a sign that management was willing to rethink its traditional orientation to the self-defined interests and needs of keyboarders. On a less charitable interpretation, management may have realized that the e-mail system was not simply an ineffective surveillance device. It was a stimulant to greater curiosity and interest among a larger number of keyboarders.

In either case, great changes were in the making by the time I was preparing to leave the company. The training program was being redesigned to accommodate a greater range of interests and skills; keyboarders were being invited to assist in redesigning an interface that would give them more control over the typesetting process; the scope of the job description was being broadened to encompass new functions, including some basic programming; senior keyboarders were being given the option of working at home.

Keyboarder initiative and resistance had challenged successfully the legitimacy of the organization's authoritative ideology of computerization. This challenge had called into deep question the "intrinsic" connection between the institutionally defined logics of work and of the structures and functions of the computing system, thus creating a new context for negotiations between management and labor about the meaning and the uses of computing tools.

I present this brief anecdotal sketch of one case of effective resistance to an authoritative ideology of computerization because I suspect that various forms of resistance and subsequent negotiation play a much more important role in directing and shaping sociotechnical change than many critics of computerizing organizations have allowed.

The critical case studies of computerizing organizations found in Wilkinson (1983), Hirshhorn (1984, 1989), and Zuboff (1988), for example, all present a very different picture from the one I have just painted: Management unilaterally defines the structures and functions of computerized systems in ways that serve managerial definitions of "productivity" and "effi-

---

virtually impenetrable from a "dumb terminal." Because I was never more than a marginal member of this keyboarding group, I was not aware of any such inside collusion. Too bad, for if my colleague is right, then there is without doubt a much more interesting story of resistance to tell than mine.

ciency"; workers, such as our keyboarders, ultimately have very little effect on management's technological definitions and choices. Thus, these studies conclude both that workers are harnessed to tools over which they have no control and that only management can take the initiative in redefining the character of the relationship between specific tools and their uses.

In most case studies the possibility of end-users initiating effective redefinition of dominant ideologies of computerization is not seriously considered. According to Hirschhorn (1984, 1989) and Zuboff (1988), this is because management will initiate a restructuring of the tool–work relationship only when they come to "realize" that increasing costs and relative declines in efficiency and productivity are due to "suboptimization of computing technologies" (Zuboff, 1988, p. 220).

Ultimately, Hirschhorn and Zuboff believe that neither management nor labor in many computerized organizations understands the "true logic" of computing technologies and the "rational" uses to which such technologies should be put. In their analyses, management and labor appear as locked into reciprocally reinforcing modes of what the neo-Marxists would call "false consciousness." The managerial understanding of computerization is thus wholly determined by Tayloristic assembly-line attitudes toward labor and technology; the nonmanagerial understanding of end-user/workers is thus wholly determined by their institutionally structured uses of specific computing tools.

However, as my keyboarders' challenge case illustrates, end-users' understandings of the nature and uses of computing tools can transcend institutionally specific definitions and structures. I have already discussed in detail one obstacle to taking this possibility seriously in such analyses as Zuboff's and Hirschhorn's: the common ideological presupposition that some presumed essential logic of computing tools determines or shapes the patterns of thought and action of their end-users. In other words, end-users in structured computerized settings are viewed as having no knowledge that would permit them to reconceptualize the institutionally defined character of their tools.

The second obstacle is based on pervasive neo-Marxian assumptions that the authority of management is absolutely coercive and, furthermore, that this managerial coercion is ultimately grounded in management's perceptions of labor as simply one form of productive technology among others to be exploited instrumentally.[8] In other words, even if end-users did have access to forms of knowledge that would permit redefinition of their tools, management would not allow the realization of end-user-initiated changes that

---

[8]Feenberg (1991) points to the formative influence of Braverman's (1974) classic neo-Marxian thesis of the "capitalization of labor" on much recent critical analyses of sociotechnical change, including Zuboff's and Hirschhorn's.

were not based exclusively on managerially defined criteria of "productivity" and "efficiency."

Although no one would deny either the importance of hierarchy or the continuing relevance of a long history of adversarial management–labor relations in the development of capitalism, our analyses of computerization must acknowledge that many managers today, perhaps the majority, have been trained in human-relations ideologies that are highly critical of Taylorism and other exploitative and coercive styles of managerial decision-making (cf. Attewell, 1991; Morgan, 1988). Furthermore, increasing numbers of corporations are adopting programs to redesign and "humanize" traditional assembly-line types of operation, as well as to foster the conditions for effective "participatory management" (cf. references in Morgan 1984, 1988, and Attewell, 1991). At the very least, all of this suggests that critical analyses such as Zuboff's and Hirschhorn's may be informed by simplistic and reductionistic notions of the character and role of both managerial motivations and end-user initiatives in determining the direction and shape of sociotechnical change in corporate settings.

Ultimately, Hirschhorn and Zuboff merely substitute one type of ideology of computerization they believe is more rational on technical grounds and more enlightened on organizational grounds for other types they find to be irrational and exploitative. However, because their own descriptions and analyses are informed by an ideology of computerization they take for granted as an absolute standard for evaluating processes of computerization in specific contexts and settings, they fail to conceptualize adequately the great range of shifting conditions, conflicting interests, and diverse motives that may serve to promote within the same setting one type of authoritative ideology now but quite a different type later. In other words, they do not acknowledge the essential contingency of all ideologies of computerization, including their own.

CONDITIONS AND CONSEQUENCES OF IDEOLOGIES OF COMPUTERIZATION

It is well known that technological choices can be motivated by an extremely wide and complex array of shifting political, economic, cultural, and technical factors variously constitutive of diverse contexts and settings of computerization (cf. Attewell, 1991; Forester, 1989; Kling, 1980; Kling & Iacano, 1989). Because of this immense complexity, the literature on computerization has yet to produce a useful general model of change that theoretically specifies the relationship between conditions motivating technological choices and the consequences of those choices for either individually or collectively defined patterns of action.

Quite apart from the considerable substantive problems of explaining computerization as a process of change, there are a number of formidable theoretical and philosophical obstacles to the construction of any such useful general model, all of which involve chronic, perhaps insurmountable, difficulties in adequately theorizing the character and role of meaning and interpretation in social action (cf. Giddens, 1976, 1979, for comprehensive overviews). Because even a brief outline of these difficulties is far beyond the scope and intent of this chapter, I rely tacitly on the critical work of such contemporary social-process theorists as Anthony Giddens to claim that failure to examine carefully and to treat seriously the situated understandings of social actors constitutes the foundational weakness of both the social realists' and the neo-Marxists' systems-analytic attempts to explain computerization as a determinate process of sociotechnical change.

Because ideologies of computerization, as structured sets of presuppositions about the relationship of particular forms of technology to the character of social action, frame and inform the situated understandings of all social actors involved directly in processes of computerization, we should acknowledge their centrality to processes of sociotechnical change. At the very least, ideologies of computerization can provide us, as they do the social actors we study, with the conceptual resources for constructing richer understandings of the diverse but structured ways in which social actors actively forge interpretive links between the conditions and consequences of technological choices in concrete settings.

Although such an interpretive approach can no more predict the shape and direction of sociotechnical change than can the social realist or neo-Marxist explanatory approaches, it has a distinct advantage over those latter approaches—by its insistence on the centrality of situated understandings, an interpretive approach never presupposes that either radical sociotechnical change or maintenance of the status quo must theoretically typify computerization. In direct contrast to "social realist" and neo-Marxist explanatory approaches, the interpretive approach seeks a clearer understanding of the dynamic of both change and continuity by focusing on the contingent construction of technologically mediated meanings and definitions that is central to all processes of computerization.

As the following case study of a university library in the early stages of the development-implementation process illustrates, administrators responsible for computer planning and implementation may have very good grounds for believing in and arguing that the specific conditions for computerization require the development of a particular form of technology and, furthermore, that this technological choice must result in the restructuring of the organization of work. At the same time, end-users may respond to this technologically mediated interpretation of the link between conditions and consequences of technological choices by challenging, on equally good grounds, the legitimacy of the institutional definition of "conditions," "consequences," or the concretely proposed "link" between them.

Case 2: Response to a Dominant Ideology of Sociotechnical Change

In an ethnographic study of work and information technologies in the Brown University Library system, Bader and I found that library administrators had begun instituting organizational changes and restructuring work practices before their new centralized record-keeping system had actually entered the workplace (cf. Graves & Bader, 1988, for the original ethnographic study). This computing system was still in development and no one could be certain about its direct effects on the character and organization of library work.

Nevertheless, systems developers, administrators, and supervisors very early envisioned the ideal system as a centralized, multifunctional information system that would allow for the electronic consolidation of all types of records throughout the library system. Behind this vision of the ideal system was a long-range strategic mission shared by many university libraries—to provide and to gain immediate access to up-to-date library data and information anywhere inside or outside the wall of the library (cf. Sack, 1986) and to develop universal standards of electronic data classification to facilitate the effective sharing of information and work among libraries (cf. Haas, 1980; Jones, 1985).

As in numerous contexts of automation throughout America, this vision was informed by and further reinforced administrative assumptions that a comprehensive computing system would "enhance productivity" and "reduce error" by eliminating redundancies in the traditional records and, thus, "costly" duplication of effort in traditional routine record-keeping practices. In effect, a preconceived understanding of the logic of the computing technology itself would serve both as the means of and the rationale for redefining institutional structures and practices.

Even though this dominant ideology of computerization provided direction and gave shape to a number of changes in organizational structure, job definition, and record-keeping practices, when the new information system was finally implemented it was considerably more limited in scope and functionality than the administration's ideology of computerization had presupposed. Its database did not incorporate all of even the most important types of library records; the structure of its applications did not facilitate the routine tasks of most functional areas of the institution.

Nevertheless, by the time the new system was first implemented, technologically defined directions of change based on the essential concepts of *centralization*, *uniformity*, and *nonredundancy* were already clearly defined. This was as true for staff who had no direct access to the new technology as it was for those whose work would depend routinely on such access. A dominant ideology of computerization, rather than any specific properties of the form and function of the computing technology itself, had laid the foundation for the formation and legitimation of a coherent administrative logic directing the course of future change in library work.

In the absence of a major implementation of new computing tools, library staff tended to be cautiously optimistic about the new changes and plans for computerization. Nevertheless, there were early indications among nonprofessional support staff, in particular, that this administrative ideology of computerization could and, possibly, would be challenged when and if the proposed multifunctional information system became fully developed and implemented in all areas of the library. During the course of our participant-observation research with support staff prior to implementation, a number of staff members challenged the core notions of centralization, uniformity, and nonredundancy on the basis that such concepts ignored crucial features of the library-wide functional integration of work and contradicted important and valued dimensions of routine staff work.

Centralization of information and *uniformity* of record-keeping were perceived as potentially threatening to many staff because they identified the traditional information environment with its plurality of standardized and nonstandardized sources of information (both paper and electronic) as facilitating the routine independence and relative autonomy they had always enjoyed. At the same time, some staff argued that because there were significant differences among university libraries both in the structure and content of their collections and in the organization of their internal records, centralization and uniformity were very questionable goals for any general system of information sharing among libraries.

Because redundancy of information was an inevitable and systematic consequence of the library's traditional heterogeneous information environment, staff were also skeptical of the administrative concept of *nonredundancy*. Consonant with the high value they placed on independence and relative autonomy, staff saw redundancy as an inevitable consequence of the fact that every staff member maintained a private system for keeping records of their daily work flow. These private records helped them control day-to-day continuity and prevented them from duplicating their own efforts. Most importantly, almost all staff were certain that redundancy in record keeping fulfilled the crucial institutional function of guarding against the errors of any single staff member.[9]

---

[9]In 1988 we met with members of the National Council on Library Resources to discuss our first report on the Brown University Library effort. During the course of our discussion, one member claimed that both the Yale University and Columbia University Libraries had experienced a dramatic increase in the proliferation of paper files and private record-keeping activities

Building on valued understandings of their individual work routines and a sophisticated knowledge of the social organization of work within the library, a few staff members eventually concluded that any library-wide, multifunctional information system could provide each staff member with direct access to all information in the database, so that each staff member could download selective data at will into his or her own individually structured and managed working database.

Thus, in opposition to the administration's ideology of computerization, staff members were beginning to formulate an alternative ideology of computerization, one that envisioned a library-wide, multifunctional computer system that was "decentralized," "non-uniform," and "redundant." In short, they were beginning to challenge the legitimacy of the institution's claim that a new technology required new patterns of work by arguing that the logic of the system could and should support, not change, traditional patterns of work.

As this case study illustrates, technological choices are always motivated by a variety of nontechnical concerns and considerations. At the same time, specific technological choices are also intrinsic to ideologies of computerization that achieve unchallenged authority by erasing the distinction between technical and nontechnical factors and considerations. Conversely, challenges to specific ideologies of computerization can only be effective in reformulating directions of development and implementation to the extent that they successfully reinstate the distinction between technical and nontechnical considerations by calling attention to a wider range of possible definitions of the relationship between technology and work.

LOGICAL LIMITS TO EFFECTIVE CHALLENGES

To this point I have attempted to show that institutional technological choices are defined and rationalized in terms of specific ideologies of computerization that presuppose some intrinsic connection between the logic of technology and the logic of use. In the preceding section, I have tried, in particular, to show that specific ideologies of computerization are essentially contingent in that nothing intrinsic to the structures and functions of specific computing tools, the structure of institutions, the social organization of work or the character of technology-mediated understanding can prevent the emergence of opposing ideologies that effectively challenge authoritative assumptions about the connection between the logic of technology and the

---

following the implementation of the type of multifunctional information system Brown had planned to implement. At the time, it seemed to us that this was a key indication of the importance of "redundancy" to staff in those libraries, as well.

logic of use. Once they have been clearly articulated, effective challenges pave the way for unanticipated sociotechnical changes that completely escape the bounds of initially anticipated and desired changes and, thus, lead ultimately to the emergence of a new authoritative ideology.

If effective challenges were an intrinsic feature of all processes of computerization, the shape and direction of sociotechnical change would inevitably escape the normative bounds defined by specific ideologies of computerization. In fact, a number of documented cases of computerization have shown that this does not invariably occur when an institution decides to computerize. Clearly, not all computerizing institutions undergo the types of technological reformulation and sociotechnical transformation illustrated by "The Keyboarders' Challenge." Why is this?

In keeping with the great power of ideologies of computerization, there are logical limits to the types of challenges that end-users can effectively issue. These are limits that have been set as a consequence of the institution's initial decision to adopt new technologies. Thus, end-user challenges that insist on absolute distinctions between the logic of computing tools and the logic of work—challenges which, in essence, reject the basis of all ideologies of computerization—are not likely to affect the authority of the institution's ideology of computerization and, thus, will not change the prevailing shape or direction of sociotechnical change.

As Bourdieu (1977, 1991) convincingly argued for processes of social change in general, the success of subordinate views ("heterodoxa") in effectively challenging dominant views ("orthodoxa") depends on their recognizability and, thus, their potential acceptability as an alternative to holders of the dominant view. In the case of the Brown University Library, for example, staff were quite capable of arguing that there were important qualitative distinctions that distinguished the logic of electronic record keeping from the routine demands of managing the library collections (cf. Graves & Bader, 1988). Nevertheless, most staff understood that the only opportunity they would have to effect any institutional reformulation of the nature and direction of computer development and implementation would depend on their success in redefining the connection between the logic of computing tools and the logic of work.

Both the computerized publishing case and the library automation case illustrate the key role ideologies of computerization play in directing and shaping sociotechnical change. Most importantly, they suggest that successful end-user challenges to an authoritative ideology of computerization will themselves be based on an alternative ideology of computerization that seeks no more than to substitute a new set of definitions of the tool-work relationship for the authoritative set.

The keyboarders quite successfully accomplished this in the publishing company because they were able to force the organization to reexamine critically the most basic premises of its authoritative ideology of computerization. As a result, keyboarders and management began to negotiate a new authoritative ideology. The library staff were preparing themselves for similar definitional challenges to the institutional ideology at the time of our study. Whether or not they actually do choose to launch a strong challenge will depend on the extent to which the library carries out full implementation of a library-wide, multifunctional system that is centralized, nonredundant, and uniform. At the same time, the success of any direct challenge will depend on the staff's ability to convince the institution that some alternative connection between the logic of technology and the logic of work represents a "better" solution to the fundamental problems of information management. At the moment, the library straddles the fence between these two possibilities.

In stark contrast to the two cases already discussed, the key end-users in the following computerization case come to doubt or to reject a specific authoritative ideology of computerization, but they do not formulate a recognizable alternative ideology. As a result, all of their social actions and understandings serve no other purpose than to bolster the legitimacy of that ideology of computerization they individually suspect or reject. In such cases, the limits of possibilities for sociotechnical change continue to be defined entirely by the specific ideology of computerization that framed the institution's initial technological choices.

Case 3: Ineffective Challenges to a Dominant Ideology

At a private secondary school embarking on an experiment to develop and implement an innovative computer-based instructional resource, the predevelopment planning stage was quite similar to the early stages of the Brown University Library project (cf. Graves, 1989). Teachers (who were also to be the database developers), school administrators, technical support personnel, and outside consultants coordinated their diverse responsibilities in support of a single and quite specific ideology of computerization.

Self-consciously based on the computerization ideology of Brown University's earlier Intermedia Project (cf. Beeman et al., 1988, for details), this secondary-school experiment was to produce a hypertext database of historical and literary resources that would assist students in understanding the relationship between their studies of American literature and their studies of American history.

Central to this ideology of computerization was the essentialist presupposition that the logical architecture of hypertext with its "nonhierarchical webs" of electronic "links" connecting diverse textual and graphic materials would facilitate an analogous integrated mode of understanding in student-users.[10] Projecting understandings of the logic of this electronic medium onto normative ideals of the character of student understanding thus led the project team to envision as an outcome of the project a "seamless web" of historical-literary knowledge in the minds of high school students.

Although this ideology of computerization provided the initial impetus and direction for the overall design and organization of activities, some project members were cautiously skeptical of this particular ideology from the very beginning. In marked contrast to the Brown University Library project, the actual process of developing the new American history/literature database resulted in the emergence of two different challenges to the dominant ideology of computerization, each characterized by a distinct definition of the form and function of the computing technology.

On the one hand, the American history instructor/developer gradually came to perceive the computing technology as a medium for electronic storage (similar to his filing cabinet, he told us). The function of this tool was a straightforward provision of information—to provide students with independent and immediate access outside class to the diverse textual, graphic, and audio materials he had always employed as illustrations and examples to support his lectures and discussions.

This understanding was central to the ways in which he both chose to develop the database and directed students to use the technology. In his role as developer, he focused his attention on scanning pictures, charts, and maps, and digitizing songs. He then entered these into the database and subgrouped them chronologically, using the same historical time line that defined his course. In his role as a teacher, he would direct students to prepare for or to follow up specific lectures and discussions by reviewing all materials in the database found under a specifically identified chronological period of American history.

In this teacher's understanding, the computing technology was analogous in form and function to the school's library. In terms of his pedagogical objectives, the logic of hypertext with its nonhierarchical webs and linkages was largely irrelevant.[11] The logic of student learning and understanding was defined in his classes, as it always had been, by the logic of the relationship between teacher and student, rather than the logic of the relationship between

---

[10]Compare Beeman et al.'s (1988) balanced ethnographic description and critical analysis of the course of Brown University's very similar Intermedia Project with the unqualified endorsements of one instructor/developer of Intermedia who became convinced of the validity of this perspective on the analogous relationship between the structures of hypertext and the structure of student understanding (Landow, 1990).

[11]In the course of one interview towards the end of the first year, this teacher told us that he was "not concerned about linkages" and "cared very little" about when, where, or how they were introduced into the database.

computing tool and student use. By the end of the first year of development-implementation, we found no evidence to suggest that this had been changed by the development or use of hypertext.

The American literature instructor/developer, on the other hand, gradually came to perceive the same computing technology as a convenient medium for creative exploration of intertextuality and the historical contextualization of literary works. An interest in "contextualizing literary texts" inspired her to develop a rich hypertext corpus of diverse interconnected literary and historical texts and images. However, out of her year-long experiences entering texts and images and creating electronic linkages among them, a strong belief finally emerged that the electronic corpus she had constructed as an instructional resource for her students was in and of itself a "lifeless product." This belief was clarified and reinforced by her earliest experiences with student-users.

By the second semester of the first year of this project, the English teacher had begun directing her students to work with the hypertext corpora. In preparation for class discussions of specific literary texts, she would design a set of broad, sensitizing questions designed to encourage thought about the relationship between specific literary texts and their sociocultural milieus order to orient her students to the use of this new technology. However, she was not completely satisfied with the results of these assignments. Rather, she finally concluded, it would be the active process of creative research and serendipitous discovery that would constitute the desired learning goals, not the careful study of the constructed hypertext corpora themselves. Although for different reasons and with a different emphasis, she would agree with the history teacher that the logic of student learning and understanding was still the logic of the teacher–student relationship, regardless of the technology employed.

In direct contrast to the history teacher, however, the literature teacher came to see the computing technology as analogous in form and function to any tool for inscription, recording, and the organization of materials; thus, students would have to actively create hypertext databases themselves in order to gain any understanding of the conceptual relevance of webs and linkages. She did not believe that systematic study of the corpora she or others had constructed could lead students to an integrated understanding of history and literature.[12]

At the beginning of this secondary-school experiment, both teachers were quite intrigued by the apparently revolutionary potential of hypertext.

---

[12]At the end of the first year, our structured interviews and our "talk aloud" sessions with all student-users of the project database provided independent support for her conclusions. We found no evidence that these students had achieved the envisioned integrated understanding as a result of working with this new technology (cf. Graves, 1989).

Within a year of their meeting at Brown University with George Landow, however, neither teacher believed that there was any necessary connection between the logic of hypertext and the logic of either teaching or learning. For the history teacher, hypertext was little more than a convenient store-house for giving students direct access to his traditional assortment of diverse illustrative and supplementary instructional materials. For the English teacher, hypertext was a novel and interesting tool students could be taught to employ in the service of a fairly traditional academic process of creative research. However, it was decidedly not the logic of hypertext that absorbed her attention. It was the explorative nature of the research process as she had always known it that she kept in constant focus. Hypertext could provide an interesting and convenient working tool that "allowed" for this, but there was certainly nothing essential about hypertext that would, as Landow described it, "encourage" or "demand" "new modes of reading, writing, teaching or learning" (Landow, 1990, p. 407).

Each teacher's understanding and concrete uses of this new technology called into question the presupposed intrinsic connection between the logic of hypertext and the logic of student learning and understanding. Neverthe-less, neither one of these challenges had weakened in the least the legitimacy of that authoritative ideology of computerization that had provided the framework and rationale for initiating and directing this development project. This was because neither teacher had proposed an alternative ide-ology that would provide a new set of logical connections. If they had done so, they could have challenged the legitimacy of the dominant ideology of computerization, thus paving the way for a transformation of strategies for development, implementation, and use.

The fact that they did not formulate an effective challenge meant that the first year of this project ended as it had begun: Teachers, school administra-tors, technical support personnel, and outside consultants continued to co-ordinate their diverse responsibilities in support of a single and quite specific ideology of computerization. Furthermore, by the beginning of the second year of this Project, the scope of the development–implementation effort had been broadened to include the American literature and American history teachers and students at a neighboring public high school.

THE DOMINANT EPISTEME OF THE 21ST CENTURY?

The sheer ubiquity of computing tools and the accelerating interest in taking full advantage of those tools in every domain of contemporary social life could mean that we are well on the way to taking the computer for granted as an essential and unproblematic tool. In a rather limited sense we already do. Government, industry, and education continue to invest heavily in new computing technologies on the basis of explicit claims that computerization entails positive, qualitative changes in productivity, efficiency, relative cost, communication, work, teaching, learning, and so on.

At the same time, the growing record of published case studies of computerization over the last decade clearly demonstrates that the qualitative changes envisioned by designers and developers do not necessarily follow from institutional decisions to automate or to adopt new information technologies. To state the matter baldly, although institutions do make and rationalize technological choices in conformity with ideologies of computerization, the end-users of new technologies do not necessarily come to understand or to act upon new computing tools in conformity with those same ideologies of computerization.

At the same time as new consumers are being socialized into institutionally defined and structured uses of computing tools, they are most certainly subordinating these new technical definitions and experiences to a much broader range of changing motives, interests, understandings, and experiences than any designer, developer, or computing administrator could ever technologically encompass. If analysts and computing administrators paid closer attention to the phenomenology of computing experience within specific institutions undergoing computerization, they would recognize that the fundamental engine for sociotechnical change is not technical, economic, or political. It is social and it is conceptual. At the level of macroanalysis, it is the institution-specific ideology of computerization that defines and objectifies the rationale, conditions, opportunities, and limits of sociotechnical change; at the level of microanalysis, it is the character of end-user response not to the technology per se but to the institutional ideology of computerization itself that serves either to reinforce that ideology or to transform it and, as a consequence, the rationale, conditions, opportunities, and limits of sociotechnical change, as well.

As we have seen, by presupposing a determinate, intrinsic connection between the logic of computing tools and the logic of computing use, ideologies of computerization promote visions of technologically shaped or driven change. Ideologies of computerization also continue to inform public and scholarly debate over the implications of an "information technology revolution." The media, popular literature, computing journals, grant proposals, and development plans do not reject in toto ideologies of computerization. They only reject specific ideologies of computerization in favor of some alternative ideological formulation of the tool–work relationship.

What characterizes our contemporary information society is, in fact, a continuously changing contest of diverse ideologies of computerization. This contest is crucial because it ultimately prevents us from taking computers for granted by chronically reinvigorating and providing legitimacy for the skeptical denial that there is anything intrinsic to computing tools that channels, shapes, directs, or necessarily facilitates any specific pattern of usage or understanding. Ultimately, it is this belief and not the belief in any concrete ideology of computerization that ensures long-term continuous change in technical development, marketing, patterns of use, and end-user knowledge and belief. Our new information society is based on a never-ending search for the perfect fit between technically defined means and socially defined ends. It is the search to secure the unfulfilled promise of all ideologies of computerization.

REFERENCES

Attewell, P. (1991). Big brother and the sweatshop: Computer surveillance in the automated office. In C. Dunlop & R. Kling (Eds.), *Computerization and controversy* (pp. 236–256). New York: Academic Press.

Beeman, W. O., Anderson, K. T., Bader, G., Larkin, J., McClard, A., McQuillan, P., & Shields M. (1988). *Intermedia: A case study of innovation in higher education*. Unpublished report to the Annenberg/CPB Project, Institute for Research in Information and Scholarship, Brown University, Providence, RI.

Bourdieu, P. (1977). *Outline of a theory of practice*. Cambridge, England: Cambridge University Press.

Bourdieu, P. (1991). *Language and symbolic power*. Cambridge, England: Polity Press.

Braverman, H. (1974). *Labor and monopoly capital*. New York: Monthly Review Press.

Chesebro, J. W., & Bonsall, D. G. (1989). *Computer-mediated communication: Human relationships in a computerized world*. Tuscaloosa: University of Alabama Press.

Dreyfus, H. (1972). *What computers can't do—A critique of artificial intelligence*. New York: Harper & Row.

Dunlop, C., & Kling, R. (Eds.). (1991). *Computerization and controversy*. New York: Academic Press.

Feenberg, A. (1991). *Critical theory of technology*. New York: Oxford University Press.

Forester, T. (Ed.). (1989). *Computers in the human context: Information technology, productivity and people*. Cambridge: MIT Press.

Giddens, A. (1976). *New rules of sociological method*. New York: Basic Books.

Giddens, A. (1979). *Central problems in social theory*. Berkeley: University of California Press.

Graves, W., III. (1989). *Project ACCESS—Ethnographic report for year one* (Unpublished report to McDonnell Foundation and Apple Computer). Research Program in Education, Culture, and Technology. Providence, RI: Brown University.

Graves, W., III, & G. Bader, (1988). *The library as information system: Aspects of continuity and change in the staff's world* (IRIS Technical Report 87–3). Providence, RI: Brown University.

Graves, W. III, & Nyce J. (1992). Normative models and situated practice in medicine. *Information and Decision Technologies, 18,* 143–150.

Haas, W. J. (1980). Research libraries and the dynamics of change. *Scholarly Publishing, 11,* 195–202.

Hirschhorn, L. (1984). *Beyond mechanization: Work and technology in a postindustrial age*. Cambridge, MA: MIT Press.

Hirschhorn, L. (1989). Robots can't run factories. In T. Forester (Ed.), *Computers in the human context: Information technology, productivity and people*. Cambridge: MIT Press.

Ihde, D. (1990). *Technology and the lifeworld: From garden to earth*. Bloomington: Indiana University Press.

Jones, C. L. (1985). Academic libraries and computing: A time of change. *EDUCOM Bulletin, 20*, 9–12.

Kling, R. (1980). Social analyses of computing: Theoretical perspectives in recent empirical research. *Computing Surveys, 12*(1), 61–110.

Kling, R. (1987). Defining the boundaries of computing across complex organization. In R. Boland & R. Hirschheim (Eds.), *Critical issues in information systems*. London: Wiley.

Kling, R., & Iacano, S. (1989). Desktop computerization and the organization of work. In T. Forester (Eds.), *Computers in the human context*. Cambridge, MA: MIT Press.

Landow, G. P. (1990). Hypertext and collaborative work: The example of intermedia. In J. Galegher, R. Kraut, & C. Egido (Eds.), *Intellectual teamwork: Social and technological foundations of cooperative work* (pp. 407–428). Hillsdale, NJ: Lawrence Erlbaum Associates.

Morgan, G. (1984). *Sociological theory and organizational change*. New York: Academic Press.

Morgan, G. (1988). *Images of organization*. New York: Basic Books.

Nyce, J., & Graves, W., III. (1990). The construction of knowledge in neurology: Implications for hypermedia system development. *Artificial Intelligence in Medicine, 2*, 315–325.

Sack, J. R. (1986). Open systems for open minds: Building the library without walls. *College and Research Libraries*, 536–545.

Sculley, J. (1991). The relationship between business and higher education: A perspective on the twenty-first century. *Communications of the ACM, 32*(9), 1056–61.

Shields, M., Graves, W., III, & Nyce, J. (1991). Technological innovation in higher education: A case study in academic computing. In J. Morell & M. Fleischer (Eds.), *Advances in the implementation and impact of computer systems* (Vol. 1, pp. 183–209). Greenwich, CT: JAI Press.

Shields, M., Graves, W., III, & Nyce, J. (1992). Computing and the social organization of academic work. *Journal of Science Education and Technology, 1*(4), 243–258.

Suchman, L. (1987). *Plans and situated actions*. Cambridge, England: Cambridge University Press.

Toffler, A. (1980). *The third wave*. New York: Bantam.

Turkle, S. (1984). *The second self: Computers and the human spirit*. New York: Simon & Schuster.

Wilkinson, B. (Ed.). (1983). *The shopfloor politics of new technology*. London: Heineman Educational.

Zuboff, S. (1988). *In the age of the smart machine*. New York: Basic Books.

5

Stalking the Art Historian

William O. Beeman
Brown University

One of the greatest mysteries in the study of human knowledge is under-standing the praxis of scholarly work. Academics know each other by the products of research and writing, but virtually no one knows what takes place on a day-to-day basis, behind closed office or laboratory doors in order to turn ideas, hypotheses, and scholarly questions into the coin of academic productivity: finished papers, reports, articles, monographs, and books.

It is remarkable that so little effort has been expended on trying to discover what scholars do all day, because it is the habits of work carried out relent-lessly on a day-to-day basis that constitutes a good part of the stuff of which knowledge is made. The great ideas of history are the products of the thinking of great minds in conjunction with specific habits of working.

Scholars themselves are often little help in reconstructing their own work habits. The routines of scholarship are built up gradually over the years and become habituated, and then disattended. People rarely consider the strate-gies they use in carrying out the mundane tasks of everyday routine—life is too short to spend time in contemplation of such things. It is only when modification of habits (e.g., changing or eliminating snacking practices) is desired that careful attention is paid to humdrum correlations of behavior (e.g., the coincidence of watching televised sporting events and consuming potato chips).

For most scholars, their own work routines are totally uninteresting. After many years of collection, compilation, and writing it is hard for a researcher to explicate his or her strategies in using library catalogues, or the precise factors that tip the decision to work on into the night in the laboratory or at the computer terminal rather than leave at 5 p.m.

For the laboratory sciences the theoretical praxis of scholarly routine is codified in the canons of "scientific method." Even though few scientists may actually follow the routines of the scientific method in their work, textbooks inculcate the methods of hypothesis formulation and testing, careful recording of data and results on ever new generations of incipient scientists. It is only later in their professional lives that these researchers discover how widely actual scientific research practice differs from its theoretical model.

The social sciences and especially the humanities are far less routinized in accounting for the practice of their disciplines. Most scholars operate with a few standard methodological tools perhaps acquired in a single graduate course on disciplinary methodology, such as literary analysis, historiography, fieldwork methodology, or archival research methods. Most often, however, work habits are acquired through apprenticeship with senior persons in the field, or through personal trial and error over time. These work habits, however acquired, remain intensely personal, and are rarely discussed with anyone, even close associates or spouses.

It seems fair to ask: If little attention has been devoted to the study of scholarly work routines, is it because there is little benefit in doing such a study? I think there are at least three reasons why such a study is potentially important. First, as I alluded previously, such work leads to better understanding of the processes of knowledge creation. Second, understanding these processes will help scholars in discovering ways to improve them. Third, revealing these processes is instructional in training students in the field.

Understanding routine work in scholarship may help crack the mysteries of the "intuitive leap" in knowledge creation. Most scholars acknowledge that their work consists largely of "dog work"—inefficient, repetitive processes that may or may not lead to finished products of earth-shattering profundity. The really creative part of scholarship lies in the formulation of new insights and ideas. The best of these ideas force other scholars to re-examine long-held assumptions and beliefs. They are, in Thomas Kuhn's formulation "paradigm-shattering" ideas. Many of these formulations are arrived at through intuitive leaps achieved by men and women of genius who have somehow acquired comprehensive enough knowledge of the basic information of their field, combined with enough creativity to see new interconnections and interrelationships that have eluded others. Following such leaps, much work may then lapse into routine in order to demonstrate and prove the validity of the new insights.

The relationship between routine work and these creative leaps is unclear. We learn from the biographies of acknowledged geniuses that some had ruthlessly regimented work habits. Others alternated fits of creative work with long periods of inattention to scholarly matters. For others, work routines were mysterious. At irregular intervals they would emerge from their inner rooms with brilliant finished work giving the world no clue as to how it was produced.

The role of interaction and discussion in producing scholarly work is also unclear. Much cutting edge scholarship is the result of collaboration, but many works of genius seem to be the product of single minds. The humanities are particularly notable for works produced by single authors. Collaboration is the rule in many laboratory sciences, and social sciences fall somewhere in the middle with respectable work produced both by teams of researchers and by isolated scholars.

For many centuries there have been only a handful of research techniques for scholars in the social sciences and humanities. Methodologies in these fields consist of personal observation, interviewing, collection of statistical data, and archival research. Analytic techniques consist of rumination, informed personal interpretation, pattern comparisons, formalized reasoning and logic, and a few limited statistical techniques. Reporting of results follows esoteric, shifting stylistic canons for each separate discipline. In some years presentational fashion embraces a more literary approach, in other years more "hard-nosed" presentation of data.

Although understanding the patterns of the minutiae of everyday work may have been largely uninteresting for the world at large—even for scholars themselves—it is this understanding that is the key to discovering the nature of knowledge itself. Still, because the praxis of day-to-day routine scholarship was so uniform and unchanging, it has been hard to focus on the nature of that work.

Now the advent of computer use in scholarship has created a new set of possibilities for scholars. The possibility now exists, through computerization, to automate many of the hitherto tedious routine aspects of scholarly work, and to accomplish analytic and reporting tasks in a much more efficient and exacting manner.

It is this burgeoning set of *possibilities* that is allowing a clearer view of work routines. We now see that editing and rewriting of manuscripts has been made much simpler through word processing. Because of this, the processes of manuscript preparation are undergoing scrutiny in a way they never had before.

The management of scholarly qualitative data may theoretically be made simpler, but only if data management tools can be created that are truly useful for the scholars that might put them to work in their everyday routine. Because the possibility of improvement has now been made clear, scholars are beginning to ask themselves how they actually perform analysis in hopes of finding ways of speeding up some parts of the process.

Communication between scholars is already being facilitated through electronic networking, and will create even more profound changes in the ways scholars collaborate if computer-based communication tools can be made compatible with day-to-day habits of the academic workplace. Therefore scholars are beginning to look more carefully at their own patterns of correspondence and talk.

A CASE STUDY IN SCHOLARLY WORK ROUTINES

In 1985 the Getty Art History Information Program (AHIP) and researchers from the Office of Program Analysis (OPA) Institute for Research in Information and Scholarship (IRIS) at Brown University undertook a collaborative research project to create a profile of the work habits of art historians. The resulting study *Object, Image and Inquiry: The Art Historian at Work* (Bakewell, Beeman, Reese, & Schmidt, 1988) was a compendium of observations, autobiographical statements, and opinions from 18 prominent art historians, combined with a close study of two 6-month long art history research projects. The account that follows is derived from that research.

The research was carried out in the spirit of an anthropological field study. The art historians selected for interviews were chosen with an eye toward providing variety within the field. The time periods for their work ranged from medieval to modern. Subject fields were widely varied, including architecture, stained glass, photographs, and manuscript art as well as more conventional painting and sculpture.

Interviews were open-ended and lengthy, some lasting 2 days. They were designed to elucidate the art historians' work practices, but they covered a wide range of autobiographical information as well. The philosophy behind this method of interviewing was that work habits and routines are acquired over a lifetime, and are inherited from mentors, colleagues, and early life experiences.

Interview subjects were also queried on a variety of ideological themes, including their attitudes toward art history as a profession, toward their colleagues, and toward their perceptions of current trends in practice in the discipline. The philosophy behind this line of inquiry was that work routines do not exist in isolation: They are contextualized within the social and institutional fabric of the discipline as a whole and can only be understood in this full context.

The case studies were likewise set up as ethnographic observational studies with the aim of discovering the way information resources were used in "natural" context. The principal investigators of the study were furnished with graduate students who were charged with keeping close track of their activities during the project through diaries and direct accounts during periodic "debriefing" interviews. They were asked to deal particularly with their use of information resources, and their information-seeking activities. The principal investigators were also interviewed at regular interviews throughout the project.

All of these activities provided a rich, comprehensive picture of art history as a discipline, and much of the practice within the field. The study could, of course, only reflect the attitudes and practice of the specific individuals studied, but it is reasonable to assume that the particular cross-section of persons included in the study was broad enough to at least have captured some of the principal trends in the field.

ART HISTORY AS AN ACTIVITY

Art history is an academic discipline of extraordinary diversity. In general, it shares many of the features of other humanistic disciplines in its overall practice. It nevertheless has some special features that set it apart. First, I present some of the general features common to art history and other humanities disciplines.

Art history is largely a qualitative discipline. Its conclusions have to do with the descriptive nature of things. Statistics may play a role in helping art historians draw their conclusions, but they are secondary considerations, in that their use is optional depending on the problem in which the art historian is engaged, and individual predilection on the part of the researcher.

Art history is an interpretive discipline. This means that the conclusions drawn in art historians' writings are derived from expertise of individual art historians. Their individual opinions derived from long contact and experience with art objects and data concerning those objects. In principle these conclusions are limitless in their scope and quality. In practice they are limited by the community of opinion active in the overall discipline at any given moment. This contrasts with laboratory sciences and some social sciences in that in these latter disciplines, although expert opinion is also important, conclusions are constrained by canons of proof that usually depend on statistical data being marshalled to support previously stated hypotheses. There is an internal logic in the laboratory sciences that guarantees in most cases that hypotheses can be shown to be proved or rejected. In art history there are few if any definitive proofs for any conclusion. There can be, however, convincing arguments in support of an interpretive conclusion.

Art history is also a narrative discipline. Scholars present the bulk of their work in the form of discursive prose. Art historians characteristically disseminate the results of their work in the form of books, articles, and museum catalogues. This means that art historians must be accomplished writers as well as competent researchers. They must be capable of producing long works in correct scholarly format. Additionally some publishing in art history is done in semi-scholarly publications that have a large lay audience. For these periodicals it is necessary for the art historian to have adequate writing skills to compose articles in a more popular style.

Art history is a cumulative discipline. Scholars typically conduct research in the same general areas throughout their lives. Their richest and most complete work is usually completed in the final years of their careers after they have acquired a vast store of experience in dealing with the principal objects of their studies. This career pattern contrasts with mathematics and some of the theoretical sciences where aptitude for the discipline is shown through flashes of intuitive insight early in one's career, with major contributions coming at an early age.

Finally, art history is a discipline that seeks breadth in its conclusions rather than narrow focus. It seeks to make connections with other areas of knowledge, such as history, literature, sociology, anthropology, economics, psychology, and even the sciences. These connections are made both in the gathering of data, and in the reporting of conclusions. This contrasts with fields such as linguistics or mathematics where satisfactory conclusions can be drawn within intellectual frameworks which are conceptually "sealed" (i.e., isolatable from any other body of knowledge).

As I mentioned earlier, these characteristics are not unique to art history. Literature, history, classics, social/cultural anthropology, and philosophy are some of the other humanities-based disciplines that share most or all of these features.

Art history has a number of special characteristics, however. Some of these are also found in other disciplines, but are not as widely shared as the five general characteristics just cited. It is these special features combined with the five general features that combine to give art history its unique flavor.

First, art history has a strong focus on art objects. Even for those art historians who concentrate on biography, the social effects of art, or the economic history, the art object must be observed and studied in great detail. As one of the interview subjects in the study stated when asked about her work: "I memorize paintings." This requirement is so strong, that it is somewhat unthinkable to call oneself an art historian without this kind of engagement. In the discipline this intimate knowledge, when it is the principal focus of one's work, is a subdiscipline known as connoisseurship.

Related to this is the art historians' use of visual images both in research and publication. Visual images serve as *aides memoires* when the actual objects are not at hand. They are used widely in teaching. Their use is also imperative in publication. One can really not publish a book or article in art history without illustrations. This need for images often prompts art historians to develop skills as photographers.

Third, art history is done largely in isolation. Individual scholars consult very little, if at all with anyone else—even those who know a great deal about their particular field of expertise. Unlike in many disciplines, collaborative research is rare.

Fourth, art history requires juggling enormous amounts of very diverse information. Anything could and usually is of significance in trying to understand the objects and social/cultural/historical frameworks in which they are embedded.

Finally, art history usually requires "fieldwork." Because it is imperative that art historians know original objects intimately, it is inevitable that they must travel to see these objects. In order to see the complete works of some European artists, it may be necessary to undertake a worldwide excursion. Consultation of archives and libraries containing unique documents also requires travel to remote sites. This creates the need for a wide range of secondary skills related to the conduct of fieldwork. Art historians must know foreign languages, must develop "people skills" in order to deal with those people serving as "gatekeepers" to their objects of study, and must know how to organize an expedition economically and efficiently. They must also have grantsmanship skills adequate to secure the money needed to support this fieldwork.

INFORMATION RESOURCES AND THEIR MANAGEMENT

The work patterns of art historians create a number of highly characteristic patterns in the use of information resources.

First, because art historians work largely in isolation, their methods for collecting and recording data tend to be highly idiosyncratic. Some record information in notebooks using a variety of formats from random notes to highly structured data collection sheets. Some use index cards upon which information is recorded using a wide array of schemes. Some are simple random note cards with all sorts of information jumbled together. Book references, notes on manuscripts, observations of art objects, and professional contacts are all scribbled willy-nilly for later sorting. Other schemes involve elaborate marking of corners and borders to allow for a wide range of sorting strategies.

Photography plays an important role in information collecting. Schemes for taking and ordering photographs are likewise highly individualized. It is sometimes necessary to rely on commercial photographs, but in general the art historians in this study preferred to do their own photography, or at least direct the photographer creating the images. Photographic images have a dual purpose. They are used both for research and analysis, and also for publication. Both require high-quality photography, so standards for creating these images tend to be high.

It should be noted, however, that *nothing* really substitutes for the original art object in the conduct of research, with one exception: In iconography, photographic images can be useful tools to search for the existence of iconographic material. Nevertheless, photographic images of these objects are largely limited in their use to serving as *aides memoires* or as illustrative material for publication.

The use of archive material is essential to most art historical research. Using archives can be a trying and tedious process, although some of the individuals in our study found that they grew to enjoy the routine over an extended period of time. Many archives allow researchers to examine only a small amount of material at a time, and the material is often not stored in any systematic way. As a result, it is often impossible to know where important documents will be found. Moreover, it may take years to thoroughly explore all of the materials in a given archive. For this reason the researcher must keep track of the "geography" of the archive, and of the material he or she has already examined, even if it is ultimately worthless for his or her current research. Often the only recording materials allowed in an archive are pencil and paper, so many shorthand notes on unusable material are made for use as placeholders when returning to the archive at a later date.

Once information is collected, it must be stored for later retrieval. Some of the art historians in our study confessed to having no systematic filing system at all. They kept all their bits and pieces of information in boxes, on a desk, or jumbled in folders. These individuals rely on their memory, overall background knowledge, and mental organization to structure their research publications. The notes are maintained as a kind of informal "backup system" in case mental faculties failed.

When systematic filing systems are used, they tend to have two important characteristics. First, they have an "organic quality." Second, they tend to be organized by project, rather than become integrated into one compendious master file.

The organic quality of files is reflected by the way they "grow" over time. A researcher may start out with a highly structured set of categories for organization of information, only to find that, for example, two of the categories develop vast numbers of sub- and sub-subcategories, whereas others contain no information at all. Because of this, the filing system can in many cases have a direct effect on the orientation of research. When it is discovered that vast amounts of information have been collected over time on what was originally thought to be a minor aspect of a research project, the entire focus of the work may be changed.

Files of material, because they are specific to a particular piece of research tend not to be reused. Once the book or article is written, the file is usually abandoned—stored in a basement or back room never to be consulted again.

The use of contemporary published material is surprisingly limited. Most art historians are working in areas that are so specialized, there may be only a half dozen or fewer persons of equivalent expertise in the entire world. Therefore, there is little opportunity or need to use secondary sources for research extensively. Archival and other primary resources are exceptions to this general pattern. Nevertheless the conventions of academic publication require that work be referenced in order to demonstrate scholarly competence. Nonarchival published library materials are most often used for this purpose

USE OF TIME (AND SPACE)

In order to understand the use of time by art historians it is necessary to see the research process in several frames, taking place in a number of spatial frameworks. A research project can take many years to complete. During this time the art historian will usually work in a number of locations, and carry out a wide variety of activities.

Most art historians have a "home base" where they keep their libraries, photographic images, and documents. This is typically a university, but it can also be a museum, a library, a foundation, and occasionally a private enterprise such as a gallery or a publishing office. Most of our interviewees did some or all of their work in their homes.

In addition, there are a number of field locations in which most research is done. This varies widely for each individual researcher. For some the field location can be a series of European archives. For the architectural historians it is the physical location of the buildings they study.

The normal pattern for most art historians is to alternate periods at the home base with periods in the field. For academics it is typical to spend the entire summer in a field location, frequently at personal expense. Some researchers have second homes in the region of their principal research. Every 4 or 5 years it is usually possible to spend a much longer period—6 or 12 months—in this field site. For persons based at other than academic institutions this time must be found in other ways. Usually the art historian is employed by an organization in which research is part of the normal routine of activity. In this case, time in the field is part of the researcher's normal job.

It normally takes one long fieldwork period coupled with several shorter periods to gather material for a major research publication. These field periods are preceded by a planning period at the home base where the project is laid out in detail. The fieldwork is likewise interspersed with periods at the home base where notes are sorted, filed, and analyzed. Finally, the end of the project is carried out at the home base, where the final write-up is accomplished.

Given this pattern of alternating activities, it is not surprising that the art historians in our study spent the bulk of their time when at their home institutions reading and writing. This might give the impression that reading and writing are their principal activities, but this would be a mistaken conclusion. Most of the reading and writing tasks are time consuming, but they are often highly mechanical in nature. The bulk of the creative "work" in a given project is usually carried out elsewhere, and consists of a vast range of varied data collection and analytic processes. The final write-up of the project is an exception to this because it is also an important creative activity.

In the final write-up, some of the most fruitful thinking in the entire project takes place according to our interviewees. Many asserted that it was during the writing process itself that they came to their most fruitful conclusions—ideas that they had not previously articulated. This is great contrast to the laboratory sciences where the final write-up is usually a mechanical reporting of results arrived at through experimentation.

Nevertheless, the period spent in final write-up is hard won. For the art historian, because he or she is generally employed in an academic position or museum during the bulk of the year, the sustained time needed for writing is generally not available. The working day is fragmented a thousand ways through teaching, bureaucratic duties, and interruptions. For most academic art historians university vacation periods are vital for getting the work of writing done. Unfortunately, this time is also the primary time art historians have for conducting primary research. Thus there must be a great deal of juggling of resources to accommodate all phases of a research project.

USE OF COMPUTING TECHNOLOGY

There was wide variation in use of computer technology in art history among the subjects of our study. One extreme was represented by those who were hesitant in using computers for any purpose at all—even for word processing. Several persons indicated that their data collection was not at all facilitated by computer technology, nor were they comfortable composing on the computer.

It was far more common to see individuals working with computers in their projects, although occasionally they did not operate those computers themselves. Many of the scholars did use computers routinely for word processing. Some of the advantages they noted were compactness of storage of computer-based materials, the relative ease of making corrections and changing formats for publication, and the ease of sorting materials in some word processing applications.

Some of the art historians were beginning to make more demands of computer technology than just word processing. The most common set of additional applications consisted of the use of database technology. Database software proved particularly helpful in organizing information on large numbers of objects where comparison of detailed information was crucial to the project at hand.

In one of the research projects studied as part of this project, the principal investigator, Professor Rolf Winkes of Brown University, had set up a very sophisticated computerized database system designed to categorize and file information on a large base of art objects—in this case Roman coins.

The overall project was designed to demonstrate the relationship between portraiture and numismatics in Roman coinage in an exhibition and catalog. The project aimed to document and reproduce unpublished Roman coins from the collections of Brown University, and the Royal Cabinet in Sao Paolo. The project aimed to compare and bring together coins that were widely dispersed geographically for analysis and comparison.

The research was carried out by two graduate students, Kelly Kambourian and Nina Duncan. Both Kambourian and Duncan located Roman coins in collections worldwide, and entered a wide variety of information concerning each coin on a index cards: the date and location of manufacture of the coin, the name of the ruler under whose reign the coin was produced, the nature of material on the reverse side, the denomination of the coin and the name of the moneyer. Image descriptions were also included.

The information on the cards was then entered by Kambourian and Duncan into a locally produced database resident on the Brown mainframe computer. This process took approximately 28% of the total time both spent on the entire project. The database was originally designed for bibliographic references. By changing the category titles from "author," "title," "publisher," and "date" to "date," "ruler," "obverse image," and "reverse image," the project was able to use the program quite easily. Other bibliographic fields were also assigned new headings.

The use of the program allowed for a wide range of sorting operations to be carried out on the coins included in the database. It allowed for comparisons of geographically dispersed coins, and provided a useful tool in selecting the coins for exhibition. It should be noted, however, that the database did not contain all the information included on the index cards. The card system was maintained and referred to even when the database system was in place. Thus the two indexing systems were really used for different scholarly purposes.

An additional computer application which proved useful for this project was electronic mail. Brown University is part of BITNET, an electronic network linking educational institutions worldwide. Professor Winkes was able to correspond regularly with one of his Belgian colleagues who had an important interest in this project throughout its duration using BITNET. This greatly shortened the time needed for correspondence and interchange of information.

Despite the usefulness of these tools, several of the subjects in the study were frustrated at not being able to find database tools that were really adequate for their work in terms of flexibility of design. As they work with these systems it becomes clear that part of the difficulty in using database software has to do with the researcher's own conceptualization of the problems he or she is trying to solve. The software itself does little if the scholars cannot clearly conceptualize the scope of their work or the tasks involved.

It seemed clear that a number of the subjects of the study not currently using computer technology could definitely use it to some advantage. There was a great deal of frustration expressed by several subjects at the difficulty of note and record keeping. A number of art historians expressed continual frustration and self-doubt about their information organizational abilities. Many felt frustration at not being able to find things easily. Effective use of database tools might be of great help to these individuals.

A number of the subjects in the study expressed the desire for computer-based tools that do not now exist: computer-accessible tables of contents for art history journals, catalogues of archives, and sophisticated computer-aided design and drafting tools to help in the analysis of architecture. A number also expressed the need for more widespread electronic messaging and conferencing tools.

There was an almost universal cautionary note among the subjects of the study warning against heavy automation of the art historical research process. Most of the skepticism had the same theme: Doing art history is in the end an introspective, interpretive process; the computer cannot really aid in this except in mechanical filing and organization and in writing.

CONCLUSION

The study on which this discussion is based dealt with a limited number of scholars who did not represent the full spectrum of specializations in art history. However, it is unlikely that any study could really accomplish that aim. Art history shares a great deal with other humanistic disciplines in its individualistic orientation. Art historians share a common set of orientations in their work as witnessed by the products of their research. Art history publications seem largely to deal with common themes and similar approaches to analysis.

The uniformities that are seen in art history publications mask the extreme individuality of art historians' research methods, however. Based on our small survey, there are as many approaches to doing art history as there are art historians. Moreover, art historians themselves appear to cherish this aspect of their discipline; indeed they jealously guard their prerogatives to pursue their own line of research in precisely the way they see best illuminates the nature of the art objects in which they are most interested.

The conditions under which art history is carried out constitute a common denominator for most art historians. These therefore serve to give some common shape to the research process. Among the most important factors are:

1. The need for direct inspection of actual art objects.
2. The alternation of periods of fieldwork with periods of writing.
3. Overall lack of collaboration in research and writing.
4. Difficulties arising from the organization and tracking of disparate information.
5. Interpretation as a primary process in producing scholarly products from research.

These parameters are all factors that must be taken into consideration in attempting to make any improvements or modifications in the enterprise of art historical research. The factors just cited are common to many, but not all humanistic disciplines as well, and might serve as a rough guide for interventions in these other intellectual activities.

Let us for a minute speculate on some of the ways that interventions might be introduced in the aforementioned parameters to improve or modify the art historical work process.

The need for direct inspection of objects implies a need for travel. The most obvious intervention that could be made here would be to provide increased funding for travel to collections and to view art objects. Alternatively, funding for exhibitions that would collect widely dispersed materials of scholarly interest in one spot might be money extremely well spent. There is currently no easy source of funding for the temporary assembling of collections for scholarly research purposes aside from the public exhibition of those objects. Reproduced images seem to be useless for primary scholarly purposes in most cases in art history. For the few areas they *are* useful, such as in iconography and historical architecture (where images of plans, charts, and areal photographs are important), improved funding for the creation and distribution of these kinds of images would be helpful, particularly if they were linked through a computer database system.

The large blocks of time for travel and writing needed for art history can be provided through increased funding for release time. In particular, unrestricted release time for primary research would be of great value to established scholars whose "track records" as researchers are well established.

The lack of collaboration in research and writing in art history is not seen as a great problem by the subjects of our study. Indeed, many indicated it was a virtue of the discipline. Nevertheless, one intervention that could make a real difference in scholarship in the field would be improved international electronic communications, and increased education of art historians on how to use it. The use of BITNET has greatly aided scholars in many disciplines. Art history could also benefit from its use.

Help in managing disparate information can be provided through development of improved computer software. In particular, free-form text databases with sophisticated bibliographic management features geared specifically for art historians would make a great difference for many persons in the field. Such tools would need to combine great ease of use with great flexibility in defining and manipulating the parameters of information storage and retrieval. Some of the textual databases, such as tables of contents of major journals, or indexes to archive contents would also be widely used.

It is hard to know how interpretive processes could be much improved or changed through institutional or technological intervention. "Thought processors" in computer software have been of some use to scholars as organizational tools, though we had no indication that these were widely used by art historians. The art historians who expressed skepticism about technological aid for this part of their scholarly activities may ultimately be right. Interfering with the art historian's interpretive processes may well be detrimental to the field.

REFERENCE

Bakewell, E., Beeman, W., Reese, C. M., & Schmitt, M. (Eds.). (1988). *Object, image and inquiry: The art historian at work*. Santa Monica, CA: Getty Art History Information Program.

6

Computers and Pedagogy: The Invisible Presence

Patrick McQuillan
University of Colorado

Whether computers enhance learning in some cognitively unique fashion in courses using computer-based education (CBE) materials or whether new content and instructional innovations tied to developing CBE materials represent the real source of improved student performance is an issue widely debated in the field of educational computing. In criticizing studies on the impact of CBE, Clark (1983, 1985a, 1985b) argued that metaanalyses reporting "small but significant contributions to course achievement" (Kulik, Kulik, & Cohen 1980, p. 525) and "positive effects on student learning" (Kulik, Kulik, & Bangert-Drowns, 1985, p. 385) are flawed. One factor confounding these studies, he maintained, is the "same-instructor" effect, derived from Clark's critique of Kulik, Kulik, and Cohen (1980). Their metaanalysis of 59 CBE studies in higher education found that when different instructors teach conventional and computer-based sections of the same course, the impact on learning (measured by differences in exam scores) is more pronounced than in cases where the same instructor teaches both sections. Kulik et al. (1980) suggested that this "same-instructor" effect can be explained by the standardization of performance brought about by developing the CBE materials that "may help teachers do a good job in their conventional teaching assignments" (p. 539) as well. In their view, "[o]utlining objectives, constructing lessons, and preparing evaluation materials (requirements in both computer-based and personalized instruction)" (p. 539) may lead to better teaching.

103

Rather than attributing the consistent performance of computer-based and conventional classes taught by the same instructor to an unspecified notion of "improved instruction," Clark argued that when the same instructor both develops CBE materials *and* teaches the traditional course, "the content and instructional method [of both courses] is more likely to be held constant and the effect of computers in the resulting achievement is negligible" (1985a, p. 139). Thus, he suggested that innovations in any aspect of a course arising from the CBE development process are likely to affect both CBE and non–CBE sections. In a later study, Kulik et al. (1985) acknowledged Clark's hypothesis that instructional innovation and strategies tied to CBE design may "[diffuse] . . . to the control condition," (p. 385), that is, the convention- ally taught course. Extending the implications of this interpretation, Clark (1985a) claimed that although computer attributes, for example, "zooming or laying out objects from three to two dimensional space or learning the reasoning steps required to program in LOGO" (p. 143) may cultivate certain cognitive skills, "the resulting skills could be cultivated with any number of nominally different, non-computer related treatments that serve the same necessary cognitive function" (p. 143). For instance, citing Bovy- Clark (1983), he noted that "irising," gradually enclosing a cue in a circle similar to the iris of a camera shutter, was just as effective as zooming in cultivating "cue attending." Furthermore, "[T]here simply are no unique contributions to learning that can unambiguously be traced to the construct computer" (1985a, p. 140).

Many educational researchers accept both Clark's (1985b) claim that "in- structional methods, [not media], influence achievement gains"[1] (p. 393) and his general skepticism regarding the unique educational impact of computers. For example, comparing the effect of computer-based lessons with conven- tional instruction in a music fundamentals course, Greenfield and Codding (1985) concluded that "instructional strategy, not technology, influences learning" (p. 110). Examining computer use in a bilingual classroom to assist poor readers, Moll and Newcombe (1985) voiced a similar conclusion, "It is the [instructional] system and not the machine that is responsible for change or maintenance of the status quo. Computers are no solution to difficult instructional problems and do not replace teachers" (p. 225). Reviewing the

---

[1]To understand Clark's distinction between media and method it is useful to examine two studies considered in his rexamination of Kulik, Kulik, and Cohen's (1980) meta-analysis (Clark & Leonard, 1985). The first involved a physics course in which one group of students carried out a simulated lab on a computer and a second group conducted the same lab in a traditional form. In this instance, the lab and associated procedures and goals constituted the method whereas the computer and traditional laboratory materials constituted differing media. In the second exam- ple, students who had used drill-and-practice programs to review their math skills were compared with those who did not. Clark and Leonard maintained that though the media varied (computer vs. pencil and paper), the method (drill and practice), remained the same.

trends in research on instructional technology, Gerlach (1985) stated that "media, at best, establish different learning conditions; media, at worst, do nothing or even inhibit learning" (p. 21). Summarizing this perspective in his research on computers in classrooms, Mehan (1985) stated succinctly, "Teachers teach; machines mediate" (p. 276).

Although these researchers and Clark argued that computer innovations in education are not restricted to the computer medium, an integral piece to this puzzling debate remains missing. As Clark (1985b) explained, "What is still unclear is the exact source of the achievement gains in the computer treatments which 'diffuses' to the control treatments when the same instructor teaches both. What teaching methods were powerful enough to cause such large effects?" (p. 390).

Addressing Clark's question, this chapter investigates the same-instructor thesis by comparing instructional methods and student learning in a conventional college English literature course (hereafter English 32A) with those of the same course after hypertext-based[2] CBE materials[3] had been designed but were not implemented (hereafter English 32B). Because the computer medium was absent (though intended) in English 32B, I was able to assess the effects of developing CBE materials on teaching and learning without the confounding influence of the computer itself.[4]

In line with Clark's same-instructor thesis as well as Kulik et al.'s (1985) notion regarding the "diffusion of innovation," this chapter contends that as a consequence of developing materials for the Intermedia hypertext system, the instructor refined and expanded his instructional strategies and goals that in turn, led to improved student learning and appreciation for course materials. Moreover, the instructor achieved some of what he hoped the computing component would accomplish, even though its "presence" in the classroom remained "invisible." Although these developments occurred in the absence of the computer, it was the model this medium embodied—specifically, Intermedia's ability to link diverse materials—that invited manipulation and thereby stimulated pedagogical innovation on the part of the

---

[2]*Hypertext* is a term coined by Ted Nelson (1967). Specifically, hypertext systems "allow users to link information together, thereby creating trails through associated materials. A link connects words or sentences in one electronic document to related information in another document" (Smith, 1988, p. 32).

[3]Specifically, these CBE materials were developed for a hypertext system known as Intermedia designed by the Institute for Research in Information and Scholarship (IRIS) at Brown University.

[4]This research design arose as follows: (a) a semester of the class in its conventional mode (English 32A) was studied as part of a project to compare the course before and after the development and implementation of hypertext-based CBE materials; (b) the instructor developed these materials in conjunction with a team of software technicians while teaching both semesters of the course; but (c) hardware problems prevented the use of computers in the subsequent semester (English 32B).

instructor and later helped students think more creatively about course materials.

METHODOLOGY

An extensive ethnographic study of two semesters of the same English literature course (English 32A and 32B) and of the CBE design process provide the data for this chapter. Specifically, five main types of data were collected:

1. interviews with the instructor (five times per semester), teaching assistants (three times), and student volunteers (three times);
2. classroom observations;
3. standardized surveys of students in both classes at the beginning and the end of each semester;
4. student diaries in which they outlined daily activities and recorded general impressions about the course for the entire semester;
5. course-related materials (e.g., assignments, course evaluations, syllabi).[5]

In many respects, this research design diverges from traditional CBE research. For instance, rather than focusing on quantitative pre- and postassessments of a predetermined conception of student learning, my research orientation allowed me to adjust to significant course-related developments as they emerged and thereby to emphasize the complexities of classroom life. Thus, the descriptions of student learning and pedagogical innovation that appear in this chapter focus heavily on qualitative data—the instructor's evaluations of his instruction and students' work, students own assessments of the class and their learning, and ethnographic observations in the classroom—as well as a series of surveys.

This combination of quantitative and ethnographic methods has generated a classroom-oriented, multidimensional perspective on university instruction and learning that allowed me to identify specific pedagogical innovations, to relate these innovations to CBE development, and to understand their influence on student performance. Consequently, although the qualitative nature of the data used to support these assertions precludes a direct,

---

[5]Although I tried to maintain consistent research designs for both classes, they differed in two respects. First, the number of students who kept diaries and were regularly interviewed varied. Five English 32A students volunteered to participate, whereas 32B had nine. Second, because English 32A was not selected as a research project course until a month into the semester, we were able to observe 65% of classroom hours in the first phase of this study as compared with 82% in 32B.

numerical comparison with the works of Kulik et al. (through evaluating student learning in terms of performance on pre- and postexams), these data offer understandings that may be even more valuable to the educational community as they detail the process that led to improved student performance—precisely what Clark (1985b) sought: "the exact source of the achievement gains" (p. 390). And as House (1980) explained, although ethnographic research cannot offer "compelling and necessary conclusions. . . . it can provide the credible, the plausible, and the probable" (p. 72). Thus, this research design offered insight into precisely those processes that were connected to change in the classroom, an especially significant finding given that technology has been seen historically as a means to reinforce the status quo rather than to alter it (e.g., Cohen, 1990).

THE STUDENT POPULATION

Students in English 32A and 32B were self-selected into each course. Prior to the start of class, they did not know that the course was part of a software development project, nor were they required to meet any criteria defined by the study. Consequently, there were differences in the student composition of each course. For several reasons, it seems unlikely that these differences would have a demonstrable effect on pedagogical outcomes in either course.[6]

ENGLISH 32A: "A SURVEY OF ENGLISH LITERATURE— 1700 TO THE PRESENT"

In a Brown University student publication entitled *Critical Review*, the instructor described English 32A as a course:

---

[6]But the question is: Do these differences confound the central argument?—namely, that developing Intermedia courseware led the instructor to refine his pedagogy and that these refinements had a positive influence on student learning. As this thesis relies on a qualitative comparison of student performance in English 32A with 32B, maintaining that students in 32B developed a greater appreciation for multicausal reasoning than did those in 32A, a key issue concerns whether the differing student compositions in English 32A and 32B constitute the source of improved student performance. Table 6.1 reports survey data on the distribution of students in each course by gender, undergraduate year, and academic concentration. Although differences between English 32A and 32B are apparent, in no case do they seem important. For instance, more arts/humanities majors enrolled in 32A than in 32B, suggesting a possible advantage for 32A in terms of performance (assuming they would have had more exposure to literature because of their concentrations). Yet, because students in 32B performed better overall, this advantage actually provides indirect support for the thesis that instruction as well as student performance improved in the second course. Other noticeable differences concern gender and the relative distribution of sophomores and juniors. In courses as small as these two, moreover, the presence of a few unusually engaging students may influence the nature of classroom dynamics and outcomes far more than nominal demographic categories could reveal.

TABLE 6.1.
A Demographic Comparison of English 32A and 32B

	English 32A (n = 29)	English 32B (n = 26)
Gender		
Men	48%	39%
Women	52	61
Class		
Freshmen	41%	35%
Sophomores	24	50
Juniors	28	4
Seniors	7	11
Concentration		
Arts/humanities	51%	31%
Life sciences	14	15
Math/physical sci.	7	4
Social sciences	7	27
Combined majors	14	19
Undecided/unknown	7	4

intended for . . . those not concentrating in English who would like both an overview of British literature and samples of its major writers. The course, therefore, is intended to teach beginning students of literature both rudimentary factual information about basic authors and periods (e.g., Neoclassical and Modern) and ways of thinking about relations among individual works and between individual works and their nonliterary context.

Although two thirds of this description reads like a standard English literature survey course, the instructor's intent to teach "ways of thinking" needs elaboration. During the early stages of CBE development, the instructor defined this goal as enabling students to "make connections between works rather than focusing on content or how to read individual works." He termed this *multicausal reasoning*. The next time the course was taught (English 32B), a handout included with the syllabus detailed and emphasized this way of thinking:

If this course has one central idea, it is that no literary phenomenon—no work, part of a work, or idea about one—can ever be explained by a single fact. All literature . . . is multi-determined, by which we mean that multiple causes impinge upon each fact. Dickens may write a particularly great novel in a certain way because 1) he needed money, 2) he worked out his own psychological problems in writing it, 3) he confronted and challenged past and contemporary novels and novelists, 4) he wished to convince his readers to think about the world in a certain way—and so on. All are explanations, and they don't conflict with one another.

These two examples of the instructor explicitly defining ways of thinking are significant because they provide a comparison (the first from the initial stages of CBE development and the second after a full year of design work) of how he refined, expanded, and clarified the notion of multicausal reasoning throughout the CBE design process.

To promote multicausal reasoning among his students, the instructor relied heavily on group discussion.[7] As he regularly emphasized, rather than "spoon-feeding students," he wanted a communicative process that encouraged students to "hazard ideas." Outlining the rationale behind this approach, he explained:

> I have always felt that I learned best when I discussed things, when I answered questions. I have always bought as a pedagogical device that you only understand something when you reach the stage at which you can express it. Therefore, if you want to teach students to develop a way of thinking, you have to put them in a situation where they can comfortably be led or prompted to start talking about things on their own.

To create this discursive learning environment, the instructor and his teaching assistant often sat silently for 15 or 20 minutes at the start of a class as students worked through their ideas on the latest readings. To guide reading and structure discussion, the instructor provided a list of questions he considered integral to understanding the assigned material.

Though never implemented, the hypertext-based CBE materials designed by the instructor were intended to facilitate appreciation of multicausal analysis as well. By combining visual models of multicausal reasoning and extensive timelines with an exploratory learning environment that allowed students to easily browse through an array of subjects, these materials were to operate like an "electronic encyclopedia" that provided the learner with cross references to the topic being investigated. For instance, when first logged on, the reader would be presented with a menu of folder icons representing either authors (e.g., Browning, Dickens, Pope, Lawrence), literary periods (Neoclassicism, Modernism), or literary techniques (see Fig. 6.1).

After selecting an author (e.g., Browning) by clicking on that folder with a mouse, a web of interrelationships—a *concept map*[8]—would appear with the author at the center encircled by blocks of subtopics such as "religion," "technology and science," "literary relations," "biography," and "works" (see Fig. 6.2). Clicking on a link marker within a subtopic (e.g., biography;

---

[7]This emphasis on group discussion represented a shift in the instructor's original course conception. Its implementation and effect on student learning are discussed later.

[8]Novak and Gowin (1984) defined *concept map* as a visual model intended to "represent meaningful relationships between concepts . . . [and] to make clear to both students and teachers the small number of key ideas they must focus on for any specific learning task" (p. 15).

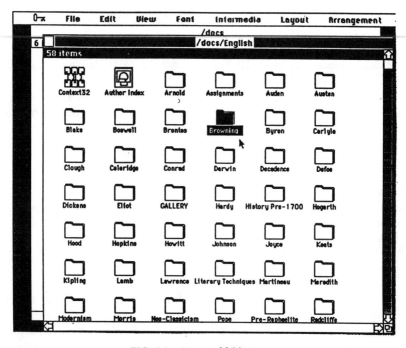

FIG. 6.1.   Menu of folder icons.

see Fig. 6.2), would call up an essay on the selected subtopic (see Fig. 6.3) or another concept map arranged with appropriate subtopics.

The essays within this hypertext database ranged from relatively brief one-or two-paragraph descriptions of particular subtopics that were de-signed to enhance students' understanding of the historical context within which the various authors wrote (e.g., Darwin's theory of evolution) to more extended, two- or three-page discussions of literary periods or biographical essays, for example. In addition to the historical and literary information contained in these essays, the readings posed questions of students, often with the intent of provoking them to consider some broader ramifications implied by what they had read. For instance, within the essay on the "Doctrines of Evangelical Protestantism" (see Fig. 6.4), the reader is asked, "What effects would you guess Evangelicalism had upon fiction?"

Within these texts there were additional link markers that could cross-reference the user to an essay or diagram related to the linked subject. For example, in Browning's biography the term *evangelical* appears with a link marker attached. If interested in learning more about this subject, a student could click on the link marker to access a corresponding essay (see Fig. 6.4).

During one interview, the instructor tied together the technical strengths

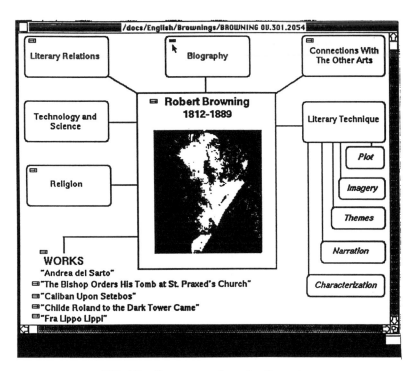

FIG. 6.2.   Concept map for author Browning.

of Intermedia as well as the value of hypertext's linking capabilities as a cognitive model for multicausal reasoning:

> The whole idea of the system is that one can have the kinds of information that one might have in a large number of books or an encyclopedia—but you could move back and forth. So, this is a new way to think . . . a new type of information technology. More to the point, it is going to allow students to develop habits of linking things . . . of making connections, of making comparisons, drawing discriminations, and formulating problems. Most important for us . . . formulating multiple explanations of complex phenomena.

The remainder of this chapter examines the role of multicausal reasoning in both English 32A and 32B as the basis for understanding how instructional innovations tied to developing Intermedia-based materials diffused into a course having no computing component. Specifically, I consider how the instructor presented multicausal analysis differently in the two courses and how his students did or did not bring this concept to bear on course materials. I also link both instructional innovation and improved student performance in terms of multicausal literary reasoning to developing CBE materials.

```
┌─────────────────────────────────────────────────────────────┐
│ □  ▓▓▓▓▓▓▓  /irwin/inter/docs/English/Browning_Bio.300.9 ▓▓▓ │
│  Robert Browning - Biography                               ⬆ │
│                                                              │
│    Robert Browning was born on May 7, 1812, In Camberwell (a suburb of │
│  London) the first child of Robert and Sarah Anna Browning. His mother was a │
│  fervent  Evangelical and an accomplished pianist.  The poet's father had │
│  angered  his own parent and forgone a fortune:  When the elder Browning │
│  arrived in  the West Indies to manage a family sugar plantation, he found │
│  slavery so abhorrent that he abandoned wealth earned from it, returned home, │
│  and became a clerk in the Bank of England.  On his very modest salary he │
│  married, raised a family, and  acquired a library of 6000 volumes. │
│      Indeed, most of the poet's education came at home, and  Browning's │
│  father, a well-read man, recreated the seige of Troy with household chairs and │
│  tables for the benefit of his inquisitive son. As a child Robert Browning was a │
│  voracious  reader (he  read  through  all fifty volumes of the  Biographie │
│  Universelle) and learned Latin, Greek, French and Italian by the time he was │
│  fourteen.   He attended the University of London in 1828, the first year it │
│  opened, but left in discontent to read at his own pace.  His extensive but │
│  idiosyncraticlearning  creates  difficulties for  his  readers,  since  he did not │
│  always realize how obscure were his references. │
│      In the 1830s he met the actor William Macready, who encouraged him │
│  write verse drama for the stage.  Browning's lack of success In writing drama │
│  effective for the theater led to his recognition that his real talents lay in taking a │
│  single character and allowing him to reveal more of himself in his speeches │
│  than he suspects—the characteristics of the dramatic monologue. Although │
│  he began his career as a poet with moderate success--reviews of Paracelsus │
│ ◁                                                          ▷ │
└─────────────────────────────────────────────────────────────┘
```

FIG. 6.3.   Essay on selected subtopic "biography."

While teaching these courses and developing his Intermedia corpus, the instructor's sense for how to present multicausal reasoning continually evolved. As this occurred, he changed both what he taught and how he taught. Though change was most evident in the second year (English 32B), signs of this influence appeared during the early stages of developing the Intermedia-based materials.

ENGLISH 32A AND ENGLISH 32B COMPARED: "CLASS DISCUSSION"

One of the first signs that the instructor was rethinking his course emerged in his increased emphasis on class discussion. For the first 5 weeks of English 32A, instruction was dominated by lectures interspersed with instructor-initiated questions. Instances of active student involvement—questioning the instructor, applying personal interpretations to the readings, or answering questions—were relatively infrequent and involved few students. The instructor developed his hypertext corpus, then he began to consider how best to integrate these materials into a course structure that facilitated multicausal

```
/irwin/inter/docs/English/Evangel_Doctrine.300.36
```

The Doctrines of Evangelical Protestantism

The Evangelical party of the •Church of England, the established church, flourished from 1789 to 1850, and during that time increasingly dominated many aspects of English life and, with its •dissenting or nonconformist allies, was responsible for many of the attitudes today thought of as •"Victorian." These heirs of the seventeenth-century Puritans believed:

1. that human beings are corrupt and need Christ to save them----thus the emphasis upon puritanical morality and rigidity;

2. that the church hierarchy and church ritual are not as crucial to individual salvation as a personal conversion based on an emotional, imagination comprehension of both one's own innate depravity and Christ's redeeming sacrifice -- thus the emphasis upon an essentially •Romantic conception of religion that stressed imagination, intensity, emotion, and also upon the •Bible, which could provide such imaginative experience of the truths of religion. What effects would you guess Evangelicalism had upon fiction? poetry?

3. that converted believers must demonstrate their spirituality by working for others -- thus Evangelical zeal in missionary work, Bible societies, •anti-slavery movements, and many social causes.

4. that the converted will be persecuted and that such persecution indicates the holiness of the believer (since Satan has much power over man and his world; see 1 above) -- thus Evangelical willingness to speak on behalf of unpopular causes, and rather annoyingly to many contemporaries, to take any political, social, or religious opposition as a martyrdom.

5. that God arranged history and the •Bible, of which every word was held to be literally true, according to elaborate codes and signals, particularly in the form of •typology, an elaborate system of foreshadowings (or anticipations) of Christ in the Old Testament -- thus Evangelical emphasis

FIG. 6.4.   Sample essay from the hypertext database.

analysis and encouraged greater student involvement. Five weeks into English 32A, these concerns prompted him to shift his instructional emphasis to discussion—hoping to create a community of discourse where students could broaden, refine, and verify their proficiency with multicausal analysis. Realizing that he would sacrifice some background knowledge previously provided in lectures, he felt he could still integrate adequate extraliterary information in a classroom focused on promoting student discussion. In the future, he planned to use the Intermedia materials as the primary source for this contextual information. The remaining classes of English 32A, then, became a testing ground for a future, discussion-oriented English 32 in which a hypertext database offered the background knowledge needed for sophisticated discussion and where class served as the arena for discussion. Reflecting on this shift, he noted:

> When I began to consider what a computer could do for my class, I began to
> realize that lecturing was a lot less efficient, and a lot less effective for what I
> hoped to accomplish. . . . But I realize, as I think most teachers do, that if
> students can work something out for themselves, it sticks with them. So,
> perhaps I can give them ten bits of information and they can, in a discussion,
> work out two [by themselves]. Those two are likely to stick with them, but
> maybe only one of the [ten] things that I've given them.

After shifting the course format in English 32A to encourage open discussion, a number of changes became evident. Rather than standing in front of class to lecture rows of neatly arranged students, the instructor and his teaching assistant sat (sometimes silently for extended periods to "force" student engagement) in the same desks as students, now seated in a circle for discussion. Whereas the instructor's voice had previously signaled the start of class and dominated classroom interaction, classes now began most often with an uneasy silence punctured by nervous students working through their own ideas and interpretations of the latest readings. In effect, what had begun as an undergraduate survey course had evolved a pedagogical format more like a graduate seminar.

Aside from these more obvious changes, subtle differences emerged as well. Students became more actively engaged in class—not merely answering more questions but devising questions of their own, proposing interpretations drawn from the readings, and challenging or extending their classmates' ideas. The instructor's role shifted from that of expert lecturer to more of a "coach," guiding students in their skill development. Whereas class direction had been determined by the instructor's lectures, discussion now drove class and lecturing became a more peripheral element.

This shift to a discussion format in English 32A helped the instructor achieve his aim of increased participation. After adopting this format, the average number of times students actively participated in class increased from 42 participations per class to 127; the percentage of students who participated at least once during a class period increased as well—from an average of 51% prior to the format shift to 70%.[9]

INSTRUCTIONAL USE AND STUDENT APPRECIATION OF MULTICAUSAL REASONING IN ENGLISH 32A: "I FAIL TO SEE THE POINT OF IT"

Two key differences between English 32A and 32B concern the manner and regularity with which the instructor employed and made reference to multi-

[9]A *participation* was defined as answering a question, asking a question of the instructor or another student, or making an observation on a topic being discussed.

causal reasoning as well as the extent to which students understood the value of this approach to literary analysis for ordering this literary corpus. Unquestionably, multicausal analysis was evident in 32A. For example, in summarizing Joyce's *Ulysses*, the instructor explained that "[l]iterature works many ways. It's multideterministic. It never has a single meaning. The cuckoo clock in this story suggests the vulgarity of its surroundings but it echoes a Shakespearian sonnet as well." Telling students he wanted them to develop "habits of mind," the instructor emphasized, "There is no one single explanation for the works we've read. . . . You should see influences from the previous authors and poets." In the final exam review, he was even more explicit, "There are two things you should take from this course: One, that no fact has one explanation. It is never impinged upon by a single force. Two, every work is as much about other works as it is about reality."

Besides these explicit references to multicausal reasoning, this analytic orientation implicitly pervaded his teaching. When discussing Joseph Conrad's *Heart of Darkness* in English 32A, for example, he interrelated ideas and built on the understandings created by connecting ideas to encourage further analysis. He began by discussing how most Europeans fared in the Congo (horribly) and how those in Conrad's writing fared (similarly). Using this idea as a base, he extended this reasoning to suggest the inevitable fate of European colonialism in Africa and to tie this with Conrad's beliefs about the ultimate fate of all economic and political imperialism. Conrad's attitude toward imperialism was then considered in terms of the author's past experiences with Russian and German totalitarianism. This led to an analysis of basic notions concerning liberal and conservative sensibilities—whether man is inherently evil and must be controlled, as conservative totalitarian regimes believe, or whether evil is a product of society and can be eliminated by changing society, the liberal explanation. Bringing these tangents to bear specifically on *Heart of Darkness* raised the question whether the "heart of darkness" resides in everyone or is created by society. In terms of multicausal analysis, this series of interrelated ideas illuminates Conrad's writing from a variety of perspectives. Moreover, following this progression from topic to topic reveals how the instructor's classroom methodology paralleled the design of the Intermedia system. That is, one could imagine a biography of Conrad containing links to African colonialism, totalitarianism, liberalism, and conservativism.

A variety of qualitative measures demonstrate that some students appreciated this approach. For example, one assignment required students to "make a timeline which dates the most important events we have covered . . . looking for interrelationships." One student drew the timeline as a tree, "a living, growing entity in which previous development influences later developments. Movements are not neatly divided but overlap and grow together." Another diagrammed two interconnected stars "to illustrate how political, social, philosophical, religious, economic, and scientific themes contribute to the development of literary forms . . . and the interlocking debt relationship each genre owes other genres and each author, other authors."

Student feedback in the course evaluations also showed an appreciation for multicausal analysis. Asked whether English 32A allowed one to analyze course material in a new way, one student said, "Yes, this appeared to be the somewhat doggedly-pursued aim of the instructor—connections, connections, connections." Another wrote, "This semester has been a total revelation in reading and analyzing. . . . We've looked at works from a different perspective—always with the goal of integrating them to a central work or theme."

Other evidence, however, strongly suggests that only a limited number of students achieved a solid understanding of the course's central principle—multicausal analysis. For instance, student commentary on the timeline and an assignment that asked students to create graphic representations of the relationship between Dickens' *Great Expectations* and other works showed a lack of enthusiasm for this analytic approach. Questioning the academic rationale for the *Great Expectations* diagram, one student wrote in her diary that she felt as if she were merely "indulg[ing] the professor's artistic interests." The most positive comment described the assignment as "enjoyable, but odd and eccentric." The timeline received similar criticism. In a survey, one student commented, "I don't feel I got anything out of the assignments. Anyone can do a timeline! I couldn't understand why we were doing a timeline!" Another found the assignment "tremendously frustrating to make coherent"—so much so that he vowed never to take another survey course.

In response to a survey question asking students what they disliked about English 32A, one wrote, "The emphasis on tying it all together—making each work tie in with the others." Though implying some understanding of multicausal reasoning, he added that he had trouble determining course themes and that the entire course "seemed a little incoherent." Yet, for the instructor, "trying it all together" was precisely the means for making the course coherent.

This lack of coherence constituted the single most prevalent criticism directed at English 32A—resonating throughout the diaries, interview sessions, surveys, and course reviews. In diaries students wrote:

> Notes from class again proved insufficient as material to establish a coherent order among the works. I need this badly. Also, some good definitions and examples in some ordered format.

> We are reading works not for their individual merit but to see how they fit with the time. I mean this isn't a "history of literature" course; it's not a "history and literature" course; it is a literature course. We are reading these works and

thinking that they are all related to each other, which I am sure they are—but to emphasize that so much? I fail to see the point of it.

Others felt there should be "more structured assignments to help us understand the material," believing the course needed "more unity."

In addressing different concerns, these criticisms all contend that students lacked a way to organize course materials. Although the instructor viewed multicausal analysis as precisely the means to order this body of literature, and some students had a sense for this analytic process ("connections, connections, connections"), many were uncertain how or why to apply multicausal reasoning to a literary corpus.

The final survey, completed by 29 of the 31 students enrolled in English 32A, made it clear that many lacked this understanding. Of the 29 respondents, 17 said the course "lacked coherence." Two responses typify this perception: "Not organized coherently enough. Themes weren't clear. Would have liked more direction from the professor." And, "The course seemed a little incoherent. I tried to grasp it myself, but it was hard to organize."

Though the instructor had increased student involvement in class, like many of his students he, too, had a sense of dissatisfaction with student appreciation for multicausal analysis. As he explained shortly before the final exam, "Thus far, we have failed in that we have not been able to get them to actually stop every week and say, 'What the hell does this week have to do with every other week?' It's been like an intellectual massage—it was a nice experience but it hasn't stuck with them."

This assessment epitomized the problem many students encountered trying to grasp the instructor's goal for the course. Failing to see multicausal analysis as a means to structure this (or any) body of literature through interrelating works, many students viewed the course as a series of isolated texts with specific meanings—thereby limiting their ability to order this literary corpus—rather than as a complex, reader-generated web of interrelated works. Through examining how English 32B students grasped multicausal analysis more comprehensively than those in 32A, the following section details how further pedagogical refinements aided students in developing a greater sense of coherence for course materials.

INSTRUCTIONAL USE AND STUDENT APPRECIATION OF MULTICAUSAL REASONING IN ENGLISH 32B: "LEARNING THE TECHNIQUES EQUALLY AS MUCH AS THE CONTENT"

In English 32B, students came to appreciate multicausal analysis much more than in 32A. In part, this can be attributed to pedagogical developments related to multicausal reasoning. As noted earlier, English 32B was intended to have an Intermedia component but due to technical complications, the technology was never available. Yet, as a consequence of the instructor's involvement in the courseware design process, the invisible presence of CBE-related innovation manifested itself in a variety of ways and led students to appreciate the practicality of multicausal reasoning for organizing a literary canon. Pedagogically, four main differences between English 32A and 32B stand out:

1. The use of multicausal analysis was encouraged and made explicit;
2. This approach to literary analysis was presented as a skill with wide applicability;
3. Graphic models reinforced the concept of multicausal analysis; and
4. A teaching assistant versed in multicausal analysis helped teach the course.

The first significant pedagogical difference between English 32A and 32B concerned a simple but effective instructional shift. Whereas in 32A multicausal analysis implicitly structured much classroom interaction, in 32B the instructor frequently and explicitly identified his own as well as student use of multicausal analysis and encouraged his class to apply this analytic approach to their readings. For example, during the first class discussion, he posed the following question about the day's reading: "Why tell such a sordid story?" and immediately followed his query with a reminder that set the tone for the entire semester: "Remember, there'll be a lot of answers to this question." After describing one of Jane Austen's characters in *Pride and Prejudice* as a "nightmare version of everybody's mother," the instructor went on to ask, "By what process does Austen characterize the mother?" After students responded, he summarized their answers, emphasizing the variety of ways one makes literary characterizations. While discussing John Keats, both the instructor and teaching assistant emphasized that one could analyze poetry, or any literary form, more effectively if biographical information on that author could be brought to bear in one's analysis—clearly implying the value of multicausal reasoning. When a student suggested that William Yeats' "Easter 1916" portrayed a longing for the past characteristic of Romanticism, the instructor asked the entire class to assess this point by seeing how many ways this work could be considered Romantic. Thus, by emphasizing that a range of explanations can all illuminate a single issue—thereby providing a means to organize as well as understand a literary corpus—and calling explicit attention to student and his own use of this technique, the instructor initiated one important pedagogical difference between English 32A and 32B.

A second key innovation in 32B linked to increased student appreciation for multicausal analysis was the *concept map*, a visual model the instructor designed "to show interrelationships in the least difficult way possible" (see Fig. 6.2). Although designed for the hypertext database, the instructor found concept maps appropriate for the blackboard as well as computer screen. For example, when discussing the first novel of the course, Graham Swift's *Waterland*, the instructor mentioned how Western culture could be understood as an interaction of music, art, literature, and philosophy. Seeking an analogue to this model, he asked his class to identify a similar body of influences for *Waterland*. Students answered "other works," "historical circumstances," "other writers," and so on. As they answered, the instructor drew a concept map on the board with *Waterland* in the center surrounded by these influences—exactly like that from Intermedia.

A similar approach was applied to Dylan Thomas' "Fern Hill." Here, boxes representing various literary influences on Thomas, specifically, stylistic parallels between this work and others authors—such as "use of vowel sounds/Keats," "subject matter/Wordsworth," and "stanza form and rhythm/Swinburne"—fanned out around "Fern Hill." In both cases, although the intent varied, the pedagogical strategy remained the same: Concept maps provided graphic reinforcement for a way of understanding and ordering literary relationships. By converting an abstract concept into a concrete model of the mental process critical to grasping multicausal reasoning—a model totally absent from 32A—the instructor felt he could enable students to better understand the concept. Moreover, this visual model was reinforced in 32B with handouts taken directly from Intermedia.

A third pedagogical difference between 32A and 32B involved how the instructor portrayed multicausal analysis. In 32A, there were occasional allusions to this analytic process and it implicitly structured a great deal of classroom instruction, but the practical value of this approach remained unclear for many students. In contrast, while teaching 32B, the instructor presented multicausal analysis as a broadly applicable academic "skill." In an interview conducted during the first weeks of 32B, he articulated this new emphasis, "The purpose of a course like this is learning the techniques equally as much as the content. If students just give back the content on the exam, you're not sure that they really learned." Throughout the semester, he reinforced this point. Explaining the intent of an upcoming exam, the instructor told the class, "It's not to see how much reading you've done, but how much thinking you've done. I want to see how you can synthesize the material you've read . . . find connections between authors. You'll be surprised at how many similarities there are, even with the most dissimilar authors."

His last words of advice before the final exam echoed the same point, "I'm trying to get you to find ways to organize the course. We're not looking for some absolute truth."

A final instructional difference between English 32A and 32B involved the teaching assistants. In 32A, the teaching assistant was more lecture oriented and had a less interactive role in class. In 32B, the teaching assistant was a proponent of multicausal reasoning, had written substantial amounts of the text for Intermedia and helped develop the concept maps (suggesting that he, too, was influenced by the CBE materials development process), and took an active role in conveying this approach in class.[10] As outlined in an interview, his instructional goals paralleled the instructor's:

> Theoretically, students should have a much more sophisticated approach to dealing with fiction and poetry . . . a much stronger sense of what it is to analyze—a sense that the world is a lot more complex than they might have thought when they went in, and that this complexity is implicit in the literature as well . . . and that there are different people with different perspectives who can all contribute to one whole.

In terms of instruction, English 32B differed from 32A in four significant ways:

1. The use of multicausal reasoning was encouraged and made explicit;
2. This analytic approach was presented as a skill with broad applicability;
3. Graphic models were employed to enhance student learning; and
4. There was a teaching assistant committed to this approach to literary analysis.

Besides these instructional changes, the curriculum for English 32B differed from its predecessor in the addition of one text, Graham Swift's *Waterland*. Perceiving a need to stress the value of identifying interrelationships as a means for bringing coherence to a literary canon, the instructor felt this contemporary British novel—with its emphasis on how the present can be influenced by a web of historical factors—was ideally suited to the task.

---

[10]It should be noted that the teaching assistant for English 32A was also involved in the materials development process and he, too, was influenced by this process. (A quote concerning this influence occurs later in this chapter.) Nevertheless, I feel justified in maintaining that the teaching assistant for English 32B was influenced more and influenced the students more based on two observations. First, the second teaching assistant developed more materials for the Intermedia corpus and was integrally involved in identifying links between these materials. The first teaching assistant wrote far fewer files, and a great deal of his writing was not completed until after the course ended. Second, the second teaching assistant was far more involved in classroom interaction. On four separate occasions, he was solely responsible for directing classroom instruction, and even when his role was secondary, he contributed to what occurred in class. In English 32A, the teaching assistant lectured the class briefly on two occasions, but other than that had little active involvement in the classroom.

Whereas few students in English 32A expressed an appreciation for multicausal reasoning and its potential for ordering and adding coherence to course materials, in 32B students widely appreciated the technique. Signs of this understanding appeared in student assessments of the instructor's pedagogical approach and of their own learning. For instance, contrasting English 32B with other literature courses she had taken, one student wrote,

> You realize that writers' lives definitely relate to their works. You see how Shelley relates to Keats in one poem and how they relate to different genres, consequently leading to a better appreciation of the poet. Things are linked together. In other poetry classes I've taken, I didn't remember what we did because we did isolated poems—they weren't linked to one another in any way.

Another noted in her diary that a recent discussion of Tennyson "put a slant on the readings. By knowing something of his life, I'll look for reflections in his work." In a similar vein, one student noted the effect of the instructor's dogged emphasis on making connections between readings, "It made my mind get into that shift of always looking for comparisons. So I would be saying, 'How does this compare with Keats?' 'How does this compare with Woolf?'"

Beyond a theoretical understanding of multicausal reasoning, students in 32B recognized its value as a generalizable intellectual skill. Commenting on his own skill development, one student wrote, "The professor doesn't teach facts—it's ideas and ways of thinking. He shows you how to analyze literature rather than merely what somebody said. . . . He makes students come up with their own ideas and then asks, "How do you prove it?" He teaches you to think about literature in its context."

Appreciation of this skill led to an intellectual empowerment for many. As another student remarked:

> One thing that I have gotten better at is pulling together a lot of different time periods, different works, and different authors. And not in the sense that you have a little paper that says, "Compare this and this." In the paper we did on the three poets, I talked not only about Swinburne, Tennyson, and Browning but I included Yeats and another poem of Browning's, Tennyson's "Ulysses" and "Morte d'Arthur." I talked about early Romantics. I pulled together a lot of different things.

Besides empowerment, these remarks suggest a sense of improvement—a logical development when multicausal reasoning is viewed as a generalizable skill. That is, practicing the skill improved performance. The instructor, teaching assistant, and other students all found this to be true. In an interview just before the final exam, for example, the instructor said, "I think there really has been an improvement. I don't think I'm fooling myself. I think a large number of students have learned something about the techniques of literary interpretation. They have learned to think in complicated terms; that is, multiple causality."

Although attributing part of this skill development to the nature of the students' latest readings, the teaching assistant concurred, "I don't know if it is because what we are reading now is more meaningful or students are becoming more sophisticated in their analyses. It is probably a combination of both—they are more sophisticated and the literature is more readily accessible."

Implicitly concurring with the teaching assistant, a student wrote in her diary, "Either our confidence in our interpretive abilities is growing or we just like Tennyson and Browning, because class seems to be getting more lively." Another student recorded this same point, "Lately, I've been leaving class feeling very good. I might not understand it all, but I feel like I've really learned something. This didn't happen as often early in the semester. Early discussions were too undirected and made me insecure."

Another connection between multicausal reasoning and enhanced student learning concerned the extent to which students understood the validity of varying perspectives. Whereas in 32A interpretive differences between the instructor and the teaching assistant confused students, in 32B one student viewed the fact that the teaching assistant "doesn't always agree with the professor" as a benefit. Another characterized class discussion as "a great way to learn—exchanging ideas and seeing what you saw that other people didn't and what they saw but you didn't." After completing the *Great Expectations* assignment, one student who worked with a friend having a "totally different view on class" nevertheless felt she benefited because "it's good to get another view."[11]

This *Great Expectations* assignment provided an especially revealing instance of 32B's enhancement of student appreciation for multicausal reasoning. Far from the "enjoyable, but odd and eccentric" review this assignment received in 32A, many students in 32B felt they benefited from constructing the diagram. One was encouraged to discover "interrelations I didn't see before." Another found that drawing the interrelationships extended her sense of literary history—how "existing literature affects a work and how that work has effects on others." Another commented that this was "a neat way to organize things. I hadn't thought of it before. I realized that there are relationships between all we read. This teaches you to organize them better." Even one student who considered the assignment "vague," in a later diary

---

[11]The instructor endorsed this approach as well. For instance, when discussing the possibility of the teaching assistants each producing different interpretations of course readings for the Intermedia materials, he stated, "It is perfectly all right for the . . . TA's to do different solutions to the same problem because then we can ask the students which they find more effective."

entry, expressed an understanding of precisely what the instructor hoped the assignment would accomplish. For her, *Great Expectations* took on greater significance "when you compare it to Romanticism. You see how Dickens tried to react against all the excesses of the Romantics. . . . It makes his style and content more justified when looking at the Romantic 'reaction.' "

Contrasting reactions to a common problem signaled another difference between the two courses. In the case of both 32A and 32B, the course anthology arrived late, thereby preventing strict adherence to chronological order. As discussed previously, many students felt 32A "lacked coherence," and one found the course hard to organize, specifically "because it did not go chronologically." Yet, in 32B, no student expressed difficulty with this "disorder." Assessing the effect of this delay, one student noted how he was nevertheless able to perceive key interrelationships, "We never read any works in chronological order so they were isolated and we thought we should be able to understand them on their own. Now, however, I can really make connections to historical background and to other poems that came before and after. . . . I appreciate a poem a lot more."

Data from the student surveys also suggest important qualitative differences between the courses. Comparing 32A and 32B to other courses they had taken (*not* to each other), students found 32B more interesting, felt they participated and learned more, and rated the course higher overall (see Table 6.2). Once again, appreciation of multicausal analysis may have played a role in shaping their opinions. Provided with a means to imaginatively interrelate an extensive body of literature, students in 32B would likely have found the course more interesting, learned more, and, in general, evaluated the course more positively. Furthermore, when listing problems with the course, 17 of

TABLE 6.2.
Students' Assessments of English 32A and 32B

		English 32A (n = 29)	English 32B (n = 26)
Compared to other courses you've taken in college . . .			
How INTERESTING was this course?	MORE	38%	58%
	AVERAGE	34	35
	LESS	28	8
How much did you PARTICIPATE in class?	MORE	24	50
	AVERAGE	45	19
	LESS	31	31
How much did you LEARN in the course?	MORE	19	54
	AVERAGE	54	35
	LESS	27	11
How would you RATE this course overall?	BETTER	31	54
	AVERAGE	35	31
	WORSE	34	15

29 students in English 32A thought the course lacked coherence; in 32B, 26 of the 31 students completed a questionnaire on the course, but none mentioned a lack of coherence.

As for student engagement during class, an open discussion format, once again, proved more effective than lecture-oriented instruction for encouraging student engagement. In English 32B, students averaged 71 participations per class with 59% of the class participating at least once.

This multidimensional body of data provides compelling evidence that students in 32B grasped the instructor's goals and pedagogical model and felt empowered by multicausal analysis much more so than did students in 32A. Moreover, interviews and classroom observations reveal that the instructor and his teaching assistant also had a clearer sense of their pedagogical goals as well as appropriate means to reinforce these goals—and this factor must be considered central in any attempt to explain improved student performance.

EXPLAINING DIFFERENCES IN STUDENT PERFORMANCE

In the research cited earlier, a central problem Clark found with the metaanalyses of Kulik et al. (1985) is that they attribute "small but significant" improvements in student achievement to computer-based education. Clark argued that this overstates the value of CBE. He contended that the computer is merely an instructional medium; it is the process of designing CBE programs—a process requiring "more systematic thinking about information organization, examples, and requirements for active responding" (1985a, p. 140)—which, in part, brings about improved student performance. Throughout the development process, the English 32 instructor affirmed this assertion: designing computer-based materials had a powerful effect on his teaching. During the first English 32B class, for example, he told his class outright that authoring and organizing files for Intermedia's linked database had made him and the teaching assistant "rethink what we want to have happen in this class." Moreover, in an interview he commented that "the expectation of having the computer has led me to rethink the way I teach and then actually change the course radically."

Examining the materials development process reveals how pedagogical innovations associated with this process diffused to a noncomputing environment. First of all, the process demanded a more comprehensive understanding of course materials—especially their interrelationships—to make intuitive knowledge and assumptions explicit. This stage of the development process is probably one of the more pedagogically significant because it represents the point at which an instructor systematizes previously taken-for-granted knowledge. Reflecting on this process, the instructor elaborated:

This is forcing me to do the things I usually do on the spur of the moment in a more deliberate fashion. Suddenly, instead of being concerned with just one [interrelationship], I have to do about 60 of these things and get them all down. . . . Not only that, but you have to know it in a different way than when you teach it because you are writing it down. . . . You have to be more precise about it in a way that is not necessary when you are making suggestive ideas in class.

In addition, editing the Intermedia corpus, written by three different teaching assistants as well as writing his own contributions, led the instructor to reconceive the organization and goals of the course. To guide their writing, the instructor provided the teaching assistants with questions related to the readings. Even so, to achieve these new goals the resulting texts often required rewriting because "they did not tie in adequately to what I thought the discussion would be, based on what it had been for the last couple years . . . that therefore limits and shapes what [I would] put on the computer."

As part of this project, the instructor gave a number of talks about his work and was regularly interviewed by a team of ethnographers. These opportunities for further reflection also influenced his work. Describing public presentations, he stated, "It is true that I have been changing what I emphasize. . . . These talks force me to take a much more skeptical view because I have to explain to people who aren't familiar with the project, what is going on. So I have to go back to square one. It is always a good experience."

Even spontaneous conversations about the project affected his thinking, "A lot of times describing the project, I will take it further because I articulated it just one more time." Reflecting on ethnographic interviews as another stimulus for reassessing his hypertext database and rethinking the course, the instructor observed, "The fact that you are asking these questions has led me . . . to think about what I am doing and try things I might not have thought of."

Besides influencing his pedagogy, the instructor felt that the teaching assistants were "forced, in a way you never do in grad school, to think about and synthesize the basic parts of their field." Supporting this assertion, the teaching assistant from English 32A described his experience:

I suppose to some extent there were new ways of conceiving things—forcing myself to think about . . . literary relations that had been a little fuzzy before. For instance, I added an essay on the imagist poets to the database because I saw relationships between them and [Gerard] Hopkins. I would have said that they were alike before, but now I had to make it clear.

Directly assessing the link between his shift in teaching style and designing a hypertext database, the instructor attributed priority to his pedagogical reconception:

Because I had planned the course this way, to try and teach multiple explanations of things, when we discussed I tried to point out, "You see, that is what you are doing now. That is [multicausal reasoning]. . . ." But I am not so sure that it was the software that did it. It was the conception of the course, if anything. So, both the style of teaching and the software came out of this original shift in thinking . . . the decision that this is what I want to do educationally.

CONCLUSION

This chapter has examined the arguments that Clark, Kulik, Kulik, Bangert-Drowns, and Cohen made about the same-instructor effect as applied to a two-semester comparison of an English literature course. The evidence from this study overwhelmingly suggests that innovations from a course employing CBE materials diffused to a course with no explicit computing component as a consequence of the same instructor critically rethinking his goals and course organization as part of the CBE materials development process. This rethinking led him to clarify his notions of multicausal reasoning, to present the concept as a general intellectual skill applicable to a variety of contexts, to design a visual model of the thought process embodying this skill, to add readings that emphasized interrelationships to his curriculum, and to stress this entire process throughout his teaching. Moreover, these materials were designed to be used without faculty present. Knowing that students would be on their own, the instructor could not "on the spur of the moment" direct students to appropriate literary links. Instead, he had to make myriad connections explicit, and this process reinforced his previous understandings of these connections, revealed interrelations that before may have been overlooked, and generally led to a deeper understanding of course materials. Given Clark's assertion that a narrow preoccupation with the role of the computer has caused many CBE researchers to overlook such potentially confounding influences as different content and instructional innovation and thereby to attribute improved student performance solely to the computer, the research design for this study provided an opportunity to assess the effects of developing a CBE corpus without the computer's physical presence blurring other relevant factors (although it is argued that the computer's invisible presence had a significant effect on this course).

The evidence also lends support to Clark's related contention that although certain computer attributes may cultivate skills, "the resulting skills could be cultivated with any number of nominally different, non-computer related treatments that serve the same necessary cognitive function" (1985a, p. 143). The English 32 instructor had predicted this likelihood while developing his Intermedia materials, "It is very possible that there will be computer to non-computer reinforcement. In other words, one can learn certain fundamental ways of doing things without any mechanical or electronic help whatsoever."

Moll and Newcomb (1985) felt the same holds true for pedagogical innovation. They noted that the mere presence of a new technology "will not produce major changes in instruction." But they added, "It is equally clear . . . however, that computers afford teachers a medium, a novel way, an opportunity, an excuse, if you will, to question the status quo" (p. 225). In a deeper examination of this "excuse . . . to question the status quo," Turkle (1980) found that the computer is "an exemplary 'constructed object' . . . which different people and groups of people can apprehend with very different descriptions and invest with very different attributes" (p. 15). She continued:

> Although airplanes can come in all shapes and can be described in all sorts of ways, there is no conceptual problem in stating their essential function: they fly. There is no equally elegant, compelling, or satisfying way of defining the computer. Of course, one could say that it computes, that it executes programs. But the execution of a program can be described on many levels: in terms of electronic events, machine language instructions, high-level language instructions, or through a structured diagram which represents the functioning of the program as a flow through a complex information system. (p. 19)

By appreciating the metaphorical power of the computer as well as its technical capabilities, these authors recognized that the computer is more than merely a sum of its component parts. It has become an "object-to-think-with"—stimulating thought and providing a new medium of expression (Turkle, 1984, p. 22).

Though the instructor maintained that his pedagogical reconception drove the materials development process, not vice versa, it was this technology's linking and storage capabilities that afforded him the luxury of relying on computer-based materials to supply the background information integral to this instructional reorientation. Moreover, Intermedia's linking capabilities reinforced this pedagogical reconception and led to extensive refinements throughout the development process. Finally, the potential practical benefits to scholarship offered by the system's permanence and widespread accessibility provided further impetus for innovation—that is, the instructor had a sense that his work would endure and could be made widely available because of its computer-based nature.

With this in mind, when Kulik et al. (1985) concluded that "[m]ost CBE programs have had positive effects on student learning" (p. 385), one should not forget the evocative power of the computer as a medium of expression inviting manipulation. Implicit in this consideration is the obvious necessity that in order to have a course with CBE materials, materials must be developed. This assumes—and the research with English 32 supports the contention—that when CBE materials are developed, it is possible that some innovations will occur that lead to "improved student performance." Thus, though Intermedia as a *computer tool* did not produce pedagogical innovation, Intermedia as a *conceptual tool* did. The question then arises whether computer-induced innovation could have occurred through other means. In support of Clark, unquestionably, it could have occurred; but in support of Kulik, Kulik, Bangert-Drowns, and Cohen, whether or not it would have occurred and to what extent is uncertain.

Moreover, in this instance the computer helped to create a learning context that promoted change in both curriculum and pedagogy, in effect, altering the classroom status quo. Because Cohen (1990) detailed how technology has historically served the interests of the status quo and often strengthened normal classroom routines, it seems noteworthy that in this classroom there were discernible shifts in curriculum and pedagogy. In part this appears to have occurred because change involved multiple dimensions of the schooling process—the role of the instructor, the expectations for students, course materials, and so on—rather than being targeted at a particular component of the course. Change may also have been promoted by the processual nature of the software design process. That is, designing the computer-based course materials was an iterative process in which the instructor regularly assessd and revised aspects of his teaching and materials development—then reassessed their effectiveness and made further changes he considered necessary. Thus, from the outset, the nature of the CBE materials required that the instructor continually reassess his work by considering how the materials he had written thus far would relate to what he planned to add. In many instances, this not only led him to think differently about what he was adding to the database but also to revise that which he had already created. And in many ways it was this process of continually rethinking the value of the materials he was creating that led him to reassess both how he taught and what he taught.

This chapter first appeared in the *Journal of Curriculum Studies*. I would like to gratefully acknowledge the *Journal* for granting permission to reprint this piece. I would also like to thank the editor of this volume, Mark Shields, for the editorial assistance he provided and I would like to thank George Landow, David Cody and Glen Everett for their cooperation in this research project.

REFERENCES

Bovy-Clark, R. A. (1983, April). *Defining the psychologically effective features of instructional treatments designed to facilitate cue attendance*. Paper presented at the annual meeting of the American Educational Research Association, Montreal, Canada.

Clark, R. E. (1983). Reconsidering research on learning from media. *Review of Educational Research, 53*(4), 445–460.

Clark, R. E. (1985a). Confounding in educational computing research. *Journal of Educational Computing Research, 1*(2), 137–148.

Clark, R. E. (1985b). The importance of treatment explication: A reply to J. Kulik, C. L. Kulik, & R. Bangert-Drowns. *Journal of Educational Computing Research, 1*(4) 389–394.

Clark, R. E. & Leonard, S. (1985 March). *Computer research confounding.* Paper presented at the annual meeting of the American Educational Research Association, Chicago, IL.

Cohen, D. (1990). Educational technology and school organization. In R. Nickerson & P. Zodhiates (Eds.), *Technology and education: Looking toward 2020* (pp. 231–264). Hillsdale, NJ: Lawrence Erlbaum Associates.

Kulik, J. A., Kulik, C-L., & Cohen P. A (1980). Effectiveness of computer-based college teaching: A meta-analysis of findings. *Review of Educational Research, 50*(4), 525–544.

Kulik, J. A., Kulik, C-C., & Bangert-Drowns, R. L. (1985). The importance of outcome studies: A reply to Clark. *Journal of Educational Computing Research, 1*(4), 381–387.

Gerlach, V. S. (1985) Trends in instructional technology research. In J. Brown (Ed.), *Educational media year book* (Part I, pp. 21–29). Littleton, CO: Libraries Unlimited.

Greenfield, D. G., & Codding, P. A. (1985). Competency-based vs. linear computer instruction of music fundamentals. *Journal of Computer-Based Instruction, 12*(4), 108–110.

House, E. R. (1980). *Evaluating with validity.* Beverly Hills, CA: Sage.

Mehan, H. (1985). Introduction: Computers in classrooms. In H. Mehan (Ed.), *Computers in classrooms: A quasi-experiment in guided change.* Final Report to the National Institute of Education, Interactive Technology Laboratory, LaJolla, CA.

Moll, L. C., & Newcomb, A. (1985). Computer activities in a bilingual setting. In H. Mehan (Ed.), *Computers in classrooms: A quasi-experiment in guided change* (pp. 201–228). Final Report to the National Institute of Education, Interactive Technology Laboratory, La Jolla, CA.

Nelson, T. H. (1967). Getting it out of our system. In G. Schecter (Ed.), *Information retrieval: A critical review* (pp. 17–33). Washington, DC: Thompson Books.

Novak, J. D., & Gowin, D. B. (1984). *Learning how to learn.* Cambridge, England: Cambridge University Press.

Smith, K. E. (1988). Hypertext and information retrieval. *ONLINE, 12*(2), 32–40, 42–46.

Turkle, S. (1980). Computer as Rorschach. *Society, 17*(1), 15–24.

Turkle, S. (1984). *The second self: Computers and the human spirit.* New York: Simon & Schuster.

7

To Move Away From Meaning: Collaboration, Consensus, and Work in a Hypermedia Project

James M.Nyce
Gail Bader
University College
Ball State University

In 1988, a research project was initiated to enhance students' understandings of the relationships between American history and literature using hypermedia computer technology (American Culture in Context: Enrichment for Secondary Schools [ACCESS]). The purpose was to provide students and faculty with a hypermedia resource that would promote greater awareness of the historical nature of American literature and the literary nature of American history. Thus, the project was intended to support the creative exploration of relationships that exist between history and literature. The project was shaped around the development and use by high school teachers in two different schools of a hypermedia corpus for their Grade 11 high school classes in American history and literature.

This project was founded on and driven by the idea of a collaborative, interdisciplinary corpus. In essence, the idea was that American history and literature teachers would create materials for a corpus that they would then link thus showing relations among these materials, disciplines, and subjects. One of the project's most striking characteristics was that this collaboration occurred more in technical domains than it did in intellectual domains. The most explicit form of "group" collaboration was typically seen (although not exclusively) at ACCESS Project meetings, and for the most part, these meetings did not address substantive intellectual or interdisciplinary issues. Instead, technical issues became the arena to which group discussion and decision making was applied.

In this chapter, we look at why collaboration took the form that it did in this project. Collaboration could have focused on interdisciplinary issues, and group work could have taken the form of group discussions and decisions about the relationships to be illustrated and materials to be included in the corpus. However, interdisciplinary work in this project was not as much a group activity as it was an activity undertaken by the individual teacher/developers. That work on this project was so loosely coordinated, we believe, reflects some central problems with hypermedia as technology for collaborative work.

We begin by looking at how the participants perceived the difficulties they faced working collaboratively. We suggest, however, that the problems as they understood them do not tell the complete story and that it is necessary to look at the issues this project raised regarding consensus and meaning. We focus on two issues. First, we argue that links or the machine-based ties and the connections or associations thought to be embedded in those ties are not the same. Further, we suggest that the initial basis for consensus, the shared belief that significant relationships between history and literature existed and needed to be taught to students, changed over the course of the project to one based on technical work. This was different than the initial conception of the project and the teacher/developers' role in it. Finally, we suggest that these issues and problems have implications beyond the project itself.

PROJECT DESCRIPTION

ACCESS, a 3-year research project, called for an American literature teacher and a history teacher at one school to work together creating materials (including textual, pictorial, audio, and video materials) for their courses during the first project year.[1] During the second project year, these teachers were joined by two more teachers (one in history, the other literature) from another school. Data for this chapter is drawn from material collected during the project's second year. During this year, the corpus was developed and used by these four teachers in two high schools, Wilson School, a private girls school, and Trust High School, an urban public school.[2]

In this project, the roles of teacher and developer were not separate. The four teacher/developers themselves were responsible for the kinds of materials entered into the corpus, how the materials would be presented there, and the kinds of links made between them. What was also important is that from the beginning this project was seen by its participants and portrayed to others

---

[1]This project was funded by James S. McDonnell Foundation, the U. S. Department of Education Center for Technology in Education and Apple Computer.

[2]For reasons of confidentiality, the names of the high schools have been changed.

as a collaborative effort that crossed two disciplines and subjects and that hypermedia, here HyperCard, could help them achieve this. In the project, Macintosh SEs with a 20 MB hard disk and 2.5 MBs of RAM were used. In each school, these computers were networked via AppleTalk to utilize a central laser printer.

The Ethnographic Effort

This research effort made use of a series of standard ethnographic data collection methods. Ethnographic methods attempt to elicit what is significant and important to the individuals and organizations we study. In particular, they allow us to pick up and understand concepts, principles, and relationships that are often taken for granted by the participants themselves in their everyday lives.

During the second project year, we looked at how the development and implementation of ACCESS affected learning and teaching in four 11th-grade American history and literature courses at two high schools. Individual structured and unstructured interviews (some 95 hours) provided the bulk of the data we collected. These interviews included school and district administrators, department heads, teachers, and students. On-site visits, formal and informal observations of activities, and primary documents (class schedules, quizzes, papers, and text) provided additional data from both schools. At each school, ACCESS class and laboratory work (about 85 hours) was also observed. As well, we drew upon ethnographic research conducted in the project's first year (Graves & Palombo, 1989).

DESCRIPTION OF COLLABORATION

From the onset, Project ACCESS was predicated on a particular set of beliefs: that there were significant relations between history and literature; that understanding these relations would benefit the study of both literature and history; and that these relationships were things students needed to learn to come to a better understanding of these two subjects. All the teacher/ developers selected for the project had prior to the project attempted in a variety of ways to build these understandings into their teaching of history and literature. In fact, they joined this project, in part, because it offered them an opportunity to use hypermedia technology to help them achieve this. These beliefs formed the initial basis for consensus and helped the teacher/ developers define their role in the project.

Before discussing the nature of the collaboration, it is important to understand how the teacher/developers went about creating the ACCESS materials. In this project, collaboration and work typically took the form of individual teacher/developers creating materials and links they saw as relevant and important. The extent to which this work was explicitly coordinated varied among developers and from school to school.

At Wilson, a model of development (and collaboration) had been established in the first year in which each teacher/developer worked fairly independently based on what each of them perceived their own pedagogical needs and goals to be (Graves & Palombo, 1989, p.34). For example, whereas the Wilson history teacher/developer entered materials into the database that he routinely used when teaching his history course, the literature teacher/developer chose to develop new materials that she saw as challenging her notion of how to teach literature. At Wilson then, link making did not seem to emerge from any explicit, prearranged agreements. Instead, it emerged more from each developer's sense that the other developer had important or relevant material they could make use of. However, at Wilson both teacher/developers decided to organize their materials chronologically. Although this may have made coordination between them easier, it tended to separate the Wilson and Trust teacher/developers because the Trust teacher/developers had chosen to organize their materials thematically.

At Trust, the notion of "values" provided the development effort with a thematic focus. Further, they made an effort with HyperCard to graphically represent history and literature and their respective materials as a single domain. This suggests that at Trust, unlike Wilson, there were some generalized agreements regarding materials and links. Further, because they could draw on their history of team teaching, Trust developers seemed to be able to agree upon what constituted major themes and/or important materials. This helped to coordinate their development work. However here, as at Wilson, creating materials and links was work done by the individual developers.

During the second year of the project then, each teacher/developer alone linked his or her materials to that of the other teacher/developers. This is not to say that the teacher/developers did not, at times, work with each other. For example, they did work over the telephone, over lunches, and through visits to each other's classes. Nor is it to say that they never discussed substantive interdisciplinary issues with each other. However, the collaboration that did develop tended to be one in which the teacher/developers worked together on technical issues, and then each developer went on and created those links and materials that best reflected and supported his or her particular corpora. Even for the Trust developers, who had in the past coordinated many aspects of their courses, the making and defining of specific links in HyperCard remained an individual activity.

The teacher/developers themselves were, at some level, aware of this. For example, one of the Wilson teachers questioned early on whether the developers were indeed "integrating" these materials. This teacher/developer felt that because each of them tended to work separately finding materials and putting them on ACCESS, they were not mutually developing connections between the materials.

MODELS, EXPLANATIONS AND DIVERGENCE

By the second year, the most explicit form of group collaboration was seen (although not exclusively) at ACCESS Project meetings where discussions and agreements for the most part reflected and dealt with technical issues. In short, "collaborative work" was not focused on shared understandings or developing shared understandings about the nature of the corpus. It is necessary to ask why collaborative work on this project came to focus on the technical.[3]

One of the important differences that separated the Trust and Wilson teacher/developers was that, to some extent, they held divergent understandings about what constituted history and literature. At Trust, an effort was made to include a broad range of perspectives and historical "voices" not always found in high school American history and literature courses. The Wilson developers chose a different route. At Wilson, there seemed to be more of a concern with understanding historical "flow" and contextualizing a "classic" body of knowledge. In short, the Wilson teachers were more concerned with an established canon and developing materials that feed back into that canon. Concerns about what materials and links should be in the ACCESS corpus came to be tied to (and expressed in terms of) concerns about what constituted the particular subject. As one developer said, "Every one has their own view of the subject."

Differences in classroom practice also tended to divide teachers, and this influenced their views of the kind of resource ACCESS was to be. Here, discussion and debate focused on the extent to which the corpus should reflect each instructor's view of what should be taught to their students and how it should be taught. For example, both the Trust and Wilson history teachers seemed to see ACCESS as a resource they themselves had to mediate. Although each stressed interaction between themselves and students as where the interpretation of class materials (ACCESS being only one of these) should occur, they wanted to remain the final arbiters of what constituted "correct" interpretations of these materials. On the other hand, the Wilson literature teacher/developer wanted her students to be able to use ACCESS

---

[3]The technical background of the teacher/developers ranged from little or no experience with personal computers (when the project began, one teacher did not even know how to type) to those who were familiar with and had used personal computers for a number of years. This range of technical knowledge and competence (and the lack of any programming skills on their part) is one reason why HyperCard was chosen for this project.

outside the classroom with little or no help from her. The Trust literature teacher/developer wanted her students to use ACCESS in class but hoped students would choose materials in ACCESS with as little mediation from her as possible.

The individual project members' beliefs about teaching and their subjects and the nature of their particular schools and their students worked against the emergence of a common social process and a series of shared understandings. Further, because each teacher's corpora reflects his or her own view of what should be taught and how it should be taught, creating linkages within ACCESS also became problematic. Ultimately, the focus of group work shifted from a shared, socially expressed concern with "what are we doing" to "how are we going to do it."

The factors the teachers themselves were aware of do not, by themselves, explain this shift. To understand why the shift occurred, it is necessary to take a closer look at the relationship between "links" as the machine-based ties and "connections" or the associations thought to be embedded in these ties. The idea of connections (as association) was central to the ACCESS Project and to these teachers' work as developers. In this project, the ability to make links in HyperCard between corpus materials was the technological embodiment of that idea. However, the ability to make machine-based ties (links) was seductive and to some extent misleading because it hid, as it turned out, the need to agree on the meaning (or associations) embedded in those ties. Ultimately, this led to a shift in the nature of consensus.

LINKS, MEANING, AND SIGNIFICANCE

Many who have studied and developed hypermedia technologies have argued that links by themselves create meaningful associations. As Virginia Doland (1989), has pointed out, "A 'link' posits a relationship between two nodes containing information, and thus creates new intellectual entity, an assertion about reality which, accepted or not, does not leave the reader unaffected. Simply to create a linkage is to create a unit of meaning" (p.10). In fact, it is this characteristic of hypermedia that these researchers and developers believe separate hypermedia from other such applications and technologies. In other words, the "promise" of hypermedia lies in its potential to reconfigure and even create knowledge in meaningful and personally satisfying ways through this linking.

Links, as Doland pointed out, can indeed be seen as assertions about reality. However, this really says very little, for it leaves unanswered the question of what particular assertions are being made. Nor does it tell us if the reader's interpretation of any link/assertion is the same as that intended by its author. In short, Doland's assessment of links, that links by themselves are assertions about reality, tells us little more than that readers and authors claim their link/assertions are meaningful in someway.

However, for individuals attempting to work collaboratively with hypermedia, the idea that links are assertions about reality lies at the heart of the matter. Following Kenneth Burke, we argue that links, like words, are indeed assertions about reality. Burke (1966) argued that terminologies (words) are necessarily "selections" of and thereby constitute reality (p.45). Through one's choice of words, one is directing attention and implicitly framing the world as one thing or another. For, when Kenneth Burke (1966) spoke of the "persuasive" or rhetorical nature of language and words, he reminded us that they force people to take stances about the world, because they make particular arguments about the nature of things (p.45). It is here, we believe, at this fundamental level, that the teacher/developers ran into trouble because making links forced them to make arguments and take stances on the nature of things.

As these teachers began to talk about and make links, they sometimes discovered they were not talking about the same connections or associations. In other words, what they all made of the materials and links they created were not necessarily the same thing. Moreover, this was not a simple difference of training, experience, or classroom goals. We believe that they did not necessarily see history, literature, and the teaching of these subjects the same way. This is because in projects of this kind, the ability to make technical ties (links) does not simply raise issues about the basic nature of knowledge, they make particular arguments for how those objects and events a discipline claims for itself should be constituted. In short, making technical ties, in Burke's (1970) terms, meant having taken a fundamental stand on ("adopted a policy" toward [p.58]) what constitutes knowledge of literature and history and how they should be taught. However, what making technical ties demonstrated here was that agreement on the precise shape of a field of knowledge can be difficult to achieve.

As ACCESS went on, the teacher/developers could not escape questions like, "What is history/literature?" and "What do my students need to learn about history/literature?" The materials, the links, and associations they created emphasized the differences between them and the longer the development effort went on, the clearer these differences became.

SHIFTS IN THE NATURE OF CONSENSUS

If these collaborators found themselves holding differing opinions and working with a technology that made it difficult for them to avoid taking a stance, why did this not emerge as a group concern? It is striking, particularly given the importance that links and connections have for both hypermedia and this project, that the issue of how and why they created particular links never came to the surface. In other words, why did the teacher/developers never address these problems about meaning head on? We believe that the reasons this did not occur has to do with the nature of consensus. Although the belief that significant relationships between history and literature existed and needed to taught to students persisted, the basis for consensus came to rest more on technical issues. We believe that this shift insured that the project would continue.

Fernandez (1965) questioned the notion of consensus itself by pointing to the inevitable individual variations anthropologists find when those in agreement offer differing accounts of the very thing they claim to be in agreement on. He also argued that one needs to recognize that "consensus" can refer to agreement at a number of levels. For example, Fernandez believed that for consensus to occur it is not necessary for everyone to share "the same" ideas in order to work together on the "same" tasks. He, in fact, suggested that attempts to establish "shared meaning" can be problematic both for the group and their ability to carry out work.

We believe that consensus changed over the course of this project and that this shift can help us understand the course the project took. The first shift was at the level of how the project itself was defined, that is, the project itself changed from an intellectual group effort to that of a technical development project. Why was this shift important? It was important because it reframed what constituted collaboration and consensus for the project members. The need to take a stance, a need inherent in any linking or hypermedia corpus development, might have hampered the teachers' ability to work together. To explicitly acknowledge and thus have to deal with the differences that hypermedia posed may well have forced the teacher/developers to take such divergent stances that group work might not have been able to continue.

However, the teacher/developers did share a less problematic set of experiences as HyperCard developers. ACCESS required developers to create (and link) materials according to a project timetable. Thus, at one level, the project had joblike elements, and there were concerns about keeping up one's end of the job. We believe they seized upon this experience to form a different kind of consensus, one based on technical issues. Here, the teacher/developers were all novices, and while their technical work had potential for disagreement, neither this work nor these disagreements carried the same weight as their "real" work did. In this way, their roles and work in the project came to be redefined. No longer was the project seen as entirely a collegial, academic effort. Rather, the teacher/developers began to focus on their status as employees and the technical tasks they shared as employees in a project.

We believe that over time this shared work experience provided a basis for a less problematic kind of consensus to emerge. In this project, consensus came to be expressed through technical idioms and the shared work and experience of being a HyperCard developer and a project employee. The collaboration that began as one of academic colleagues thus became a collaboration among developers that focused on technical issues.

CONCLUSION

What this project raised were a set of issues about meaning and significance. Ideas about discipline and classroom were deeply held by the teacher/ developers and reflected well thought-out understandings about the nature of their subjects and disciplines. However, the possibility exists, when meaning and significance are probed deeply, for negotiations and understandings to break down and even fail. We believe that these problems may arise, as they did here, when experts are asked to develop a corpus together around their areas of expertise. In situations like this, one is asking people with the greatest stake in a subject and the most developed set of understandings to agree on what, for them, are the most central and fundamental of issues. As simple as this point is, it is one that really has not been dealt with in respect to hypermedia and hypermedia development projects.

The ACCESS development effort did not address these issues head on. For example, project meetings became arenas in which technical issues like how HyperCard stack icons should be represented were discussed. Issues about which materials should be in the ACCESS corpus and which links should be made there for the most part never became project issues. Instead, when questions of this order arose, they were either masked or reworked into technical idioms.

In this hypermedia project and we suspect in others (if the literature on hypertext is any indication), issues about meaning, significance, and the constitution of knowledge are avoided, if not essentially trivialized. By this we mean they are reduced to essentially technical discussions about application-specific issues such as linking protocols. In short, we do not believe that this project was in any way exceptional. Further, we do not believe that the project would have worked if only the participants had shared similar ideas and stances. We suspect that collaborative, hypermedia projects may always exhibit these kinds of divergences in understanding and that this needs to be both recognized and taken into account in these development efforts.

REFERENCES

Burke, K. (1966). *Language as symbolic action.* Berkeley: University of California Press.
Burke, K. (1970). *The rhetoric of religion.* Berkeley: University of California Press.
Doland, V. D. (1989). Hypermedia as an interpretive act. *Hypermedia, 1*(1), 6–19.
Fernandez, J. W. (1965). Symbolic consensus in a Fang reformative cult. *American Anthropologist, 67*(4), 902–929.
Graves, W., III, & Palombo, M. (1989). *Project ACCESS at Lincoln School: Ethnographic Report for Year One.*

8

The Social Ecology of Student Life: The Integration of Technological Innovation in a Residence Hall

Kenneth T. Anderson
Anne Page McClard
Brown University

James Larkin
Cosmopsis Communications, Inc.

Of the numerous studies on computing in academic settings, few have examined the use of personal computers in a residential environment (Butler-Nalin & Goodrich, 1987; Jackson, 1987; Palmer & Harnisch, 1987). Instead, most research has focused on the use of computers in public computing facilities on campuses.

As investment in a personal computer became a consideration for every college student, we wondered what effect these machines would have on the more subtle aspects of college education such as residential life in general and the social aspects of learning in particular. Taking this question a bit further, we wondered whether a computer in every room would create a dormitory full of hermits or whether on the contrary, computers could contribute to a more collegial style of life. Or perhaps computers would have no major impact on how undergraduates live and learn.

With these and many more questions in mind, in August 1987, the Office of Program Analysis/Institute for Research and Information in Scholarship placed IBM PS/2 Model 30s in 33 of the 34 rooms of the Littlefield residence hall at Brown University. We provided a Novell network that connected to all the computers in the residence hall, gave them access to a laser printer (located in the hall), network-based software (including electronic mail), and served as a gateway to the Brown mainframe. Of the 63 students who lived in the residence hall, 61 agreed to let us observe how they used the networked personal computers during the 1987–1988 academic year.

Because we believe that understanding the place of technology and technological innovation requires an understanding of the culture in which the
technology is embedded, we spend much of the discussion that follows
sketching the most salient features of student behavior at Brown. We use this
behavioral information to develop analytic categories as a way of describing
student culture, that we define (somewhat narrowly) as patterns of individual
and group behavior that can be linked to the status of being a student. We
then expatiate our description of student culture in terms of the technology
intervention–the network of personal computers–that we introduced into the
residence hall.

Our methodology differs markedly from previous research that focused on
the role of computing in the university setting and relied exclusively on
self-reported, quantitative, or short-term observational data (Butler–Nalin &
Goodrich, 1987; Palmer & Harnisch, 1987). By contrast, our study used a
mix of methodologies. An ethnographer lived in the residence hall, observing
and participating in daily activities for most of the academic year. In addition,
during the course of the year, we conducted formal face-to-face interviews
with all the residents, administered three questionnaires, and developed an
automated system to track network use (recording user, time of day, length of
use, applications used). In retrospect, we believe that the richness of this
approach gave us access to domains of student life that would have otherwise
gone undiscovered.[1]

Computers do not seem to revolutionize the way students live and work
but rather fit within existing individual and group social patterns. The
Littlefield students did not believe that their increased access to computers
distinguished them from other freshmen in significant ways, and our observations support this belief. Instead of isolating individuals, as computers are
sometimes thought to do, the Littlefield network reinforced community life;
the computers and the network presented a set of shared problems, the
solutions to which were discovered through a set of shared resources. In this
way, students' interaction with the computers and with each other were
typical of their behavior in other domains.

Freshmen at Brown operate with a set of common goals, namely, to learn
about things in the world through academic studies and to learn about others
by meeting people and making friends. They manipulate the conceptual
categories of time, work, and play in very specific ways to accomplish these
goals. The computer and the network quickly became integrated into the
habitual lives of the residence hall and became simply another means by

---

[1]The Program in Education, Culture and Technology (ECT) in Brown University's Department of Anthropology undertook the Littlefield Dormitory Research Project during the academic year 1987–1988. A more detailed discussion of research methodology appears in the
report, *The Littlefield Research Project*, (Anderson, McClard, Bader, & Larkin, 1988).

which to accomplish the twofold goal of learning about the world and learning about others.

THE SOCIAL ECOLOGY OF STUDENT LIFE

We call this section "The Social Ecology of Student Life" because just as individuals, groups, and societies respond ingeniously to overcome obstacles imposed by the natural environment, so do students respond to obstacles imposed by the cultural environment of the residential hall and the university through socially constructed understandings of learning, time, and play. In this section, we lay the foundation for our analysis of how the computer and network came to have meaning for the freshmen we studied. First, we discuss student goals of learning about the world and learning about others, then we discuss how these two forms of learning are accomplished by students via manipulation of the previously mentioned conceptual categories.

The Dual Goal of Learning

Most people would guess that the primary goal for students is to learn, and–not surprisingly–for Littlefielders, learning was the primary stated goal of attending college. As we found, however, learning is a huge umbrella; it can accommodate so many behaviors that the term, used alone, lacks meaning. At first, the learning seemed to be associated only with academic work. Academic work, as expressed by students, was weighted with a moral imperative; to do academic work is why they had come to Brown. We saw signs of this attitude during our first encounters with students before classes began. Students spoke consistently of wanting to do well in their academic work, and implicit in their statements was that there was a one-to-one correspondence between doing well in their work and learning.

One gets the impression, at first, that for freshmen learning is almost a form of organized religion. They have entered into the sacred halls of academe, to be cloistered for 4 years (or more), to learn the wisdom of the ancestors and the wise ones. Many of the freshmen in Littlefield did not know to which end their learning would lead them, others saw it as leading to personal enlightenment, and still others saw it as leading to specific careers. Universally students expressed the sentiment that learning needs no justification; it is in and of itself good—a kind of unquestioned faith. One student typified the belief this way, "I'm not exactly sure what I am going to do when I get done with my education at Brown. All I know is for now I have to study and study hard. I mean, that is why I am here."

Another student, while learning with a specific end in mind—to become a doctor—nonetheless saw intrinsic value in learning for the sake of itself, "It used to be that to become a doctor all one did was follow a certain set of courses. I don't like that approach. Here at Brown they allow you to take several courses that are really just as important. I'm taking a course in English literature now. . . . There is so much out there to learn that's important for life."

Many students, especially early in the first semester, saw the amount of academic work ahead as forbidding. Interaction among students during orientation week and for several weeks into the semester reflected this attitude; students talked about all of the things they had to learn and the hours of work that would be required. Many students even bought all of their books during orientation week for the courses for which they had registered, and some actually began reading them before getting their course syllabi (which contained their reading assignments). There was no time to waste. There was so much to learn; work had to begin at once.

Littlefielders in the dorm frequently communicated that learning took an overwhelming amount of time. One student expressed this by saying, "I never have enough time to do all my homework. There is just so much there." As the semester progressed, norms for the amount of time spent working began to develop as is evident by the following statement, "I *only* studied two hours last night because a friend from home called. I love to hear from them but I'm glad they don't call too often or I would be really behind."

What each student regarded as an appropriate amount of time to spend on academic work varied; for this student, 2 hours was insufficient. For freshmen, work is a catalog of requirements necessary to achieve the fulfillment of the goal of learning. The implicit relationship between work and learning for freshmen is quite direct, as the previous quotation suggests: study and one will learn.

Although commonly espoused by students, a simple cause-and-effect model of learning does not fully explain the meaning of the conceptual category learning for freshmen. The goal of learning is not as monolithic as one might think, nor is it achieved solely through academic work.

Students discovered during their first semester that there were more than just academic demands at Brown and that those demands were just as real as the academic ones. Besides the academic activities of studying and going to classes, students wanted and implicitly were expected to become involved in a variety of other activities such as extracurricular activities (e.g., intramural sports, musical ensembles, community service organizations), special events (e.g., lectures, concerts, unit meetings), student jobs, "hanging out" with friends (e.g., movies, parties, meals, study breaks, watching TV), and developing personal relationships (e.g., with members of the dorm, members of the opposite sex). These activities required an enormous amount of additional time. One way students resolved the conflicts they felt about spending time away from working, the activity that led to the fulfillment of the goal of learning, was by expanding the category of learning to include them. Thus, the goal of learning became twofold: learning about the world and learning about others. Learning about others quickly became a legitimate use of time as a secondary goal for college.

In sum, the meanings and goals of learning are quite broad. The Littlefielders expanded their conceptual understanding of learning to include activities that would have otherwise fallen outside of its scope. The reconstruction of the category learning was the logical response to the pressures exerted on the students by the implicit expectations of students at Brown and in the residence hall. Students are expected to be both fully engaged in academic activities and in community-oriented activities. The goal of learning is discussed more fully in the following section in relation to the conceptual categories of time, play, and work.

The Social Construction of Work, Play, and Time

In the previous section, we discussed the way students resolved conflicts between the ethic of work and the attraction of play by redefining learning in such a way that it could result from social and community-oriented activities as well as academic activities. For example, socializing, which was defined initially by students as a "nonwork" activity and therefore of a lower priority than work, became redefined as learning about other people, an activity that most students, in the end, considered to be a legitimate use of time and one of their primary goals in college. In this section, we discuss how the dual goals of learning are pursued by students through the organization of their everyday activities.

The allocation of time, as discussed earlier, was important to Littlefielders. The conceptual category of time is perhaps the most important one of all for students. Differing conceptions of time across cultures has been of long-term interest to anthropologists. Cultures, like individuals, are bounded by limitations imposed by their conceptions of time. The model year in the automobile industry (around which most activities in the industry are organized), the fiscal year, and the academic year—all are examples of culturally constructed units of time. Within these large categories are more granular divisions such as the benchmark 40-hour work week that define the organization of time and effort in relation to the main categories. Students generally do not refer to the 40-hour week with its explicit division of work and nonwork activities. Instead students organize their time rather intricately around conceptions of play and work activities.

Although student time revolves around the defined semester and the academic year, its most outstanding characteristic is its fluidity. For students, play and work activities are largely planned around assignment due dates. Students are concerned with what has to be done immediately on a day-to-day basis, and as a result their activities shift from day to day depending on what has to be done.

Each student's daily routine in Littlefield was different, but we did observe patterns. Nine o'clock until 11 a.m. in the morning was class time, 11 a.m. to 1 p.m. was lunch time, 1 p.m. to 3 p.m. was class time, and 3 p.m. to 5 p.m. was flexible time, depending on what was due. If a student used it as play time, then he or she was likely to take a nap or play in an intramural activity or just hang out with friends. If his or her schedule was tighter, this time would be devoted to reading, doing problem sets, writing, or lab preparation. Five until 7 p.m. was dinner time. From 7 p.m. until 8 p.m. students seemed to generally settle into studying, and from 8 p.m. until 11 p.m. was the prime study time. Students usually took a break from studying between 11 p.m. and 12:30 a.m. to get food. Late-night activities depended most directly on work due. People who had a due date the next day usually worked past 1 a.m., although they socialized quietly as well. And frequently, those individuals with more than 1 or 2 hours of work to prepare for the next day would take time off to sleep for a couple of hours sometime during the evening and then work through the late-night hours until morning.

This sketch is intended to convey only a broad patterns of daily life in the dorm. In actuality, students seldom took 2 hours for lunch or attended classes all morning and all afternoon. Lunch and class time were interspersed with various play and work activities, depending on what a student had to have done. The student day is not governed by a clock; it is governed by classes that must be attended and by what has to be read, written, or accomplished immediately in order to learn what has to be learned.

Two principles that guided student orientations to time in Littlefield were "the search for the B" and "crisis periods." Unlike Becker, Geer, and Hughes (1968), who suggested that student life revolves wholly around the grade, at Brown, where there is no grade recorded below a C, the attempt to get a grade above a C is a driving force among students because it signifies learning (typically, a B is considered the minimally acceptable grade at Brown (Anderson & McClard, 1988; Beeman et al., 1987). The nature of this relationship is not always clear; often the critical task for students pursuing the B grade was to figure out what their instructor(s) wanted them to know. They then studied in effective and economical ways to achieve these well-defined ends. Crisis periods are times when students had to give extra effort such as working through the night or foregoing other activities to meet due dates.

With the search for the B and recurrent crisis periods as driving factors, student time can be defined by what occupies it (work or play), and it can be defined by its shortage or sufficiency, that is, time wasted or time saved. Time is particularly important with respect to definitions of work and play.

Generally, time spent away from work was considered second-class time by Littlefielders, at least initially, because such time did not apparently contribute to the goal of learning; initially, freshmen conceived of play and work as mutually exclusive categories. When students talked about work, they referred to activities that would help them achieve the goal of learning. Typically, when they talked about the goal of academic learning, students referred to course requirements and all the many activities involved in meeting those requirements. Play, on the other hand, was conceived as having fun and enjoying oneself. Eventually, however, certain play activities were redefined; they came to mean learning about other peoples' viewpoints and reflecting on one's own understandings.

In this sense, play was reconstructed so that it contributed to the attainment of the goal of learning about others. Additionally, some activities that were initially considered play came to be redefined under the rubric of work. Going for a late night snack, taking a walk, socializing in the hall, even going shopping or to a movie all came to be included in a category called study break; study breaks are subsumed by the category studying and are therefore conceived as part of work.

Study breaks seem to take up the most time during the period from Sunday night until Friday around noon. Students took study breaks when they were "fed up" with working, had "had it," or were just "tired." On the other hand, a study break could be something earned by working hard. Hearing such phrases as "I deserve to take a study break" or "I have gotten to the point where I need to take a break," were not unusual. On several occasions students were known to have spent their whole night on a study break. When asked what they did the night before, their response was, of course, "I studied." During study time, students were supposed to study, and so by their way of thinking, they did.

We believe that different kinds of breaks may have been a part of student study strategies. Due dates could be important indicators of the kind of break a student might take. The choice of which kind of study break a student took—for example, going to the movies with a friend, going to get something to eat, going to hang out, or playing a computer game—most likely depended upon what the student had due immediately. A student who was writing a paper at the last minute (as many did) was less likely to go to a movie for a study break than the student who "just" had some reading to do for a class that met the next afternoon. Rather if he or she decided to take a break, it would be short. Going down the hall to say "Hi" to someone or just walking around are typical break activities (Anderson & McClard, 1988). The study break was conceived as a necessary part of studying; it offered a respite from the ongoing activity of work, allowing the student a rest and bringing the student back mentally to a place where it was possible to study again.

Thus, the activities students engaged in during study breaks were play activities, and yet they were reconstructed into work activities; play became relevant to work, furthering the goal of learning. Certainly, students did not rationalize every activity by calling it a study break, but nearly any activity *could* be one when there was studying to be done.

We do not want to suggest that this shuffling of labels was pure rationalization. A midnight pizza *could* provide the fuel for late-night inspiration; it could serve as a forum for learning about others through socializing with them; and certainly one could learn about the world—at least keep in touch with it—by going to a movie. But more subtle examples also support the validity of students' reconceptualization of nonwork activities. On one occasion, for example, a student who was discussing a paper topic over dinner with friends had substantially changed her approach to an assignment she was working on by the end of the meal, yet this interaction was not recognized explicitly as work. Clearly, much informal interaction between students in the dorm was directly related to the goal of learning, whether or not the students involved always realized it.

In short, Littlefielders defined and redefined the broad goal of learning and also reconstructed the categories of time, work, and play in response to the expectations they perceived in the cultural environment of the university. Although students are explicitly supposed to maintain a certain level of academic excellence—getting grades above C—they are tacitly expected to participate in the university community socially as well. To overcome possible conflicts between play and work, they redefined their goal of learning, the means by which they accomplish this goal through their organization of time, and the categories of work and play. In the next section, we discuss the cultural environment of the dorm and the way the computer and the network came to have meaning for the students who lived there.

COMPUTERS IN THE CULTURAL ENVIRONMENT OF THE DORM

The Cultural Environment of the Dorm

To understand how the computer was integrated into the daily life of the dorm (or residence hall, in administrative parlance), one must first have an understanding of what the dorm was for the students who lived there. Jackson (1987) maintained that residential facilities at MIT were "refuges" from academe. Littlefield was not really a refuge but a place where students spent most their lives. Most major work activities—writing, reading, reviewing—took place within the dorm, as did the major portion of nonwork activities such as socializing and game playing. Additionally, dorm residents together engaged in a number of other nonwork activities outside of the walls of the building such as intramural sports (organized by dorm units) and study breaks and meals taken with other Littlefield residents.

Littlefield was the center of all student activity rather than a refuge, as is shown by Fig. 8.1; it was much more than a place where freshmen slept or a place to which they retreated after engaging in classes and other academic activities. It was the location of the primary reference group of many of its inhabitants—students who routinely talked to one another, ate together, went to movies and parties together, and studied together. Students who lived in Littlefield shared a bond. For some, this bond was stronger than for others, but everyone had the sense that they belonged at Littlefield and that this distinguished them from students who belonged to other dorm units. Littlefield was a social system in microcosm with identifiable standards of membership, behavioral norms, and relationships of all types between its members.

Littlefield residents typically wandered in and out of each other's rooms to socialize and study (see Fig. 8.1). This study pattern was illustrated by one resident's description of his study habits, "I study here in Littlefield but not here in my room all the time. I study in the lounge a lot. I study in the room next door, I study next door [on the other] side, I will study down in Jack's room at the end of the hall. I have studied downstairs in Rachel's room, I have studied in Victoria's room. You study all over the place."

Because the dorm was a social group as well as a physical location, it was important to freshmen that they knew people in their dorm and that residents were friendly to each other. These friendships extended beyond simple peer-group recognition to encompass reciprocity, a norm of friendship based on exchange of resources. In college, friends are a primary resource for assistance of all kinds. Although there are a number of other resources set up within the institution itself to assist students—such as the library, health services, teachers, and deans—students invariably turned first to their fellow students and friends for assistance. Within the dorm, much of student life involved sharing and trading of various resources. Pragmatic exchange of resources was not the only basis of friendship in Littlefield, but friendship was the most legitimate and visible medium of exchange.

Students could offer to request two primary kinds of resources from friends in the dorm: (a) things or material objects, including such items as food, computers, televisions, or phones; and (b) services, that could range from general helpfulness to providing specific skills or knowledge. Friends

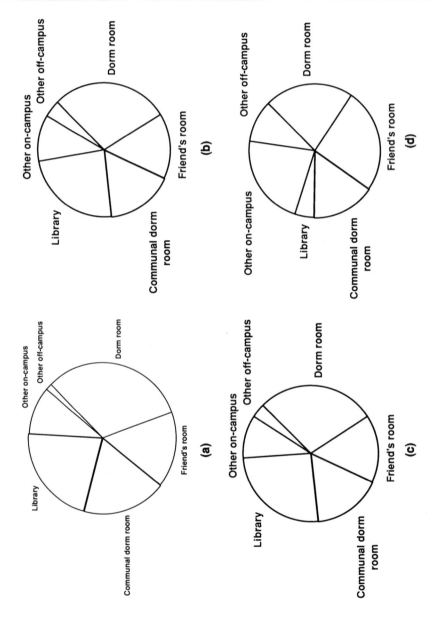

FIG. 8.1. (a) Where students write, (b) where they study, (c) where they review for exams, and (d) where they socialize.

were the people to whom students turned when problems arose or when they needed practical information. They were the people from whom one could borrow clothes or with whom one could go for a late-night snack.

Here we have sketched some of the most prevalent features of the cultural environment of the dorm. In summary, the dorm is of central importance to freshmen at Brown. It provides them with their primary reference group; a place where they can work and play; a network of people who they know and can draw on as valuable resources. In the next section, we discuss the ways in which the cultural environment of the dorm and the university contributed to shaping the way computers and the network were integrated into Littlefielders' daily lives, in short, how the computer came to have meaning for the residents in the dorm.

Computers and the Network in Cultural Context

Computing activities in Littlefield were well integrated into the routines associated with the categories of work, play, and learning. Doing programming assignments for a course was work, for example. Programming for oneself, making pretty pictures in BASIC, was viewed as play, "Sometimes when I get tired of studying I just sit and make pictures (on the computer). I need a break from work. I used to do it in the high school computer lab after school. I felt funny about it there. I love being able to sit at my own desk in my own room to create them. It's one of the best things about having the computer here."

The combined attributes of integration into student lives and the various uses to which they could be put meant the computers were both a resource and a drain on resources. Computers were a resource because they helped students meet their academic goals, fulfill requirements, and save time. They were a drain on student resources because many students were unfamiliar at first with the computer and software provided by the project, and therefore they had to devote time to learning about the computer, recovering from mistakes, and helping other students do the same. As familiarity with, use of, and dependence on the network increased during the year, it too was an occasional hindrance because of malfunctions.

As a resource, computer use in Littlefield among the freshmen related closely to the student concern with an economical approach to time, that is, the time needed to get a B grade. In relation to academic work, the computer was available when and where the students needed it. This was particularly true for students who liked to wait until the last minute and put in an "all-nighter" on a paper—a common strategy—and for students who did most of their writing in the early morning hours because of the relatively quiet work environment. In short, with the room-based computers, students did not have to change their work routines, as they would have had they used one of the public computer clusters on campus.

In addition to convenience, students believed the computers saved them time because they could work more intensively using the computer than they could working on a typewriter or on paper. For example, they said they could revise written work more quickly using a computer, and therefore they could do it more thoroughly. In addition, they believed they had to adhere to a rising set of external norms in the university for written work: A "perfect" laser-printed paper makes a better impression than an erased and corrected typewritten version.

The computers also played several other roles as time-saving resources. First, the computers were a resource for writing, one of the students' most important tasks. Students believed that computers saved them the time they would have otherwise used typing and retyping their work; thus, they had more time to spend on revision. We suspect that this represents just one cut of a deeper alteration in writing practices that computers encourage.

Aside from the computer functioning as an efficient tool, it also worked to facilitate interaction with friends. Electronic mail was used to exchange messages, arrange dorm-wide activities, and set up face-to-face meetings. When students used the network, they often checked the system to see who else was using it. Some students used E-mail to keep in touch with dorm and individual activities when their own schedule prevented them from spending time in the dorm. In all of these cases, students were conducting and orchestrating interaction among themselves. They were, in effect, making friends, helping friends, getting help from friends, and generally carrying on the everyday business of living. The computer helped them conduct these seemingly routine tasks that are so essential to acquiring knowledge and learning about others. But the network did not transform the character of these tasks or the nature of relations with others.

Finally, the computers also became a resource for controlling and allocating time as study breaks. Breaks taken without other people are more controllable breaks than those involving other people. Computer games became a primary way to take a study break in Littlefield because frequently they took less time than going out to a movie or for a pizza and were less expensive. Regardless of what games students played, they controlled the duration of play. In contrast, other types of breaks frequently lasted longer than was desirable, because the students became engaged in conversations or other activities that were not inherently time-bounded events. The types of computer games with which students took breaks usually required very little thought and yet were engaging enough to constitute actual breaks.

These game breaks differed from many other types of breaks because they represent a genuine break from academic activities, whereas other types of breaks often served as forums for discussion of academic subjects. Although

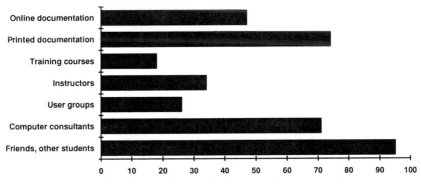

FIG. 8.2. Where students seek information about computing.

for most students games were a favored way to take a short break from
studying, some students felt computer game playing presented the danger of
getting "hooked," and so they avoided these games altogether. There were
only a few students for whom game playing became obviously detrimental to
academic activities rather than serving simply as a bounded break in their
daily routines.

There are certain costs associated with computing, and these tend to be
internalized in the group. Students count other students among the computing resources available to them; computing as an activity was strongly
supported by the presence of friends who helped. Even formal computing
help, like the two consultants hired by the project, were called upon as friends
as much or more than they were called upon as people paid to do a job (the
friendship aspect was particularly important when students woke them at
4:00 a.m to help print a paper due that day). Underlying all of the tremendous
sharing of knowledge, helping, and supporting of computer endeavors was a
norm of reciprocity that emphasized the role of friends as people who do
things for each other. This norm is evident in our survey data. Students were
asked where they went when they needed help with computing. As Fig. 8.2
shows, 95% of students at some point turned to their friends for help. This
was in sharp contrast to other sources of help such as courses on computing
(19%) or Brown's Computer and Information Services sources (27%). Further, not only were other students the primary source of information, they
were also perceived to be the most helpful of all sources, as seen in Fig. 8.3.

Sharing of computer expertise fit well within patterns of sharing other
kinds of information. Expert knowledge was usually offered on the basis of
friendship or membership in the dorm community.[2] Students helped each

---

[2]Expert knowledge was sometimes offered in exchange for goods like a date. This was not,
however, usually the case with people inside the dorm. Special rules of dating behavior seemed
to apply to "members of one's own group/dorm" (Anderson, 1988).

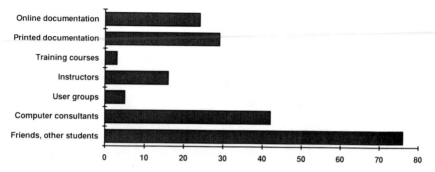

FIG. 8.3.   Percent of total sample saying the information is *quite helpful* or *very helpful.*

other write papers, do math problem sets, and design experiments. In the case of computers, peer tutoring occurred most often when people in Littlefield were first learning Microsoft Word (Anderson, Bader, & McClard, 1988).

Electronic Mail in the Student Context

This standard of helpfulness parallels another major component of group behavior that we found reflected in computing behavior: social control. Over time there emerged a consensus about what constituted appropriate uses of electronic mail (or E-mail that includes both nonsimultaneous electronic mail and simultaneous electronic messaging). At times this consensus solidified into group action to control the nature of E-mail exchanges. Initially, students often used the E-mail system to broadcast messages to everyone in the dorm. This changed when people began to feel the messages were too pointed and critical towards individual students and issues in the dorm. Although gossip and controversial issues continued in the form of private messages to selected individuals, generalized mailings containing "hot items" or "flames" tapered off. Self-expression mail such as poetry and personal thought messages also followed this pattern. Thus, the content of student expression shifted in response to ideas about appropriate uses of the network.

Much of the research on E-mail networks has focused on conferencing systems between physically separated E-mail users or on experiments where people did not know each other (Hiltz, 1982; Hiltz & Turoff, 1978; Sproull & Kiesler, 1985). In these situations, there is much concern with the issue of anonymity as a feature of the medium and the effects of anonymity on communication. In these situations, too, it is assumed (or so structured for research purposes) that there is no social world outside of the one created via the E-mail group. Indeed, much of this research is aimed at seeing how forms of interaction might change if features of the social world were somehow held in abeyance. For example, if user knowledge of the gender and status of senders and recipients were suppressed, would interaction change and, if so, in which ways?

The Littlefield context differed from this body of research in a number of ways. The dorm group was created for reasons that had nothing to do with computing. They were, first and foremost, freshmen students at a university. E-mail was in constant competition with a number of other communications media, including writing, posters (on dorm walls and doors), memo boards on doors, face-to-face interaction (including meals, word of mouth networks, casual meetings on campus), and telephones (both the intercampus system and public phones). Most importantly, students all knew each other.

We believe that Littlefield is representative of a class of E-mail use in which users know and interact with each other frequently. Because of this, we would expect the social context and the identity of users to affect use as much as, or even more than, the nature of the network medium (Anderson, 1988). Situations in which users are anonymous—if such situations truly exist— tend, we believe, to give E-mail use an unreal, game-like quality. In Littlefield, the group appeared to act fairly quickly when "the game"[3] started to get out of hand and have very real consequences for social functioning and group maintenance. We believe that the social context and social identity of users will become extremely important for understanding the development and use of electronic mail in institutional settings.

This line of thought also applies to electronic networks in general. Much of the literature on networks stresses their promise for stimulating collaboration and/or creating intellectual communities (Feldman, 1987; Oberst & Smith, 1986; Snizek, 1987). Network systems, it is argued, may encourage collaboration because they make it fairly easy to exchange materials among geographically separated people.

The Littlefield network, although used for many academic and social purposes, was not very successful in creating on-line intellectual communities. The students simply did not use the network for holding discussions on course-related topics, nor as far as we know, to exchange files serving as a basis for discussion between individuals or among groups. They did, however, use the network to facilitate face-to-face discussions, including discussions focusing on academic topics.

The Littlefield data led us to rethink our original understanding of networks. We now see networks as facilitators of discussion rather than as replacements or substitutes for face-to-face communication. Face-to-face

---

[3]"The game" was Snipes, a maze shoot-em-up game supplied with the network software that allowed up to five players in different rooms to play simultaneously, provided they all started the game at the same time. The object of the game was to wander through the maze, locating and destroying all snipes and snipe factories, although players could—and did—shoot each other as well.

interaction was the preferred means of communication among Littlefield students. However, the network did serve to keep students aware of social knowledge about the group. It allowed students to alert hard-to-reach fellow dormmates with questions that would later be discussed directly. Many students used it to keep in touch with the mood and temper of the dorm as well as actual plans and events. For individuals who shared the dorm as a reference base, the network added one more way of tracking and affecting the social group. Networks placed in situations where users share a physical location must be studied far more intensively if one is to understand for what social purposes they are used and the resulting implications for individual and group communications.

Word Processing in the Student Context

Another illustrative point of contact between computers and the student world is word processing. Word processing is the prime academic use to which the greatest number students directly put their personal computers. And paper writing, particularly at an institution like Brown that emphasizes the importance of liberal arts and social sciences for all students, is a critical educational task. It links students to the grading structure of the university and to their personal conceptions of learning. It is something they believe they "must do," and something they believe reflects their personal intellectual positions on issues from the scholarly world at large. It links personal and institutional conceptions of education in the same instructional event.

Software for writing papers, we suggest, is also educational. For students, the value of the computer as word processor emerged from the role of paper writing in their education. Yet writing technology is not critical in defining the nature of the act as educational. The elements that define paper writing as an educational process are present in writing whether one is using a typewriter or computer.

Word processing software, however, does modify this important educational process in specific ways. It allows students to assemble papers differently from the way they would if they were using a typewriter. They believe that word processing allows them to spend more time on the draft-writing stage, reallocating time away from the mechanical transfer of handwritten text to typewritten draft. They also believe that the typewriter "fixed" the text in a way that encouraged far earlier closure to the revising process than did a word processor. Overall, students claimed that a new way of assembling a paper was an educational gain because they could spend more time "up front," thinking and writing drafts. Because they saw this as a significant advantage and because students wanted to meet minimal perceived standards of acceptable written work, learning to use the word processing software was an imperative supported by the ethic of doing well. In turn, learning the software required drawing on resources (time and the help of friends).

In conclusion, the social organization of the group in which the user is lodged helps define how the user seeks help. In this freshman dormitory, room-based implementation, group life, and friends as resources were central features of daily life. Student computing and the support networks that developed in Littlefield reflected theses features; in Littlefield *anybody* was an immediate potential expert, and help with a computing problem was as close as a student's roommate or next-door neighbor. Computing knowledge was widely shared and disseminated in discussions with other dorm members. In groups or organizations that are highly structured and hierarchically organized, we would expect very different kinds of help networks to emerge.

In addition, the ability to control one's environment was a valuable feature of the room-based model. The room-based model is very flexible because it allows students to control their immediate surroundings, for example, during the writing process. In general, privacy is an extremely problematic issue for students. On the one hand, Littlefield students were surrounded by norms of group interaction and friendliness that encouraged an activity they themselves found enjoyable—talking to others. On the other hand, students routinely sought privacy to get work done or meet a due date. From an outsider's view, dorm rooms are almost public with respect to the amount of access fellow dormmates have to them, and therefore in large part, the room-based model (as opposed to, say, a cluster-based model of computing) did not solve the students' dilemma. Indeed, we think that no computing arrangement will solve students' difficulties with respect to both desiring interaction and feeling the need for privacy. However, the room-based model at least increased their ability to control how and when they worked.

CONCLUSIONS

Studies of computing technology are riddled by questions about the extent to which this new technology is changing social life. In the case of our research, our focus was on the microanalytic scale of change within the dormitory during one academic year.

One set of changes we were able to trace over the course of the year was knowledge of technology as it relates to the use of specific features and functions. This was a constantly growing and changing body of information for individuals and the group that, in turn, produced changes in the forms of technology used. By forms of technology use we mean two things. First, clearly, actual physical interaction with the technology was always changing. As one student learned to do something with the technology, such as repaginate a document, play a game, change fonts, and so on, the information spread rapidly throughout the dorm.

Second, the perceived functionality of the technology also shifted at different points in the academic year. The use of the E-mail system is the clearest example. As we discussed, when students became uncomfortable with the personal nature of E-mail messages, either because they were directed at another individual or seemed self-indulgent, the general consensus of the purpose and meaning of the network slowly changed.

This pattern of change suggests that computer uses and notions of usefulness are best looked at as situationally dependent. In the Littlefield situation, functionality and patterns of use varied with such factors as the flow of the semester and academic calendar (e.g., exams and assignment due dates), the life cycle of the group (group integration and disintegration), and the nature of group life (e.g., specific events and issues). Technologically, the E-mail system allowed all of these uses. Actual use, however, was closely linked to the demands of student life at Littlefield. Although change was characteristic of student use of the Littlefield technology, that change was more incremental than transformative in nature, and it was highly influenced by the preestablished routines of student social and academic life.

We have tried to show how the immediate social situation exerts a powerful influence on individual conduct. This is a general feature of all social life, not simply a by-product of our research setting and problem. The computer user, who like all members of society, is influenced by social pressures, collective definitions, and rationalizations of social situations will act in a way that takes all of these factors into account. Individual computing choices, as we see them, cannot be understood simply as a product of individually defined motives and interests. Although individual motives and interests do play a part in behavior, that behavior is developed and carried out not in isolation but with regard to the motives and interests of others. The aim of this chapter has been to look at the collective behavior that helped to shape computing in Littlefield rather than at an imaginary user, a user cut off from his or her social world.

Understanding computing behavior, then, can also be viewed as understanding collective responses to more general questions such as "What are we doing here at college?" "What is an education?" "How does one get an education?" Only by understanding the nature of student goals, their views of appropriate and inappropriate behavior, which rules they follow and which rules they break, and which strategies they use to achieve their goals can we understand networked student computing.

ACKNOWLEDGMENTS

This research was funded in part by the IBM Corporation. We wish to acknowledge the other primary investigator for the project, Gail Bader, as well as interviewers William Graves III and James M. Nyce, all of the Department of Anthropology, Brown University.

REFERENCES

Anderson, K. T. (1988). *An ethnography of communication approach to electronic mail: A computer science department as a case study working report.* Providence, RI: Brown University, Department of Anthropology.

Anderson, K. T., Bader, G., & McClard, A. P. (1988). *The role of social contexts in understanding technological innovations.* A report to the IBM Corporation.

Anderson, K. T., & McClard, A. P. (1988). *Study time: Temporal orientations of freshman students and computing.* A report to the IBM Corporation.

Anderson K. T., McClard, A. P., Bader, G., & Larkin, J. (1988). *The Littlefield Research project* (a report to the IBM Corp.). Providence RI: Institute for Research and Information in Scholarship, Brown University.

Becker, H. S., Geer, B., & Hughes, E. C. (1968). *Making the grade: The academic side of college life.* New York: Wiley.

Beeman, W. O., Anderson, K. T., Bader, G., Larkin, J., McClard, A. P., McQuillan, P., & Shields, M. (1987). *Intermedia: A case study of innovation in higher education.* Unpublished report to the Annenberg/CPB Project, Brown University, Institute for Research in Information and Scholarship.

Butler-Nalin, K., & Goodrich, T. S. (1987). *Computer clusters in student residences project report.* Stanford, CA: Stanford University, Instruction and Research Information Services.

Feldman, M. S. (1987). Electronic mail and weak ties in organizations. *Office: Technology and People, 3,* 83–101.

Hiltz, S. R. (1982). Experiments and experiences with computerized conferencing. In J. H. Blair (Ed.), *Emerging office systems.* Norwood, NJ: Ablex.

Hiltz, S. R., & Turoff, M. (1978). *The network nation.* Reading, MA: Addison-Wesley.

Jackson, G. (1987). *Workstations as roommates* (a report to Project Athena). Cambridge: Massachusetts Institute of Technology.

Oberst, D. J., & Smith, S. B. (1986, summer). BITNET: Past, present, and future. *EDUCOM Bulletin,* 10–17.

Palmer, C. J., & Harnisch, D. L. (1987). *Computers in residence halls: Student experiences, attitudes and expectations* (Research Rep. No. 2). University of Illinois at Urbana-Champaign.

Snizek, W. E. (1987, June). Some observations on the effects of microcomputers on the productivity of university scientist. *Knowledge, Creation, Diffusion, Utilization,* 612–614.

Sproull, L. S., & Kiesler, S. B. (1985). *Reducing social context clues: The case of electronic mail.* (Working Paper Series RP-14). Pittsburgh, PA: Carnegie-Mellon University, Department of Social Science.

9

The Legitimation of Academic Computing in the 1980s

Mark A. Shields
University of Virginia

This chapter addresses three questions: (a) Why, in just a few short years during the 1980s, did personal computers go from almost nowhere to nearly everywhere at hundreds of American colleges and universities? (b) What consequences did their rapid diffusion bring about? (c) Were those consequences revolutionary? My theoretical stance toward these questions stresses the social construction of technological realities. A starting point (but only a starting point) is one of the most powerful explanatory principles of sociology: "If [people] define situations as real, they are real in their consequences" (Thomas & Thomas, 1928, p. 572). Known as the "Thomas Theorem," it was employed by Robert Merton in a blistering critique of self-fulfilling prophecies that feed ethnic and racial conflict (Merton, 1968). But the sociological insight that underlies the theorem—namely, that reality is intersubjectively defined, not objectively given—has broad if not universal application. Within the past decade, that essential insight has been applied in counterintuitive fashion to objects of social reality that presumably were more or less immune to it, namely, technologies. The central insight of the Social Construction of Technology (SCOT) perspective is "that technological artifacts are culturally constructed and interpreted" (Pinch & Bijker, 1987, p. 40; see also Bijker & Law, 1992) The "interpretive flexibility" of technologies means not only that different groups react differently to the same artifact. It means also that the very definition of a technology—its design, content, and functionality—is itself the product of complex negotiations among networks of engaged

161

actors. I propose to use this model of sociotechnical explanation to account for a phenomenon dubbed the "academic computing revolution" by its leaders and acolytes.

Technocratic-managerial decision making models of the diffusion of innovations have limited relevance to understanding why computing captivated—and captured—academia during the 1980s. Such models stress administratively determined, hierarchical patterns of technological innovation, driven by managerial interests in rationalizing production and controlling employees (see Attewell's, 1987, critique of such models). They provide little analytical leverage for understanding the social processes through which personal computing became so widespread so quickly in higher education throughout the 1980s. Such models fail to capture the full complexity of academic computerization because they tend to reduce legitimation problems to implementation problems, rest on an inadequate concept of how technologies are institutionalized in "loosely coupled" organizations (Weick, 1976), focus more on outcomes than on processes, and may present a misleading picture of actual decision making.[1]

Far from selling itself on technical merits alone, personal computing encountered a great deal of skepticism and even resistance on U.S. campuses. Certainly, major academic computing initiatives of the kind undertaken by leading colleges and universities in the early to mid-1980s required technology, money, and administrative leadership to pull off. But these initiatives also required something else of comparable and preconditional importance: institutional legitimation. Although there are literally hundreds of studies of the implementation, impact, and evaluation of computers in higher education, the legitimation of academic computing has received no attention in the social scientific literature.

This chapter first examines the experience of one university in the vanguard of the academic computing movement of the 1980s: Brown University. Along with Carnegie-Mellon and MIT, Brown was widely regarded as one of the three pioneering experiments in campuswide computerization (Osgood, 1984; Tucker, 1983–1984; Waldrop, 1985). They shared this distinction for two major reasons: the ambitiousness of their visions and the magnitude of their projects. All three universities signed semiconfidential multimillion-dollar contracts and grants for equipment and cash with IBM and other computer vendors in the early 1980s that were intended to provide core funding for their long-term computing initiatives. Arguably, Brown's

---

[1]On both conceptual and empirical grounds, a key structural difference between most universities and most business or other complex organizations is that universities tend to be "loosely coupled" (Weick, 1976) whereas the latter tend to be more "tightly coupled." Unit autonomy in universities (e.g., among departments or schools) is often quite substantial, relative to other complex organizations, and this has a significant influence on how computing systems are deployed, used, and judged (see Shields, Graves, & Nyce, 1991, 1992; Turkle, this volume).

"computer revolutionaries" (Kling & Iacono, 1988, 1991) articulated the most ambitious vision of academic computing in the future. It was a vision that became emblematic, nationally, of the enormous potential of the new technologies, yet the vision was controversial on the Brown campus itself (Shields, 1986). Given the initial conditions, successful implementation of its bold computing strategy was hardly a foregone conclusion. Yet if the academic computing revolution were to become a reality among liberal-arts-and-sciences institutions, it probably had its best chances for success at Brown.[2]

THUMBNAIL SKETCH: 1980S VISIONS, 1990S REALITIES

What was Brown's vision of academic computing in 1983? In its cover story for the September 1983 issue, the *Brown Alumni Monthly* made this enthusiastic pronouncement: "Today Brown is poised to begin an experiment that may have as equally strong an impact on the life of the mind as the Gutenberg Press. The University has embarked on a proposal to spend $50 to $70 million in the next 6 years to equip each faculty member, student, administrator, and staff member on campus with a powerful new type of personal computer" (Hinds, 1983, p. 29).

So, beginning in 1983, the university began gearing up for a massive, long-term effort to build what its proponents called a "network of scholar's workstations" on campus. These workstations would be highly sophisticated and powerful, but easy to use; they would be a type of new computer that would functionally "leapfrog" existing personal computers; and they would revolutionize scholarly work. The scholar's workstation vision was of a campus that, by the end of the 1980s, could become a showcase for the "wired university" of the future, with 10,000 workstations linking all "knowledge-workers" (scholars) in the university community to one another. Analytically, the workstations vision simultaneously embodied a selective critique of current realities, a conception of desirable future possibilities, and a strategy for translating current visions into future realities. Normatively, the vision embraced a universalistic conception of the scholarly

---

[2]Brown, MIT, and Carnegie-Mellon also conducted multifaceted social science assessment and evaluation projects of computing on their campuses, beginning in the early 1980s. Among the three schools, I focus on Brown for two reasons: (a) Brown's academic computing strategy was considered the most promising model for other liberal arts and sciences institutions; and (b) it is the case with which I am most familiar, having been a founding member of the social science research group that did nearly all of Brown's computing project assessments and evaluations from 1983 through 1988. For accounts of the MIT and Carnegie-Mellon ventures in academic computing, see Balkovich, Lerman, and Parmelee (1985), Cohen (1987), and Turkle (this volume) on MIT; Arms (1990) and Kiesler and Sproull (1987) on Carnegie-Mellon.

community, while affirming that community's capacity to nurture the individuality and creativity of each scholar. It was a technologically driven vision, but with technology as a means, not an end. From the beginning, it was a vision that resonated with the institutional culture and identity of Brown (Beeman et al., 1988), yet also one that projected beyond its campus to encompass eventually all of higher education. Brown would lead the way by making its campus a hospitable sociotechnical laboratory for new educational experiments with scholar's workstations. Others would soon follow, it was assumed, because the vision was irresistible and its realization was within reach.

The workstations project vision was first spelled out in a March 1983 proposal to the California-based System Development Foundation (SDF) titled *Experiments with Scholar's Workstation Networks in a Wired University*. The SDF proposal was a manifesto. Its foreword described the magnitude and significance of the project: "We are planning for a social and a systems experiment: an attempt to find out what a university of the year 2001 would be like if the most modern computing were exploited to the fullest in order to augment people's thinking and learning, and if we rethought many of the ways we work, teach, and do research in the university" (p. ii). Later in the proposal, the authors pointed to the project's revolutionary implications: "At Brown we believe the actual quantum jump in education and scholarship will be the use of the computer as a pervasive, multimodal medium. If developed properly, the environment created with networks of scholar's workstations can catalyze the most fundamental change in education and scholarship since the Gutenberg press" (p. 12). The proposal listed three major "improvements" being sought through "interdisciplinary experimentation" with scholar's workstations:

1. Integrated methods for creating, accessing, filtering, synthesizing, and manipulating information;
2. More efficient processes and tools for learning, teaching, research, and the routine daily tasks that often impede or take valuable time away from the above; and
3. Enhanced group interactions with more sharing of work and more joint exploration of ideas.

. . . When these objectives are realized, students will play a much more active role in the classroom than they do now. The classroom will be extended to the dormitory and even off campus. The new dynamic media for both education and scholarship—as well as the new ways for individuals to communicate and interact with one another—will fundamentally change the university as we know it. (pp. 1–2)

The vision of academic computing in higher education articulated in the SDF proposal would in fact inspire and rationalize an experiment that sought nothing less than a sea-change improvement in the quality and conduct of academic work, employing innovative computing tools as its chief instrument. The proposed experiment, the SDF manifesto cautioned, would be a risky one, but nevertheless one well worth pursuing at Brown:

> We . . . realize that this is by far the most ambitious undertaking that we as a University have attempted, not only in terms of the impact on the entire University but also in terms of the human, financial, and material resources required. While our discussions have certainly illuminated the magnitude of such an undertaking, they have also reaffirmed the sense among the highest leadership of the University not only that Brown can do the job, but that it can do it well. (p. 32)

The proposal estimated that capital costs for the project (through mid-1985) would be $32 million, with estimated yearly fixed costs of $7 million for staff, equipment, and maintenance. In addition to requesting startup funds for computer equipment and infrastructure, the authors proposed the creation of a new campus-based organization to initiate, manage, and legitimate the Scholar's Workstation Project. In June 1983, the Institute for Research in Information and Scholarship (IRIS) was established for this purpose. SDF did not fund the proposal, but starting in 1983 both Brown and IRIS received multimillion-dollar support from IBM as well as funding from several other corporations and foundations, including Apple and the Annenberg/CPB Project. IBM's initial 3-year $15-million agreement was in fact the largest corporate grant ever made to Brown.

As Bill Shipp, one author of the SDF proposal, emphasized 3 years later in a memorandum to the faculty workstation committee, "We had to come up with *some approach that at least had the potential to benefit all of the academic disciplines*. What could we market? The concept of building a better computing environment that improved support for scholarship seemed to match both the marketing needs and the faculty's needs. We had to become leaders in academic computing" (p. 6).

When the vision was first presented to the Brown community in mid-1983, there were no prototypes of the anticipated scholar's workstation, although Sun and Apollo workstations, plus earlier Brown experiments with hypertext systems on campus, served as interim working models of some of the capabilities envisioned for future workstations. In addition, Apple Computer gave Brown 50 Lisa computers in 1983–1984 to distribute to selected IRIS staff and Brown faculty for a pilot project in the distribution, use, and support of graphics-based workstations. But it was another 3 years before a prototype (IBM's RT) was available for wide-scale campus deployment. In the meantime, as IRIS director Bill Shipp pointed out in a memorandum, "PCs and Macintoshes [would] serve as 'place holders' until *real* workstations were available and affordable" (p. 1). In the absence of "real workstations," the vision articulated in the SDF proposal helped shape campus expectations about what academic computing could eventually become. Indeed, in this capacity the manifesto embodied the reciprocal notions of technology as text and text as technology.

Three years after the proposal, and just 1 month before the installation of IBM RT workstations in two university departments, IRIS director Shipp offered an intriguing metaphor for the Scholar's Workstation Project (SWP) in a memorandum to Brian L. Hawkins, vice president for computing and information services at Brown:

> From one point of view our "experiment" is just about as much of an experiment as the electrification of rural America. Electrification did not guarantee productive uses would be made of electrical appliances, but it did offer people living in rural areas many opportunities for altering their work. Computers don't guarantee much either, but they do offer opportunities. And many believe computers offer far richer opportunities than did other technological developments such as automobiles and rural electrical distribution systems. (p. 8)

Yet the vision itself, both in its encompassing generality and in some of its specific promises, was contested for some time by many faculty and students as well as by computing services and technical staff nurtured on mainframe-based timesharing computing concepts and systems. Faculty skeptics were concerned about the possible conflicts of interest between the university's mission and IBM's research, development, and marketing needs—a concern fueled by the secrecy surrounding the initial agreement with IBM and the confidentiality provisions of proprietary information and equipment. Student opponents conjured images of an Orwellian distopia, "Brown Tech," as well as more mundane (and relevant) implications like the burden of computing costs as a looming factor in possible financial aid reductions and tuition increases.

Perhaps the sharpest, most influential student assessment of the scholar's workstation project appeared in a 1983 full-page *Brown Daily Herald* editorial, "What's Wrong With Brown's Computer Plans." The author, Jonathan Rotenberg, a Brown senior and president of the 11,000-member Boston Computer Society, criticized the SDF workstation vision for its technological unrealism, institutional inappropriateness, and elitist hyperbole: "Reading all the literature that has emanated from the project's organizers, one gets the impression that the computers will do everything. . . . They will help people in every mode of thinking and working in a college environment. In short, you name it, the computers will do it" (p. 3). Although several of Rotenberg's specific criticisms eventually turned out to be wrong (including his negative assessments of the cost and feasibility of networking and his dismissal of what he called the "extremely cumbersome and tedious" new " 'mouse' pointing devices"), his was an influential voice among the chorus of voices raising basic questions and doubts about the scholar's workstation project.

Nearly 7 years later, in its April 1990 issue, the *Brown Alumni Monthly* ("Computer Technology," 1990) reported: "In 1990, instead of using high-powered workstations, most people at Brown now write and communicate on simple personal computers such as the Macintosh and IBM PC. . . . The powerful, desktop workstations that were the focus of the 1983 feature haven't disappeared; about 500 of them are in use, most notably in the sciences where their computational capacities are needed for faculty and graduate-student research" (p. 23). Even the 500 workstations, however useful and powerful compared to those available in 1983, were a faint reflection of the scholar's workstation network of 10,000 interconnected machines envisioned in 1983. To be sure, enormous technological and administrative changes in computing took place at Brown between 1983 and 1990—initiatives that led to an academic computing environment that other colleges and universities may have envied ("Computer Technology," 1990; Shields et al., 1991, 1992). Brown's project was not alone, by any means, in falling short of its expectations, but because its vision was so grandiose, the gap seems so large.

TECHNOLOGICAL LEGITIMATION AND INSTITUTIONALIZATION

From the start, the university wide acceptance of the Brown workstation's vision was hardly a foregone conclusion. Yet even today, with historical myopia, academic computer revolutionaries may have forgotten the controversy generated in the early to mid-1980s, before computing became securely institutionalized. For some, it seems, the pervasive presence of personal computers in higher education and especially their rapid rate of diffusion during the 1980s requires no special explanation. After all, it might be argued, colleges and universities, like the rest of society, merely responded to a compelling technological imperative: the immense capacity of computers to improve productivity, efficiency, and the quality of work. By this logic, it was not only rational but also inevitable that academia would embrace computing with gusto: Investing in computers was a predictable response to technological advance. ("Academics of the world compute! You have nothing to lose but your typewriters!") And because it is a widely shared cultural presumption in the United States that technological advance is a central, indeed dominant, social force leading to other social changes, higher education's embrace of computing could be treated as simply one instance of a general process: technological innovation driving sociocultural change. Such an assumption, however, would be mistaken.

The saturated rhetoric of revolution coupled with the demonstrable technical changes that personal computers produced in academic work during the past decade obscure the fact that the first step in the institutionalization of the "new computing" (Gilbert & Green, 1986), namely, normative *legitimation*, was by no means inevitable.[3] Academic computing policies and their implementation do not operate in an institutional vacuum; they are not self-legitimating. Computing policies acquire legitimation not only through successful implementation and demonstrated effectiveness but also through their compatibility with institutional culture. By institutional culture, I mean those broadly shared beliefs about the academic mission and collective identity of a college or university—what its members value about it and which images it self-consciously projects to the outside world. Institutional culture shapes peoples' visions and expectations of academic computing in terms of an institution's mission and identity. Academic computing visions draw on key symbolic dimensions (Ortner, 1973) of institutional culture as a way of influencing beliefs about the general value of computing and the more specific translations of these beliefs into computing policies and their implementation.

Social analyses of new technologies increasingly have emphasized the indeterminancy of innovation-and-diffusion processes and consequently the necessity for innovators to "construct a meaning-framework for their artifacts to *create* a need that did not previously exist" (Pfaffenberger, 1988, p. 41), and to connect an inclusive network of inventors/designers, advocates, and potential users within a shared "technological frame" (Bijker, 1987, 1992). The legitimation of academic computing involved a symbolic reconstruction of the computer's appropriate place and function in higher education beyond the sciences, engineering, and administration. Specifically, as Pfaffenberger (1988) argued, this involved a "reconstitution strategy, promoted by the personal computer industry's founders and embraced by many of the technology's users, [that] sought to invert the equation of computers with central authority by creating a new computer that would foster decen-

---

[3]Institutional legitimation in the present context refers to the process by which a persuasive complex of symbolic and verbal rationales are invoked for justifying a pivotal role for personal computers on campus. Such rationales include but also transcend the particularistic interests of their proponents as well as values of technological rationality, cost effectiveness, and enhanced productivity. In addition, they articulate a kind of "moral vision" of the role that computing should play in academic life. A moral vision makes a normative claim, and in Brown's case the claim was that the instrumental capabilities of personal computers would contribute to building a better scholarly community by opening up new creative possibilities for each of its individual members.

tralization" (p. 42). Timing was critical, of course: IBM, the epitome of huge centralized computing, came out with its PCXT in 1983, followed within a few months by the debut of Apple's long-awaited Macintosh in early 1984.

The futuristic technological virtuosity of the Brown workstations vision therefore had to be constructed and justified not only on instrumental grounds but also on normative–ideological grounds. Academic computer revolutionaries—principally located in the computer science department and the provost's office—realized the essential connection between legitimation (the scholar's workstation vision) and implementation (the creation of IRIS). They also realized the necessity of quickly recruiting a network of supporters and experimenters in other crucial sites on campus—"building a critical mass" was the operative phrase. This was supposed to be accomplished through a two-pronged strategy: an experimental hypertext–hypermedia instructional computing project, called the Intermedia Project (see Beeman et al., 1988; McQuillan, this volume) and a project to deploy workstations (and later PCs and Macintoshes) to as many individual faculty and departments as possible, via the Faculty Workstation Project (see Shields et al., 1991, 1992).

What, then, were the decisive normative claims that helped give legitimacy to the vision? First, the very notion of a scholar's workstation served as a compelling technological metaphor (Edge, 1990) of institutional transformation. It rested above all on two crucial pillars of legitimation: universalism and pluralism. The scholarly community was conceptualized to include all knowledge-workers (essentially anyone working at a desk), each of whom would benefit from computerization. No kind of academic work, group, or discipline would be excluded. In contrast to the centralized, hierarchical, and elitist computing cultures of the past, no longer would computing—now, specifically, *personal* computing—be regarded mainly as a research machine for scientists and engineers.

The pluralism and universalism of the vision even promised to transcend the deep antinomies of U.S. society, culture, and academia: individual autonomy and communitarian solidarity. By linking thousands of desktop personal computers together over local, national, and international networks, the dream of an electronic global village seemed almost within reach. The instrumental capabilities of the powerful new technology could build new "virtual communities" both within and beyond the campus, yet accommodate the intellectual diversity and creativity that lie at the core of academic work. In short, according to the vision, a network of scholar's workstations would nurture the values of both individualism and community. It posed no challenge to core academic values or interests; indeed, it would enlarge and enliven the application of those values.

Organizational mechanisms of various kinds were established to enlarge the network of participants and to mobilize support for implementing the vision. In addition to the creation of IRIS, several university planning and advisory committees, consisting in some cases of students along with staff and faculty, were commissioned; computing-attitudes-and-experience surveys were conducted to inform the policymaking process and to reassure the campus community that there was nothing to fear; personal computers and workstations were distributed to individual faculty and departments; and "computing-across-the-curriculum" became a rallying cry, symbolized by the high-profile Intermedia Project (see Beeman et al., 1988).

Furthermore, the Brown computing vision was consistent with the university's ethos of innovation in both computing and the curriculum. It also offered the potential for enhancing the university's national and international prestige. The financial feasibility of massive computerization was vindicated by pointing to the largesse of corporate vendors (like IBM and Apple) and private foundations (like the Annenberg/CPB Project), thus muting the voices of skeptics who argued that rapid computerization would divert financial resources from crucial human needs, especially faculty and staff raises, student financial aid, and the library. The coupling of economic feasibility and academic integrity—of material and ideal interests—provided the kind of legitimation that eventually enabled proponents of rapid computerization to seize the day. Yet, all of this preceded the availability of a concrete piece of computing equipment or software, let alone an integrated network, that came close to embodying the articulated vision.

An obvious question thus arises: Was the rhetoric about an academic computing revolution mostly hype and hucksterism, as some prominent skeptics (Bok, 1985; Boyer, 1987) suggested at the time? There was certainly a great deal of that, but also a great deal more. The grandiose visions were more than empty hyperbole or self-deception. They were believed by their proponents, who regarded their visions as not only desirable and necessary but also feasible. Afterall, they were touting the potential of a powerful, fast-changing technology—a technology, moreover, that had already helped to bring about dramatic changes in the rhythm, if not the quality, of academic work. Thus, why not think that even more radical technological advances and consequent sociocultural changes would come about in the near future, as the technology moved forward inexorably? Above all, why not be an institutional agent in promoting that change? As Pfaffenberger (1988) pointed out, it was a time when innovative leaders in the personal computer industry—and, by extension, academia—were trying to redefine the symbolic meanings associated with dominant centralized computers by "reconstituting" their ideological implications through the ostensibly more benign attributes of personal computers as decentralized, democratic, and participatory technologies. "Though some industry founders advanced [a mythology of personal computing] for cynical reasons, others took it quite seriously, and saw themselves on the leading edge of a major wave of social change" (p. 40).

In short, academic computer revolutionaries were not electronic hucksters or crazed futurists. Nor, despite some of their occasional rhetoric, were they cultural revolutionaries. Instead, they might best be characterized as "instrumental idealists," based on two longstanding mainstream U.S. cultural predispositions that help to account for the subtext of the revolutionary rhetoric they employed: technological idealism-cum-utopianism (Segal, 1985) and instrumental activism (Parsons, 1977). First, their imaginations were captured by a kind of technological hubris, common to the culture generally but not historically to academia that, before the personal computer, had tended to regard things technological with an elitist cultural contempt. Academic computer revolutionaries really believed that new computing technology would transform the academic world. Yet at the same time, their technological idealism was joined and thus tempered by their instrumental activism: a means-oriented, goal-directed, technocratic realism about the need for pragmatic, strategic, aggressive leadership to bring about the envisioned transformation. It was the combination of these two rationalities—a kind of Weberian instrumental means-oriented activism coupled with a uniquely American idealistic ends-oriented technological utopianism—that led to the early successes of these instrumental idealists of academic computing. Together, moreover, the two rationalities were the foundation of a legitimation and implementation process that institutionalized a new mode of networked computing in higher education during the 1980s.

FROM LEGITIMATION TO IMPLEMENTATION

By the end of 1985, 2 years after the public announcement of SWP, the workstations vision was securely legitimated on the Brown campus (Shields, 1986). It was virtually taken for granted that networked, desktop computing was not only essential but also desirable. To be sure, the pressure for specific legitimations had not vanished. Chiefly, these focused on the need to justify the unequal allocation of computing resources to the various campus segments and the related (chronic) need to justify growth in computing expenditures in light of competing budgetary priorities.

From 1986 on, the main challenges became allocation and implementation problems—how-to issues: how to fund, deploy, and manage growing demand for more and better computing resources within existing budgetary constraints; how to persuade or convert reluctant adopters ("laggards," in Rogers', 1983, terminology); how to organize and provide access to better (decentralized, distributed, powerful) computing services. The need for gen eralized legitimation in terms of core academic values of teaching, learning, scholarship, and research had been superceded by more mundane concerns. The initial and uncertain legitimation-through-reconstitution of the campus computing revolution thus evolved into a complex but more routinized and regularized (Pfaffenberger, 1988, 1992) process of technocratic implementation and deployment—addressing how-to problems with can-do solutions. Implicitly, if not explicitly, it was now presumed that computing per se had become self-legitimating, an undeniably good thing that merely needed to be deployed to users in the right packages. The early rhetoric of legitimation, emphasizing "cutting-edge" computing, had shifted to a rhetoric of implementation stressing "appropriate" computing, and also requiring a different level and focus of justification. In the abstract, an appropriate computing policy is one that implements an affordable campus computing environment after prudently weighing the diverse costs and benefits of plausible computing packages in light of existing technological options and the university's computing needs, available resources, and other budgetary demands. Thus, a computing policy is appropriate to the degree that its implementation leads to "effective" and "successful" outcomes. This expansive redefinition of the technological frame made it difficult to oppose appropriate computing even though there was no fixed consensus about what that might be for a diverse campus user community.

The allocation of computing resources and the impact of computing on the university's budgetary priorities continued to provoke debate. Despite major equipment grants from IBM and campus computer store discounts for individual purchasers of Macintoshes and PCs, both of which contributed to the proliferation of personal computers on campus, the university spent over $6 million on computer operations in 1986. Since 1984, the need for greatly increased staff and facilities to support burgeoning campus computer use had been emphasized by high-level administrators. But the rising costs of computing were also occurring alongside rising costs of needed maintenance and expansion of the university's physical plant as well as recognized needs for increased faculty salaries and student financial aid. These fiscal constraints, coupled with the absence of expected workstation technology, meant that the vision of achieving more-or-less universal access to sophisticated computing tools for everyone on campus would remain elusive.

Nevertheless, the legitimacy and utility of distributed computing was no longer seriously contested, as it had been for some time following the announcement of the scholar's workstation project to the Brown community in 1983. Recognition that the only advanced IBM workstation available at the time (the UNIX-based RT) was not an appropriate computer system for all academic work did not produce disenchantment with computing per se. On the contrary, the campus community embraced computing more enthusiastically than ever before. "Heightened expectations are persisting," a computing administrator remarked in late 1987. Echoing this sentiment, a geology professor observed that "the RT has raised the expectations of most people in this department." The RT experience, in short, introduced a large segment of campus computer users to a new and appealing concept of computing (Shields et al., 1991 1992). The appropriate computing environ- ment came to reflect a blending of technological needs, budgetary con- straints, organizational diversity, and institutional culture. And the central mechanism for implementing this strategy was not the scholar's workstation but rather the Faculty Workstations Project (FWP) coupled with a major reorganization of computing and information services.

The implementation strategy was decided ultimately by technical con- straints and choices. From the start, the idea was that there would be a "family" of compatible (networked) workstations with different price and performance levels to serve the varying work routines and computing needs of different groups of scholars: faculty, staff, and students in all disciplines. In fact, it would be another 3 years before even a single type of workstation (the RT) was available for campus deployment. Yet, in the absence of real workstations, the vision and the symbol of the scholar's workstation helped legitimate the goals of the FWP, while also shaping campus expectations about what academic computing could eventually become. By the end of 1989, however, there was still no compatible family of workstations but rather a diverse mix of only partly compatible workstations and microcomputers.[4]

The Brown University case exemplifies and illuminates the recursive interaction between technological legitimation and implementation. Aca- demic computer revolutionaries on that campus—the instrumental ideal- ists—self-consciously and successfully constructed a broadly inclusive tech- nological frame (Bijker, 1987, 1992) around the notion of a universally accessible, decentralized network of powerful, user-friendly desktop com- puters and workstations. With substantial material inputs from large com- puter vendors, the vision animating the whole project seemed, for awhile, not merely utopian but also feasible. The shift from cutting-edge to appropriate computing—from legitimation of the vision via the Scholar's Workstation

---

[4]Nor was the hypertext–hypermedia software originally envisioned running on those ma- chines—the result of an important technical decision about the choice of operating systems. Originally the idea was that the FWP would deploy workstations that could run the hyper- text–hypermedia software known as Intermedia that IRIS was developing. Intermedia, how- ever, was designed to run on a different UNIX operating system. The decision to go with two different operating systems—one for RTs that ran Intermedia, the other for RTs deployed by the FWP—thus severed the original link between the hypertext–hypermedia software development and demonstration project (Intermedia) and the campuswide deployment of workstations to faculty and departments (FWP). Among other results, this approach to deployment signaled a new recognition of the diversity of individual computing needs and interests as well as a commitment to accommodate that diversity (Shields et al., 1991, 1992).

Project to implementation of the possible via the Faculty Workstations Project—did not delegitimate the key symbolism (Ortner, 1973) of the original vision as much as it redefined what could be accomplished under realistic constraints. In retrospect, during a 5- to 6-year period between 1983 and 1989 the academic computing "revolution" at Brown was not so much a technical reality as it was a sociotechnical construction that eventually included a diverse network of supporting actors and fellow travelers, forged ultimately by the ramifying strength of weak ties (Granovetter, 1973). But that period of spellbinding technological virtuosity was and still is a long way from having an "impact on the life of the mind" equivalent to the Gutenberg Press, let alone "the most dramatic change [for higher education] since the founding of the University of Paris and Bologna . . . some eight or nine centuries ago," as Johns Hopkins' president, Steven Muller, mused in 1984 (quoted in Boyer, 1987, p. 170).

ACADEMIC COMPUTING INTO THE 1990S: REVOLUTION OR THERMIDOR?

Brown University's experience, though unique in several respects, was nonetheless emblematic of the academic computing movement's aspirations for higher education. What, then, shall one conclude sociologically after a decade of experience with academic computing? Assessments and forecasts from academic computing proponents and interest groups now tend to be more guarded and less millenarian than those of the 1980s. Nevertheless, most academic computing analyses are still tendentious, usually authored by writers who continue to invoke a rhetoric of revolution and who, in collaboration with vendors of computing products and services, seek to sustain high levels of financial investment in and ideological commitment to computerization. "They employ a rhetorical strategy of curt confidence to communicate their viewpoint and to help inspire readers to trust in a 'computer revolution' made by acquiring and using computer equipment under commonplace social conditions" (Kling & Iacono, 1991, p. 73). The remainder of this chapter proposes some broadstroke answers to the question of the consequences of academic computing from the vantage point of the early 1990s by examining U.S. higher education at large, drawing especially on recent national data and reports about campus computing. I examine consequences for students, faculty, and administrators, with special attention to issues of cross-institutional inequalities and electronic networks. My assessment is intended as suggestive and preliminary in lieu of systematic and comprehensive social scientific evaluations.

No Social Revolution

Appropriating Marx's distinction between the means of production and the social relations of production, one general conclusion stands out: *Although there was a computational revolution in the means of academic production, it was not accompanied by a revolution in the social relations of academic production.* "Dumb" typewriters and terminals were almost universally replaced by "smart" microcomputers and workstations, laser printers replaced ditto machines, and for the first time ever mail was something you could send and receive on a screen, where "nodes" and "userids" replaced city and street addresses. These and other unprecedented technical innovations—in text production, graphics, data processing, database searching, networks, and instructional computing—were proof that the technical means of production in academic life had been irreversibly transformed within a matter of years, not decades. But the technical innovations that so transformed the means of production have not had a comparable impact on the social relations of academic life and work. The latter have resisted fundamental change, and certainly transformation, quite effectively. Indeed, computer revolutionaries' over-technicized view of sociocultural change led them to conflate technical means and social relations. They even seemed to assume that rates of technical computing innovation, measured in months and years rather than in decades and generations, could be transposed to the realm of social relations. But there was no technological imperative, no *deus ex machina*, no revolution (cf. Kling, 1991).

The structures of influence and authority within colleges and universities have remained relatively untouched, except for new administrative and technical roles and units created to manage academic computing and information services. Academic and financial administrators still control the bulk of organizational decision-making authority at most colleges and universities. For the most part, too, professors still control the content of their curricula and the evaluation of their students. Students have not, in any demonstrable way, gained more input into these matters, in contrast to the 1960s and even 1970s, when curricula and student evaluation procedures were dramatically reformed to give students more control of their academic lives. "In most respects, the social relations between teachers and students in classrooms or courses with access to computer systems are not fundamentally different [from] those without such equipment" (Kling & Iacono, 1991, p. 70). Moreover, the great debates on U.S. campuses in the early 1990s—about racism, multiculturalism, political correctness, outcomes assessment, and budgetary crises—were fueled by political, economic, demographic, and cultural currents that in general bore no direct or explicit relationship to computing technology issues (academic budgeting being an obvious and critical exception).

Nor is there much evidence to suggest that computing-across-the-curriculum has in any thoroughgoing way infused scholarship or pedagogy with a stronger impulse to reflect critically on the cultural mission of higher education (Jacoby, 1991). On the contrary, "corporatist" values coupled with an "entrepreneurial ideology of expertise" (Slaughter, 1990) have if anything become more pronounced in American higher education—not only because of computing, of course, although extensive ties with vendors have played an important part in the overall process.[5] Higher education administration in the 1980s and now especially in the 1990s seems more conservative, technocratic, and entrepreneurial than ever before. Extraordinary investments in computing-and-information infrastructure, capital, staff, and services, along with unrelenting pressures for their expansion and upgrading, have reinforced technocratic and entrepreneurial values. Campus-vendor relations are more routinely businesslike: "Campuses are investing in technology but are asking more questions before they do. Companies are giving away fewer machines and are less eager to finance projects on campuses unless the colleges are willing to invest in the efforts, as well. . . . The days of a 'higher-ed handshake with the palm up' are over, says a software executive" ("Recession Spurs Changes," 1992, p. A16; see also Green, 1989).

The role of computer vendors in higher education must be viewed within the broader context of growing ties between academia, industry, and the state that accelerated during the 1980s and show no sign of slowing down. For example, National Science Foundation (NSF) initiatives in several areas, including the establishment of university-based engineering, science, and technology centers, have been significant (Peters & Etzkowitz, 1990). In computing, the NSF established four national centers for supercomputing applications and is being advised to broaden significantly its academic support for high-performance computing ("From Desktop to Teraflop," 1993). The National Research and Education Network (NREN) program supports high-speed "test-bed" networks on several campuses. And a number of federal agencies will play major roles in developing the National Information Infrastructure. Peters and Etzkowitz (1990), referring to the spread of in-

---

[5]A special issue on "The Entrepreneurial University" (September/October 1990) in *Academe*, the main publication of the American Association of University Professors, addressed the economic risks and benefits of commercialization and technology transfer opportunities created by university–corporate ventures, including those in information technology. One contributor to the issue emphasized the risks of academic entrepreneurship: "The growing practice of selling technological advances that come out of university laboratories poses special problems. . . . [T]he corporate linkages that are necessary to transform the ideas into marketable products can have a chilling effect on traditional academic values" (Anderson, 1990, p. 14). The author warned that such ventures pose a "threat to the culture and values of the institution held by students and employees, especially the faculty" and that "increased involvement in technology transfer" may result in the "possibility of dividing faculty into classes of economic 'haves' and 'have-nots' " (p. 13).

dustry-oriented centers on U.S. campuses, remarked that "[t]he implications of [government attempts to be responsive to industry and the economic environment] are that many more research universities . . . are actively trying to integrate into the industrial technical system and to assume a role in economic development" (p. 439).

Instructional Computing: Unmet Expectations

After the early wave of entrepreneurial largesse and millenarian anticipations subsided, the academic computing movement seemed unable to attract large numbers of dedicated new cadre. The vast majority of faculty, to be sure, regard computers as indispensible for research, writing, and communication; a significant minority also use computers in teaching. But it is hard to find academics who are not themselves academic computing leaders discussing the relevance of computing to the larger cultural mission of higher education. This was most tellingly confirmed by the then Vice President of EDUCOM, Steven W. Gilbert (1990), in an "Open Letter to Ernest L. Boyer, Russell Edgerton, and other leaders in higher education," reprinted in the April/May 1990 issue of EDUCOM's *The EUIT Newsletter*:

> What prompted this letter was my recognition that even within the context of a respected higher education association [American Association of Higher Education] that is "friendly" to information technology, when it was time to discuss the future of post-secondary education and approaches to transform teaching within colleges and universities, computers and other information technologies had disappeared from the horizon. . . . This technology was not being rejected, it was simply omitted. (p. 6)

Gilbert also pointed out that "access and utilization issues for information technology are still not mainstream concerns for researchers and policy makers" (p.6).

That was not the first time he lamented the higher education community's neglect of academic computing. In an earlier newsletter, Gilbert (1988a) observed that faculty members' adoption of computing was slower than academic computing advocates expected or wanted: "[T]he number of faculty ready and eager to integrate computing into their instructional efforts is not increasing at the same rate as the development of new capabilities in computer technology and systems" (p. 8). And in the next newsletter (1988b) Gilbert criticized the higher-education publication *Change* for ignoring information technology in its special issue discussing higher education policy changes for the next U.S. president to consider.[6]

---

[6]*Change* did eventually devote an entire special issue (January/February 1991) to academic computing. But in contrast to the generalized euphoria of the 1980s, most of the academic computing leaders contributing articles to the special issue were cautious if upbeat. Brian

Gilbert was right. Faculty were not then and are not now drawn in great numbers to instructional computing or courseware development. This is the perennial teaching–versus–research bind in a new electronic guise. A 1991 national survey of about 1,100 U.S. colleges and universities, conducted by the Center for Scholarly Technology at the University of Southern California, confirmed previous reports about the difficulty of getting faculty to use or develop their own computer-based instructional tools. "[R]elatively few institutions [15%] offer any rewards or incentives to faculty to encourage the development of instructional resources" (Green & Eastman, 1992, p. 6; see also Turkle, this volume). Follow-up surveys in 1992 and 1993 found little or no change in the percentage of institutions offering professional incentives for faculty courseware development ("Academic-Computing Directors," 1993). Moreover, in 1991, less than one third of U.S. campuses had "a formal plan for integrating desktop computers into the curriculum" or "formal projects for developing desktop instructional software/courseware" (Green & Eastman, 1992, p. 16).

The clear if implicit message is that colleges and universities should be offering more incentives and rewards, but the normative claim seems to downplay a compelling sociological reality: Academic disciplines, through their professional associations, ultimately define the products that count as legitimate academic work. Disciplines are conservative social structures that resist challenges to redefine and broaden the criteria according to which their members may expect to be rewarded. The "publish-or-perish" imperative that still governs promotion and tenure decisions is not now, in most disciplines, defined expansively enough to include instructional products as publications ("Professors Report Progress," 1993). By themselves, universities have neither the incentive nor the power to alter unilaterally the enduring reward structures (and time demands) that ultimately explain why only a minority of faculty members are attracted to courseware design and development. Although influential individuals and interest groups certainly are urging that the imbalance of research over teaching be corrected (Boyer, 1990), the traditional paradigm is still dominant (Cavalier, 1992). Unless disciplinary cultures accept the desirability of courseware as a legitimate professional product for their members, there is not likely to be much

---

Hawkins (1991), former Vice President for Computing and Information Services and later Associate Provost for Academic Planning at Brown University, provided perhaps the most realistic reflections on the past achievements of and future prospects for academic computing:

> No one can debate that the 1980s were characterized by rapid technological change, but the jury is not yet completely in as to the direct benefits that these technological innovations have had on teaching, learning, and instruction. . . . While a number of very substantive advances have been made over the past decade, there remains an accompanying set of unmet expectations and unfulfilled promises associated with this explosion of technology in the campus community. (p. 24)

movement in this direction no matter how sophisticated software development tools themselves become.[7] Suggestions that instructional computing
should be used for labor-substitution—"as a way of improving [courses]
without having to shrink class sizes and hire more faculty members" ("Crucial Role," 1992, p. A22)—will not be embraced by the professoriate.

Another reason for limited faculty involvement with instructional computing and courseware development may be that the pedagogical benefits of
computer-based learning have been exaggerated ("As Instructional Technology Proliferates," 1993). There is not much evidence thus far that computing has altered, let alone transformed, the cognitive-intellectual processes
and capabilities that students nurture and develop in college. Despite
quantum improvements in the power, versatility, and elegance of instructional computing technology and software authoring tools, what Kulik,
Kulik, and Cohen (1980) concluded over a decade ago in their meta-analysis
of the effectiveness of computer-based college teaching probably is still true
today: "[F]or the most part the computer has made a small but significant
contribution to the effectiveness of college teaching. . . . Overall, however,
the accomplishments of computer-based instruction at the college level must
still be considered modest" (pp. 537–538). Another researcher (Clark, 1985)
questioned whether specific attributes of the computer per se (as opposed to
instructional methods, content, and/or novelty) explain learning gains; he
also suggested that learning effects reported in the literature may be exaggerated because journals are reluctant to publish studies that do not demonstrate
significant differences in outcomes between experimental and conventional
courses (see also McQuillan, this volume). Apparently in recognition of these
problems, in 1993 EDUCOM announced a new initiative and focus for its
Educational Uses of Information Technology (EUIT) division: "a new effort
aimed at demonstrating that computers can make instruction more effective
and more efficient" ("EDUCOM Hopes," 1993). It is by no means inevitable, however, and not even highly probable that the newest instructional
computing technologies will produce measureable learning gains that are

---

[7]In 1987, EDUCOM, an organization representing almost 600 colleges and universities,
initiated EDUCOM/NCRIPTAL Higher Education Software Awards Program to encourage
and reward innovative courseware by faculty. (NCRIPTAL refers to the National Center for
Research to Improve Postsecondary Teaching and Learning.) Robert Kozma and Jerome
Johnston, co-directors of the EDUCOM/NCRIPTAL, estimated that in 1990 "on any one
campus the [instructional computing] pioneers number less than five percent of the faculty"
(1991, p. 10). Taking for granted precisely what this chapter argues is problematic, the authors
added: "But we believe that others will follow [the pioneers'] example as they discover that the
innovations can make dramatic contributions to the discernment of complex ideas, and when
resources become available to support more computer-intensive learning environments" (pp.
11–12). (For interesting accounts of personal experiences with instructional computing by
several EDUCOM/NCRIPTAL award winners, see the collection edited by Graves, 1989.)

dramatically better than those of past experiments using older computing technologies. A healthy skepticism toward "hypermedia learning" is advisable, enthusisatic endorsements nothwithstanding (Jensen, 1993).

Inequalities in Computing Access

Many early academic computer revolutionaries believed that the spread of microcomputers would have a dramatic egalitarian effect on access to computing resources, a sentiment captured by Apple's adline billing its Macintosh "the computer for the rest of us." Instead, an unanticipated effect of computerization on college campuses probably has been to exacerbate cross-institutional technological inequalities, and hence also inequalities in the competition for other resources: students, research grants, faculty, and prestige. There is a partial, albeit important, exception: better access to computing resources by women, minorities, nonscience, and engineering majors (Shields & Larkin, 1989). Yet even their enhanced access is not universal within institutions nor equally distributed across them. Access to the Bitnet or the Internet networks, for example, is much greater for faculty and administrators than for students at most colleges and universities (Green & Eastman, 1992, p. 27). Students in every type of college or university are also far less likely than faculty and administrators to "have or own" a computer (p. 13). Moreover, Green and Eastman found, both faculty and students in business and engineering are perceived as better prepared to use computer technology more effectively than their counterparts in the humanities and the fine/performing arts.

New cross-institutional inequalities also have arisen, according to the Center for Scholarly Technology's national surveys. Green and Eastman (1992) concluded that "research institutions and more affluent campuses invest a greater proportion of their desktop computing resources in their faculty" than other institutions (p. 6). Their surveys also showed that access to networking at universities, both private and public, is significantly greater than at private and public colleges, but that students, faculty, and administrators at private universities are most likely to "have or own" a computer (p. 13). They also found that in both 1990 and 1991, financially strapped public colleges and universities were more likely to reduce their campus computing budgets than private institutions. In 1991, for example, nearly two thirds of public research universities and over one half of public 4-year colleges reduced their campus computing budgets, in contrast to computing budget increases at 45% of private research universities and 49% of private 4-year colleges (35% and 21%, respectively, reported reductions).

In light of these inequalities it is with only some exaggeration that Douglas Greenberg (1991), Vice President of the American Council of Learned Societies, wrote that "current technologies now provide only limited access to a select group of high-prestige scholars in high-prestige disciplines in high-prestige institutions" (p. A48; see also Greenberg, 1992; McNeil, 1989). Broadening controversies about funding and access to national electronic networks—the Internet, the National Research and Education Network (NREN), the proposed National Information Infrastructure (known by its metaphorical moniker as the "national data superhighway")—highlight new sources of cross-institutional and sectoral inequalities ("Campus Officials Pleased," 1993). The NREN—a multibillion-dollar joint private- and public-sector project to develop a super-high-speed electronic network linking educational institutions, libraries, businesses, and laboratories—requires participating organizations to upgrade their network hardware systems. For some campuses, the costs are prohibitive, thereby leaving them behind in this latest venture in electronic leapfrogging ("Compromise Reached," 1993; "High Cost," 1991; "Promoters," 1993). The Telecommunications Policy Roundtable, a group of nonprofit organizations formed in 1993 to represent the interests of the "technologically disenfranchised," is "afraid that a national network [the "data superhighway"] developed by market forces would not reach the poor and minority communities or include the services that educators, librarians, people with disabilities, and others want" ("Guaranteeing Access," 1993, p. A23). Such expressions of escalating concern for equity issues were highlighted in a 1990 report by the Congressional Office of Technology Assessment (OTA). "OTA found that changes in the U.S. communication infrastructure are likely to broaden the gap between those who can access communication services and use information strategically and those who cannot" (p. 11.)

On balance, then, despite unprecedented technical innovations in the means of academic production, the diffusion of microcomputers on American campuses has scarcely reformed, let alone revolutionized, higher education. Instead, probably the net effect thus far has been to reinforce prevailing stratification systems, institutional values, and hierarchies of authority. "Computer-based ways of work and new services sometimes overturn specific practices, but they do not readily overturn key social relations . . ." (Kling & Iacono, 1991, p. 74). Nevertheless, there is no doubt that academic computer revolutionaries successfully constructed the idea of a computing revolution in higher education, engaged in persuasive technological framing to legitimate and implement it, and even now continue to characterize what happened (and what can occur in the future) as revolutionary. The Thomas Theorem coupled with the socially constructed character of technological realities aptly account for the self-fulfilling prophecy "academic computing revolution." Yet an alternative interpretation, presented in the preceding pages, certainly lends support to Kling and Iacono's (1991) assessment: "Instructional computing has not yet revolutionized the social organization of schooling in any meaningful sense. And we do not see substantial changes from computerization likely in the near future because computer-based systems have been adopted in ways that fit pre-existing relationships between students and teachers, curricular arrangements, etc." (p. 71; see also Kling, 1986).

CONCLUDING REFLECTIONS: REVOLUTION, ROUTINIZATION, REALISM

My examination and assessment of the putative academic computing revolution has not been an exercise in mere historical exegesis and critique. Despite the evidence of experience from the 1980s, the computer still serves as a key symbol (Ortner, 1973) of transformation and transcendence through technology. To cite just three typical expressions of the recent hubris: "Exploited to the full extent of its potential, information technology can literally give every scholar a global reach, almost instantaneously placing him or her beside any desired collaborator anywhere, or in direct contact with any storehouse of knowledge" (Langenberg, 1989, p. 16). In October 1990, the theme of EDUCOM's annual meeting in Atlanta was "Preparing for the Renaissance." And in 1993, writing about the emerging potential for "hypermedia learning," a professor concluded: "A great new force will, in the years immediately ahead, change the nature of learning and what it means to be a faculty member" (Jensen, 1993, p. 13). The visions of the early 1980s may have passed, but others—equally far-reaching and arguably utopian—have arisen to take their place into the 1990s.

Above all, now the new visions seem to be animated by the idea of something like a "virtual academy," integrated by super-high-speed networks in seamless local environments of "ubiquitous computing" ("And Not a Personal Computer in Sight," 1991) stretching around the world—a true electronic global village, presumably ushering in a new era in human history. According to *The Chronicle of Higher Education* ("Presidents," 1993), a report issued by the Higher Education Information Resources Alliance argues that "[n]etworks allow users to communicate inexpensively, unconstrained by time-zone differences, distance, or location" (p. A34). The report goes on to suggest that "geographical and cultural barriers between departments are being broken down by the ease and cultural neutrality afforded by networked communication" (p. A34). Invoking an unqualified logic of technological determinism, one background paper for the alliance's report claims that there is "no way to predict where and how far technology's evolution will take us . . . but this is a given: It will be extensive, expensive . . . and inevitable" (p. A34). Contrary to the effusive technophilism of the report, networks are no more "culturally neutral" than interstate highways, and both are extremely expensive to build, maintain, and extend. There is no doubt that the importance of networking issues is growing throughout academia, and that more colleges and universities are offering networking services each year. But one should not forget that administrators and faculty (especially in the sciences, business, and engineering) have better access to these networks than students (Green & Eastman, 1992); and that in 1993 over one third of all U.S. higher education institutions still had no campus network whereas 30% lacked access to Bitnet or Internet ("Academic-Computing Directors," 1993). Even when (if ever) universal access is achieved, transformation of the social relations of academic production, including equal access to network services by students, will not necessarily follow. There is no technological imperative.

I have criticized the hyperbole and utopianism of academic computer revolutionaries, but they have certainly not been, in the main, unsophisticated "technological somnambulists" (Winner, 1986, p. 10) who unreflectively believe that computers are morally or politically neutral tools. On the contrary, they have been acutely aware that academic computing was a technological means for realizing nontechnological ends. Yet collectively they embraced an implicit belief in the notion of a technological imperative—and hence, at least a "soft" technological determinism. According to the imperativist presupposition, the "promiscuous utility" (Winner, 1986, p. 6) of personal computers—of information technology generally—is so manifestly obvious and compelling that they can sell themselves on technical merit alone. Such a view, implicit in the notion of "technological impacts," attributes a monolithic, socially decontextualized causal force—and thus really a sense of agency—to tools themselves, while denying agency to their human users. In the case of academic computing, at least, this chapter and others in this volume have pointed to the theoretical and empirical fallacies of this way of thinking.

As Jeffrey Alexander (1992) observed, "Expectations for salvation were inseparable from the technological innovations of industrial capitalism. . . . In this technological discourse, however, the machine has been not only God but also the devil . . . The computer is the newest and certainly one of the most potent technological innovations of the modern age, but its symbolization has been much the same" (pp. 307–308). What is perhaps most striking about the symbolization of academic computing has been the virtual absence of distopian or satanic discourse. Yet now, in addition to the hubris, there are signs of a cautious instrumental realism about academic computing from some of its most thoughtful leaders (see, especially, Hawkins, 1989, 1991). The new realism, driven largely by budgetary stringencies and post-revolutionary ideological thermidor, was reflected in several presentations given at the 1993 EDUCOM meeting in Cincinnati. The keynote speaker, Blenda J. Wilson, president of California State University at Northridge, emphasized the urgency for a "very disciplined approach" toward computing and other technologies on college campuses. "I hope we will be guided by the maxim, We don't *have* to do everything that is possible to do" (quoted in "Colleges," 1993, p. A21). Might this be a new phase in higher education's reception of computing, one characterized by a deflationary rhetoric, a contingent pragmatism, a strategy of "situational adjustment" (Pfaffenberger, 1988, 1992) and its accompanying resymbolizations (see Graves, this volume). Alexander (1992) detected such a shift in today's popular discourses about the computer, what he termed its "routinization" (p. 313). Yet as the current debate about electronic networks shows, routinization is by no means an all encompassing theme of contemporary discourses about computing. The present phase does not signify the end of instrumental idealism even if it does seem to command a need for instrumental realism. In all likelihood, instrumental idealism and instrumental realism will coexist in dialectical tension as alternating currents of discourse in the social construction of academic computing.

ACKNOWLEDGMENTS

I am grateful to JAI Press and Plenum Press for permission to draw on material from Shields et al. (1991, 1992, respectively).

REFERENCES

Academic-computing directors give low priority to developing instructional software, survey finds. (1993, October 20). *The Chronicle of Higher Education*, pp. A26–A27.

Alexander, J. C. (1992). The promise of a cultural sociology: Technological discourse and the sacred and profane information machine. In R. Munch & N. J. Smelser (Eds.), *Theory of culture* (pp. 293–323). Berkeley & Los Angeles: University of California Press.

And not a personal computer in sight. (1991, October 6). *New York Times*, pp. F1, F6.

Anderson, R. E. (1990). The advantages and risks of entrepreneurship. *Academe, 76*(5), 9–14.

Arms, W. Y. (1990). Reflections on Andrew. *EDUCOM Review, 25*(3), 33–43.

As instructional technology proliferates, skeptics seek hard evidence of its value. (1993, May 5). *The Chronicle of Higher Education*, pp. A27–A29.

Attewell, P. (1987). Big brother and the sweatshop: Computer surveillance in the automated office. *Sociological Theory, 5*(1), 87–99.

Balkovich, E., Lerman, S., & Parmelee, R. P. (1985, November). Computing in higher education: The Athena experience. *Computer*, pp. 112–125.

Beeman, W. O., Anderson, K. T., Bader, G., Larkin, J., McClard, A. P., McQuillan, P., & Shields, M. A. (1988). *Intermedia: A case study of innovation in higher education*. Unpublished report to the Annenberg/CPB Project, Brown University, Institute for Research in Information and Scholarship, Providence, RI.

Bijker, W. E. (1987). The social construction of Bakelite: Toward a theory of invention. In W. E. Bijker, T. P. Hughes, & T. J. Pinch (Eds.), *The social construction of technological systems: New directions in the sociology and history of technology* (pp. 159–187). Cambridge, MA: MIT Press.

Bijker, W. E. (1992). The social construction of fluorescent lighting, or how an artifact was invented in its diffusion stage. In W. E. Bijker & J. Law (Eds.), *Shaping technology/building society: Studies in sociotechnical change* (pp. 75–102). Cambridge: MIT Press.

Bijker, W. E., & Law, J. (Eds.). (1992). *Shaping technology/building society: Studies in sociotechnical change*. Cambridge, MA: MIT Press.

Bok, D. (1985, May/June). Looking into education's high-tech future. *Harvard Magazine*, pp. 29–38.

Boyer, E. L. (1987). *College: The undergraduate experience in America*. New York: Harper & Row.

Boyer, E. L. (1990). *Scholarship reconsidered: Priorities of the professoriate*. Princeton, NJ: Princeton University Press.

Campus officials pleased but worried by Clinton plan for "information superhighway." (1993, March 31). *The Chronicle of Higher Education*, pp. A17–A18.

Cavalier, R. J. (1992). Shifting paradigms in higher education and educational computing. *EDUCOM Review, 27* (3), 32–35.

Clark, R. E. (1985). Confounding in educational computing research. *Journal of Educational Computing Research, 1* (2), 137–147

Cohen, K. C. (1987). *Project Athena—Year 3.5 student survey findings, 1986–1987.* (Project Athena Impact Study Report No. 7). Cambridge: MIT Press.

Colleges told to take "disciplined approach" to technology. (1993, October 27). *The Chronicle of Higher Education*, pp. A21, A23.

Compromise reached on legislation leading to national information network. (1993, June 23). *The Chronicle of Higher Education*, pp. A15, A17.

Computer technology is reshaping the university. (1990, April). Interview with Vice President for Computing and Information Services Brian Hawkins by Managing Editor Anne Diffily. *Brown Alumni Monthly*, pp. 23–29.

Crucial role seen for technology in meeting higher education's challenges. (1992, September 25). *The Chronicle of Higher Education*, pp. A21–A22.

Edge, D. O. (1990). Technological metaphor and social control. In L. A. Hickman (Ed.), *Technology as a human affair* (pp. 79–89). New York: McGraw-Hill.

EDUCOM hopes to demonstrate how computers can improve instruction and save money. (1993, July 14). *The Chronicle of Higher Education*, p. A25.

Experiments with scholar's workstation networks in a wired university. (1983, March 28). Proposal to the System Development Foundation. Providence, RI: Brown University.

From desktop to teraflop. (1993, October 27). *The Chronicle of Higher Education*, A20, A22.

Gilbert, S. W. (1988a, September/October). Asking the right questions. *The Software Initiative Newsletter*, p. 8.

Gilbert, S. W. (1988b, November/December). Message from ESI director Steven W. Gilbert. *The Software Initiative Newsletter*, p. 1.

Gilbert, S. W. (1990, April/May). Tomorrow's faculty and information technology: An opportunity lost? *The EUIT Newsletter*, p. 6.

Gilbert, S. W., & Green, K. C. (1986, May/June). New computing in higher education. *Change*, pp. 33–50.

Granovetter, M. S. (1973). The strength of weak ties. *American Journal of Sociology, 78*(6), 1360–1380.

Graves, W. H. (Ed.). (1989). *Computing across the curriculum: Academic perspectives*. McKinney, TX: EDUCOM/Academic Computing Publications.

Green, K. C. (1989). A perspective on vendor relationships: A study of symbiosis. In B. Hawkins (Ed.), *Organizing and managing information resources on campus* (pp. 89–113). McKinney, TX: EDUCOM/Academic Computing Publications.

Green, K. C., & Eastman, S. (1992). *Campus computing 1991*. Los Angeles: University of Southern California, Center for Scholarly Technology.

Greenberg, D. (1991, October 23). Information access: Our elitist system must be reformed. *The Chronicle of Higher Education*, p. A48.

Greenberg, D. (1992). Technology, scholarship, and democracy: You can't always get what you want. *EDUCOM Review, 27* (3), 46–51.

Guaranteeing access to the data highway. (1993, November 3). *The Chronicle of Higher Education*, p. A23.

Hawkins, B. L. (Ed.). (1989). *Organizing and managing information resources on campus*. McKinney, TX: EDUCOM/Academic Computing Publications.

Hawkins, B. L. (1991, January/February). Preparing for the next wave of computing on campus. *Change*, pp. 24–31.

High cost could deny big computer advance to some colleges. (1991, December 4). *The Chronicle of Higher Education*, pp. A1, A32.

Hinds, K. (1983, September). The computer and education at Brown: Symbols of a changing time. *Brown Alumni Monthly*, pp. 28–32, 41–45.

Jacoby, R. (1991). The greening of the university. *Dissent, 38*, 286–292.

Jensen, R. E. (1993, July-August). The technology of the future is already here. *Academe*, pp. 8–13.

Kiesler, S. B., & Sproull, L. S. (Eds.). (1987). *Computing and change on campus.* New York: Cambridge University Press.

Kling, R. (1986, Spring/Summer). The new wave of computing in colleges and universities: A social analysis [Commentary]. *Outlook*, pp. 8–14

Kling, R. (1991). Computerization and social transformation. *Science, Technology, & Human Values, 16* (3), 342–367.

Kling, R., & Iacono, S. (1988). The mobilization of support for computerization: The role of computerization movements. *Social Problems, 35* (3), 226–243.

Kling, R., & Iacono, S. (1991). Making a "computer revolution." In C. Dunlop & R. Kling (Eds.), *Computerization and controversy: Value conflicts and social choices* (pp. 63–75). San Diego: Academic Press.

Kozma, R. B., & Johnston, J. (1991, January/February). The technological revolution comes to the classroom. *Change*, pp. 10–23.

Kulik J. A., Kulik, C-L. C., & Cohen, P. A. (1980). Effectiveness of computer-based college teaching: A meta-analysis of findings. *Review of Educational Research, 50* (4), 525–544.

Langenberg, D. N. (1989, January). Supporting the global scholar. *Academic Computing*, pp. 12–16.

McNeil, D. R. (1989, June 7). Technology is a hot topic, but its impact on higher education has been minimal. *The Chronicle of Higher Education*, p. A44.

Merton, R. K. (1968). The self-fulfilling prophecy. *In Social theory and social structure* (pp. 475–490). New York: The Free Press.

Office of Technology Assessment. (1990, January). *Critical connections: Communications for the future.* Washington, DC: Author.

Ortner, S. B. (1973). On key symbols. *American Anthropologist, 75*, 1338–1346.

Osgood, D. (1984, June). A computer on every desk. *Byte*, pp. 162–184.

Parsons, T. (1977). Comparative studies and evolutionary change. *Social systems and the evolution of action systems* (pp. 279–320). New York: The Free Press.

Peters, L. S., & Etzkowitz, H. (1990). University–industry connections and academic values. *Technology in Society, 12*, 427–440.

Pfaffenberger, B. (1988). The social meaning of the personal computer: Or, why the personal computer revolution was no revolution. *Anthropological Quarterly, 61*, 39–47.

Pfaffenberger, B. (1992). Technological dramas. *Science, Technology, & Human Values, 17*(3), 282–312.

Pinch, T. J., & Bijker, W. E. (1987). The social construction of facts and artifacts: Or how the sociology of science and the sociology of technology might benefit each other. In W. E. Bijker, T. P. Hughes, & T. J. Pinch (Eds.), *The social construction of technological systems: New directions in the sociology and history of technology* (pp. 17–50). Cambridge, MA: MIT Press.

Presidents on 5 campuses urge colleagues not to miss benefits offered by computer networks. (1993, October 13). *The Chronicle of Higher Education*, p. A34.

Professors report progress in gaining recognition for their uses of technology. (1993, March 3). *The Chronicle of Higher Education*, pp. A19, A21.

Promoters of plan to create a national "data highway" turn to "thorny" policy issues and legal questions. (1993, July 21). *The Chronicle of Higher Education*, pp. A17, A20.

Recession spurs changes in college market for computer technology. (1992, December 9). *The Chronicle of Higher Education*, pp. A15–A16.

Rogers, E. M. (1983). *The diffusion of innovations* (3rd ed.). New York: The Free Press.

Rotenberg, J. (1983, December 7). What's wrong with Brown's computer plans. *The Brown Daily Herald*, p. 3.

Segal, H. P. (1985). *Technological utopianism in American culture*. Chicago: University of Chicago Press.

Shields, M. A. (1986). Computing at Brown—An ongoing study. *Perspectives in Computing*, 6(2), 57–62.

Shields, M. A., Graves, W., III, & Nyce, J. M. (1991). Technological innovation in higher education: A case study in academic computing. In J. A. Morell & M. Fleischer (Eds.), *Advances in the implementation and impact of computer systems* (Vol. 1, pp. 183–209). Greenwich, CT: JAI Press.

Shields, M. A., Graves, W., III, & Nyce, J. M. (1992). Computing and the social organization of academic work. *Journal of Science Education and Technology, 1* (4), 243–258.

Shields, M. A., & Larkin, J. (1989). Gender and class-year differences in undergraduate computing experiences and attitudes. In T. J. Kozik & D. G. Jansson (Eds.), *The worker in transition: Technological change* (pp. 301–306). New York: The American Society of Mechanical Engineers.

Slaughter, S. (1990). *The higher learning and high technology*. Albany: The State University of New York Press.

Thomas, W. I., & Thomas, D. S. (1928). *The child in America: Behavior problems and programs*. New York: Knopf.

Tucker, M. S. (1983–1984). The star-wars universities: Brown, CMU, MIT (Computers on Campus: Working Papers). *1983–84 Current Issues in Higher Education, 2*, 3–24.

Waldrop, M. M. (1985, April 26). Personal computers on campus. *Science, 228*, 438–444.

Weick, K. E. (1976). Educational organizations as loosely coupled systems. *Administrative Science Quarterly, 21* (1), 1–19.

Winner, L. (1986). Technologies as forms of life. *The whale and the reactor: A search for limits in an age of high technology* (pp. 3–18). Chicago: University of Chicago Press.

Author Index

Page numbers in *italics* denote complete bibliographical references

Subject Index